THE PROFESSION AND PRACTICE OF EDUCATIONAL PSYCHOLOGY

Also available in the Cassell Education series:

P. Ainley: *Young People Leaving Home*

P. Ainley and M. Corney: *Training for the Future: The Rise and Fall of the Manpower Services Commission*

G. Antonouris and J. Wilson: *Equal Opportunities in Schools*

L. Bash and D. Coulby: *Contradiction and Conflict in Education: The 1988 Act in Action*

N. Bennett and A. Cass: *From Special to Ordinary Schools*

D. E. Bland: *Managing Higher Education*

M. Booth, J. Furlong and M. Wilkin: *Partnership in Initial Teacher Training*

M. Bottery: *The Morality of the School*

L. Burton (ed.): *Gender and Mathematics*

C. Christofi: *Assessment and Profiling in Science*

G. Claxton: *Being a Teacher: A Positive Approach to Change and Stress*

G. Claxton: *Teaching to Learn: A Direction for Education*

D. Coulby and L. Bash: *The Education Reform Act: Competition and Control*

D. Coulby and S. Ward: *The Primary Core National Curriculum*

C. Cullingford (ed.): *The Primary Teacher*

L. B. Curzon: *Teaching in Further Education* (4th edition)

J. Freeman: *Gifted Children Grow Up*

B. Goacher *et al.*: *Policy and Provision for Special Educational Needs*

H. Gray (ed.): *Management Consultancy in Schools*

L. Hall: *Poetry for Life*

J. Nias, G. Southworth and R. Yeomans: *Staff Relationships in the Primary School*

A. Pollard: *The Social World of the Primary School*

J. Sayer and V. Williams (eds): *Schools and External Relations*

B. Spiecker and R. Straughan: *Freedom and Indoctrination in Education: International Perspectives*

R. Straughan: *Beliefs, Behaviour and Education*

H. Thomas: *Education Costs and Performance*

H. Thomas, G. Kirkpatrick and E. Nicholson: *Financial Delegation and the Local Management of Schools*

D. Thyer and J. Maggs: *Teaching Mathematics to Young Children* (3rd edition)

M. Watts: *The Science of Problem-Solving*

J. Wilson: *A New Introduction to Moral Education*

S. Wolfendale (ed.): *Parental Involvement*

The Profession and Practice of Educational Psychology

Future Directions

Edited by

Sheila Wolfendale,
Trevor Bryans,
Mark Fox,
Alan Labram and
Allan Sigston

CASSELL

Cassell Educational Limited
Villiers House
41/47 Strand
London WC2N 5JE

First published 1992, Reprinted 1993

British Library Cataloguing in Publication Data
The profession and practice of educational psychology.
 I. Wolfendale, Sheila
 370.15

 ISBN 0-304-32540-6
     0-304-32347-0 pbk

Typeset by Colset Pte Ltd, Singapore
Printed and bound in Great Britain by
Dotesios Ltd, Trowbridge, Wiltshire.

Contents

Section III – Focus on Community

The Editors

Trevor Bryans is Principal Educational Psychologist in the London Borough of Brent. He has been a teacher and educational psychologist in several local education authorities and a polytechnic lecturer in special needs. He has written widely on special needs, on the assessment of and intervention in cases of learning difficulty, and on behaviour management.

Mark Fox trained as an educational psychologist at Exeter University before working in Solihull and Bromley, where he was in charge of the School Psychological Service. He has a particular interest in working with pre-school children and their families and with children with severe and complex difficulties. In the past five years he has had a combined post for Professional Development in Essex and is a tutor for Advanced and Initial Training of EPs at the Polytechnic of East London (PEL). He is Course Tutor for the MSc in Educational Management at PEL, which is for practising educational psychologists.

Alan Labram is a Senior Educational Psychologist in the London Borough of Newham and Associate Tutor to the MSc course in Educational Psychology, the initial professional training course at the Polytechnic of East London. Alan's interests include the management of educational psychology services and professional development for educational psychologists.

Allan Sigston has worked as an educational psychologist for thirteen years in several local education authorities. He is currently a Senior Educational Psychologist in the London Borough of Waltham Forest and Associate Tutor to the MSc course in Educational Psychology, the initial professional training course at the Polytechnic of East London, where he is also component leader on the MSc Management programme for educational psychologists. Allan has written and published on Portage, and applications of organizational psychology in education.

Sheila Wolfendale has been a remedial and primary teacher and educational psychologist in several local education authorities and currently is Tutor to the MSc course in Educational Psychology, the initial professional training course at the Polytechnic of East London. She is author, co-author and editor of books, booklets, articles and manuals on a range of special educational needs and parental involvement. In 1988 she was awarded a Professorship at the Polytechnic of East London.

The Contributors

Billy Conn is an educational psychologist with eighteen years' experience in a number of local authorities and in independent practice. He specializes in cases of child abuse and neglect, a role which inevitably involves many court appearances as an expert witness. Research interests include, besides child abuse and neglect, the areas of stress and developmental disorder.

Tony Dessent is Principal Educational Psychologist in Nottinghamshire. He has wide-ranging interests in the field of special educational needs and related services and writes regularly on matters relating to integration, support services, working with parents and the needs of pre-school pupils. He is author of *Making the Ordinary School Special* (Falmer Press, 1987) and is currently involved in the implementation and development of 'Children First', which is Nottinghamshire's strategy for meeting special educational needs in the 1990s.

Geoff Lindsay is Principal Educational Psychologist for Sheffield LEA and Associate Tutor to the professional training course in educational psychology at the University of Sheffield, where he is also co-director of the Special Needs Co-ordination and Research Group. Geoff is the co-author or editor of ten books and collections of papers. He is a past Chair of the British Psychological Society's Division of Educational and Child Psychology, currently Chair of that society's Professional Affairs Board and a member of other society committees.

Marianne McCarthy is currently Principal Educational Psychologist in Hammersmith and Fulham LEA, having previously worked in the London Borough of Waltham Forest and in Derbyshire. She is interested in integrating the knowledge and skills established in social and community psychology into the practice of educational psychology, and has published articles on working with secondary schools and developing a coherent curriculum planning and assessment framework in the context of the National Curriculum.

Philippa Russell is Director of the Voluntary Council for Handicapped Children at the National Children's Bureau and currently seconded, part-time, to the National Development Team for People with Mental Handicap at the Department of Health as an Associate Director with reference to services for children and young people with mental handicap/learning difficulties. Major areas of current work include a DES funded project on partnership with parents and the implications of the Children Act 1989 for children with special needs. Philippa has written many articles, chapters and books on subjects relating to disability and special needs.

Gary Thomas is a Senior Lecturer in Education at Oxford Polytechnic. He has worked as an educational psychologist in Manchester and as a Senior Educational Psychologist with two London boroughs, providing advanced training for educational psychologists at University College London. He is co-editor of *Planning for Special Needs* (1988), author of a number of articles and on the editorial board of the journal *Support for Learning*.

Preface

What we have tried to do in this volume is to make a coherent statement about the contemporary practice of educational psychologists in various domains and to address a number of current issues which have a bearing on educational psychologists' own work and which are relevant, too, for those other professionals who come into contact with educational psychologists.

Our task has been one of selection and, thereby, inevitably omission. We have had to exclude potential contributions from educational psychologist colleagues who are doing exemplary work in academic and field settings. We wanted to establish certain parameters and contexts for this book which would particularly reflect practice at the individual organizational and community levels; for there is a potent mix of traditional and innovative, of established and emerging work. Thus we want to broadcast how 'mature' professional activities can effectively be set alongside newer activities that are borne out of legislative requirements or needs analysis by family, school, community members as well as by educational psychologists themselves.

Our authors are 'reconstructionists' but in no sense have we wanted to demolish erstwhile practice. Our contention is, first, that 'bad' practice will fade away, become extinct, as practitioners and recipients realize and feel its limitations, and secondly that professional activity, at any one time, provides the building blocks for future practice.

So we invite readers to be reflective, with us, about the issues, ideas, practices described in this book. We hope that our readers will include not only educational psychologists themselves, in training and in practice, but also colleagues in education such as teachers, advisers, inspectors, administrators, educational welfare officers, and tutors and students in colleges of education. We would like to think that professionals from other services and disciplines who come across or work with educational psychologists could find it useful, informative and relevant.

Chapter 1 is intended to be a 'scene-setter' and ranges across a number of areas and issues that have a bearing on each of the other eleven chapters. These are divided into three sections, each one exploring a major domain within the practice of educational psychology.

SECTION I: FOCUS ON INDIVIDUALS AND CASEWORK

Most of the educational psychology texts of recent years have paid scant attention to matters of casework practice. As Tony Dessent points out in Chapter 3, this is also a feature of job advertisements. The emphasis on policy and systems in these earlier works seems in stark contrast to the day-to-day experience of educational psychologists in the field, who are likely to spend 60 per cent or more of their time addressing the needs of individual children. This suppression or devaluing of an evident 'core' activity represents an obvious inherent paradox of the type described by Mark Fox in Chapter 8. In planning this book we as editors quite deliberately sought to redress this imbalance. In our view the chapters in the section not only reassert the importance of casework as a vehicle for change for individual children but also as a basis for a fuller contribution by educational psychologists to the enterprise of school improvement. All three of the chapters emphasize the complexity of casework and the need to depart from conventional thinking of the past, where children's problems could be regarded as *objective* and *divorced from the contexts in which they occur*.

Gary Thomas (Chapter 4) considers classrooms, and the patterns of behaviour of the inhabitants, in terms of nested interrelating systems. The problems of individuals can only be understood, therefore, within analyses that embrace these different systems. Allan Sigston (Chapter 2) notes that concerns about a child emanate from adult observers of the 'problem'. As a result educational psychologists acting as consultants work with adult constructions of problems, and ignore at their peril the phenomenological features of problem solving. Tony Dessent (Chapter 3) stresses the interactional and relative aspects of the definition of special education needs. The complexities described by these different authors indicate the important psychological dimensions of casework and the unexplored potential of practitioners' parent discipline.

All three chapters, either explicitly or by implication, make a case for the privileged and unique perspective available to educational psychologists on organizational functioning, gained through their work with teachers, parents and children about the needs of individuals, a view echoed by Mark Fox and Allan Sigston (Chapter 7).

It is hoped that the chapters in this section go beyond a reaffirmation of casework, offering readers models of practice (e.g. 'the problem-solving alliance'), broadened frameworks for analysis (e.g. 'the ecological viewpoint') and useful appraisals of the profession's relationships with other parts of the education system in the post-1988 Education Reform Act era.

SECTION II: FOCUS ON ORGANIZATIONS   *SYSTEMS APPROACH*

One of the major criticisms of psychology is that its focus on the individual negates the importance of organizational or institutional factors when explaining how change occurs. Educational psychology has not been immune to these criticisms and over the last few decades has begun to address the importance of understanding the organization. Nevertheless in practice much EP work is still driven by an individual perspective no matter how much a systems approach is espoused. One of the reasons for this may be the gradual realization that organizations are notoriously difficult to change, and the more educational psychologists understand their complexity the more unsure they become about the simplistic approaches to change that are sometimes advocated in the educational world.

This section addresses how educational psychologists' different ways of working affects schools as organizations. In Chapter 5 Alan Labram examines the complex and rapidly expanding area of consultancy work, suggesting that educational psychologists need to develop a different set of consultancy skills if they are to move from their individual casework. Marianne McCarthy in Chapter 6 asserts the importance of individuals as an organization's central resource; educational psychologists therefore need to use their 'people' skills to help the development of organizations through ensuring that people develop. Mark Fox and Allan Sigston in Chapter 7 outline different explanatory frameworks that can be used to help explain organizational behaviour, and suggest that educational psychologists' inability to effect change may stem from their being locked into a psychological explanation of organizations rather than acknowledging the economic and political realities of the external environment. Mark Fox in Chapter 8 explores the inconsistencies and paradoxes contained in educational psychology services as organizations and suggests that the way forward may be for educational psychologists to work on their own systems before working on schools' organizational change.

By taking an organizational perspective the focus on the individual is shifted rather than lost. In many ways the individual comes more clearly into focus as the key to understanding how educational psychologists will need to work in the 1990s. It is a focus that rejects disenfranchisement and disillusionment and emphasizes empowerment of the individual at every level within the system.

SECTION III: FOCUS ON THE COMMUNITY

The four chapters in Section III provide an opportunity for the authors, and the reader, to 'peer over the parapet' and look to the horizon. While the sheer pace of change within education during the last decade of the century is sufficient to cause professional head-spinning, the context is clearly addressed by Trevor Bryans in acknowledging that educational psychologists cannot work in blissful isolation from those conditions of society which hinder many of our children and young people from fulfilling their educational potential. Professionals ignore these issues at the peril of colluding with the problem.

While several of the authors in this section address the issue of who is the client, society is moving by way of legislation towards the notion of children's rights, and William Conn and Philippa Russell explore the undoubted impact that the Education Reform Act 1988 and the Children Act 1989 will have on practice. Less parochially, Geoff Lindsay examines the effects of European legislation which allows professionals to practice in any part of the European Community.

These are exciting and challenging times for a profession which now has unprecedented opportunities to establish a secure niche within national and international communities.

Sheila Wolfendale, Trevor Bryans, Mark Fox, Alan Labram, Allan Sigston

London, March 1991

Chapter 1

Applying Educational Psychology: Locations and Orientations

Sheila Wolfendale

PREAMBLE

This introductory chapter aims to deal with a number of themes and issues which impinge on or inform present and emerging practices, some of which are described in this book. All initiatives can be located in their uniquely apposite time and place; in other words, there is a context, if not an explanation, for the origins and justifications of practices identified as 'new', 'different' and 'innovative'. Between and among them the chapters describe contemporary practice located at various stages of development at levels that encompass child, service and policy foci. Where we can confidently prognosticate the future orientations of the profession, we do so: where we cannot, we may only speculate. Our definitions of what educational psychology *is* lie in our descriptions of what educational psychologists *do*.

INTRODUCTION

There have been few published texts about a profession which has pervasive influence at most levels of the education service locally, and which, via educational psychologists employed by local education authorities, fulfils a range and diversity of statutory and other duties.

Although the number of articles by educational psychologists themselves, published mainly in the two journals *Educational and Child Psychology* and *Educational Psychology in Practice*, is legion, the number of books about the practice of educational psychology is so small that each one is perceived as a kind of landmark. Of these an even smaller number, one or two at most, would be regarded as seminal and influential, judging by citations alone. While their pronouncements and prescriptions cannot be proved to be definitive in the longer term, the views expressed by their authors may be at least heeded and debated, in part because of the very paucity of core texts.

In all there are half a dozen or so books on the profession, spanning no more than twenty years, and each has attempted to describe contemporary (at those times) educational psychology practice while simultaneously taking a forward-looking approach. This is not only because the publishers of these volumes sought sales beyond the (relatively) small number of active educational psychologists. The writers have wanted to describe, inform and influence those within and those outside the education service whose own work and remit are in some ways significantly related to those of educational psychologists.

At a deeper level, the rationales for these texts, including this one, invariably include reference to their unique contemporary contexts, which are perceived to be significant for various societal, educational, political and economic reasons. In particular they cite professional justifications, such as: '[this book] has been prepared because the authors feel that texts of this kind will be needed to meet the demands of the increasing numbers of psychology graduates who train as educational and child psychologists' (Chazan *et al.*, 1974, from the foreword), and later 'during the last ten years there has been, among educational psychologists, an increasing questioning of their role and of . . . job descriptions' (Gilham, 1978, from the foreword), and recently 'Here we are addressing a further range of topics, outlining their psychological basis and exploring their application in educational psychologists' work with teachers in ordinary schools' (Jones and Frederickson, 1990, from the editors' introduction).

In this volume we would claim, similarly, to take an overview, but additionally to proclaim and describe a number of quite distinctive and emerging models of practice. Although it may be perceived as platitudinous to say, at the time of writing, that this is a critical time for the profession, in fact this is demonstrably so. The profession cannot be exempt from the changes and uncertainties within education, and the effects of the provisions of the Education Reform Act 1988 will continue to reverberate and have impact on recruitment, patterns of employment and type and style of service delivery. The very basis of applied psychology within education may and probably will continue to shift, as already noted by Jones and Frederickson (1990).

Whether or not this volume represents a celebration of practice that is perceived to be effective is for readers to judge—we are in no way arrogant or complacent about what might be claimed as modest successes, but nevertheless eschew being 'cautious experts' (Quicke, 1982) and have tried to approach the issues in a spirit of critical appraisal. The complexities of the phenomena with which we are engaged preclude gratuitous prescriptions and militate against unidimensional solutions, in the way, indeed, that Quicke identified when he explored the apparent tensions between the status-quo-maintaining and the change-oriented practices of educational psychologists.

The sections in this book have been chosen to reflect the various facets and levels of practice that represent the bedrock of the profession. This is hardly a novel formulation, but it does acknowledge the reality that educational psychologists operate at these levels and in these activities simultaneously. The danger of over-promoting one approach is that it will inevitably be construed as being at the expense of another, and in this way they become construed as being mutually exclusive, bipolar practices.

What many educational psychologists have learned from their hypothesis-testing exercises in the field is to follow situation-specific, problem-solving strategies, and to apply hard-won professional judgment as to when micro or macro approaches are applicable, or indeed when a 'mixed' response is called for. So each chapter within each section addresses itself to *current* approaches and issues arising within the time-honoured overall frameworks denoted by the three sections.

A corps of requisite knowledge and basic skills seems to have been transmitted across generations of educational psychologists, judging by the kinds of activity undertaken by them, as reported in various surveys from the 1940s onwards (the Summerfield Report, 1968; Freeman and Topping, 1976; DECP, 1980). An historical analysis, based on these sources, confirms the enduring nature of a number of core activities, even if their frequency and function change over time (for instance, home visiting, family counselling, assessment and one-to-one child contact). These activities act as constant markers to more recent spheres of professional activity (such as INSET involvement, governor training, curriculum design and systems approaches).

core activities

In sum, survey data and function checklists confirm an evolving and maturing profession which could and should be equipped to respond positively to new and changing demands. The particular kinds of challenge facing educational psychologists come from various sources, societal, economic and political. These are embodied particularly in recent legislation, most notably the Education Act 1981, within which framework educational psychologists are now used to operating. Other legislation is calling for reappraisal of working practices, because the provisions contained in legislation such as the Education Reform Act 1988 and the Children Act 1989 demand varying degrees of service restructuring, reformulation of funding mechanisms, and role and function reappraisal.

While this kind of external momentum forces educational psychologists to respond rather than to initiate, nevertheless, the legislation does open up windows of opportunity for them to be constructively creative rather than simply responsive out of necessity. The time and tide are such that forced reappraisal (for example, that rendered essential by the advent of local management of schools, and its implications for educational psychology services that have up to now been retained centrally by the LEA) is also an opportunity to reappraise fundamental theory and practice issues. So in this volume the spotlight is turned on:

(a)   professional–consumer/client relationships;
(b)   broader environmental forces that operate upon and influence educational psychologists' work in schools and with families;
(c)   constructs of handicap and disability;
(d)   efficient ways of delivering services commensurate with the self-expressed needs of users and consumers;
(e)   the maximization of human resources as the major asset of any organization;
(f)   the possible integration of other branches of applied psychology (for example, organizational psychology) into practice that up to now has emphasized the pedagogical and the pathological.

ALIGNING PRACTICE WITH PRINCIPLES

On matters of principle educational psychologists may be seen to have been less forthcoming than when they write about their practice. Statements of intent, or 'mission statements' (Reason and Webster, 1990) are beginning to creep into the jargon as part of an educational psychology service (EPS); acknowledgment that public proclamation of what it has to offer is all part of the new, finance-driven, competitive orientation within education. Perhaps educational psychologists have felt that they were always too minor a part of the education service to have espoused operational principles of their own. Indeed many educational psychology services have nestled under the broader umbrella of locally articulated educational principles, in particular that of commitment to equal opportunities (Wolfendale *et al.*, 1988).

A chapter in Section III of this book deals with the question of bias and justice. Implicit in educational psychologists' work, enduringly, has been the humanitarian or benevolent intent to give, to provide, to ease burdens on a self-selecting basis; that is, with clients who offer themselves up for such help, or who are persuaded by educational psychologists or other agents that they need it. Client-receivers have first to demonstrate eligibility for professional help; that is, to be assessed on a criterion of need, commensurate with greater or lesser degrees of urgency. Thus the 'opportunity' is not equally available to all potential users of a psychological service.

Although many educational psychology services are now reconsidering their referral and access routes, they need to acknowledge soberly that a service of the future, under full delegation and possibly reliant on ability to pay, cannot at the same time be accessible and equally available to all.

The contributors to this book share a fundamental commitment to and aspiration for the continuation of free and universally accessible psychological services. This principle has to be a lodestar to keep educational psychologists on course to a central principle, even at the same time as it becomes eroded in practice. Otherwise profit margins become the dominant goal. The tradition of 'free' services differentiates practice in the United Kingdom from those alternative models that have operated on a larger scale for longer in other parts of the world; that is, models of parallel state and private provision (an issue explored later in this chapter).

There is sufficient evidence from national surveys such as the DECP one cited earlier and local ones reported in journals that schools continue to value educational psychologists' services and that, as one principal educational psychologist expressed it, 'the order books remain full'. So it is likely that the needs for such a service will continue, but whether these can still be met under possible alternative arrangements in the future is unclear at present.

Mission statements, product portfolios and service aims (Watts, 1990) are realistic responses to a market-forces model of service provision, but an aspect of quality on offer to consumers (explored below) must surely be corresponding statements of and commitment to a number of key principles, if only to distinguish educational psychological services from other competing services. The HMI Report (1990) points to the fact that during 1988–9 few services had policy statements, though they noted that a number of services were in process of developing these at the time of their visit. What is advocated in this introductory chapter to a book on directions of change within educational psychology services is the formulation of a set of core principles that inform policy and practice.

The area of equal opportunities and its ramifications into issues of race, disability, gender, sexuality and social class is one already cited and on this book's agenda (see Chapter 9). It would certainly form an integral part of an articulated set of principles that a service could develop, along with statements about rights and responsibilities to protect providers and users of the service (the notion of a code of practice is mentioned later in the chapter).

The enumeration of a number of basic rights has been a major feature of recent formulations of principle by various groups concerned with disability (Rieser and Mason, 1990). A main motivation has been to do with redressing the power balance between professionals and 'consumers'; that is, children and their families. This has certainly been an unresolved, not to say thorny, issue for educational psychologists, who have on many occasions felt squeezed between their duties to their employers (overwhelmingly LEAs) and moral/professional obligations towards their clients. It has not been easy for educational psychologists, placed in such situations of conflict of loyalty, to act unequivocally either as parent-advocate or as bureaucrat upholding procedural matters. Nor does adherence to 'technocracy' necessarily help, since to maintain a stance of objectivity based on assessment evidence may only exacerbate this conflict (and see Chapter 8).

Perhaps educational psychology services can only gain from setting out a list of rights as part of a set of principles, whether or not they remain part of an LEA or become independent. Modelled on the kind of citizens' bill of rights proposed by Rieser and Mason (1990) or Cameron and Sturge-Moore (1990), which essentially safeguards children and their families, educational psychology services could adopt a number of reciprocal rights designed to protect providers and users on a basis of equality. Components of such a list could include:

(a) participation by all in referral and decision making;
(b) access by all to all information, reports and documents;
(c) enabling self-expression and freedom of expression by all;
(d) empowering providers and users to explain and defend their interests;
(e) acknowledging: each other's needs and situation; the potential of as well as limits to action;
(f) proper representation of users and providers at all levels of discussion and decision making.

For the child-focused services likely to remain a key feature of EPS, few would deny the paramountcy of the rights and interests of the child. In that connection, it is suggested that the underpinning right to be incorporated into rights principles is indeed that of the child.

The United Nations Convention on the Rights of the Child, passed in 1989, entered into international law in September 1990 and by the early part of 1991 had been signed by sixty countries, not including the United Kingdom. The Convention provides a universal framework, which could be adapted to fit particular children's services. Of the fifty-four articles, a number are of special relevance to an educational psychology service. These are:

Article 2   Non-discrimination
Article 3   Best interests
Article 5   Parental guidance
Article 12   Children's right to express an opinion
Article 13   Freedom of expression
Article 16   Protection of privacy
Article 18   Parental responsibility
Article 19   Protection from abuse and neglect

Article 23   Handicapped children and rights
Article 28   The right to education
Article 29   The aims of education
Article 30   Children of minorities and indigenous populations.

Other relevant articles deal with: separation from parents (Article 9), protection of children without families (Article 20), adoption (Article 21), health and health services (Article 24), periodic review of placement (Article 25) and administration of juvenile justice (Article 40). Some of these rights are now covered by the Children Act 1989 (and see Chapters 10 and 11 in Section III).

For an educational psychology service to incorporate the views and rights of children into its stated provisions would in fact be consistent with the review of children's rights currently being undertaken by a substantial number of local education authorities in connection with the United Nations Convention. (For the availability of the Convention see 'References' under Amnesty International.)

GUARANTEEING QUALITY IN EDUCATIONAL PSYCHOLOGY SERVICES

The framing of principles for services is an idea that is gaining credibility (Hanvey and Russell, 1990), for a public statement of principle can be a yardstick against which to measure quality. The measurement of quality service is inherent in the Education Reform Act 1988 and made explicit through the mechanisms of the National Curriculum and assessment systems. Quality assurance and quality control are nowadays perceived as a bedrock of any service in the public and private domains, but the means for defining, achieving and guaranteeing quality are by no means agreed.

Promises of quality are part of advertising rhetoric and all of us, as consumers who are bombarded with choice, face the task of trying to assess and differentiate between goods and services. But whereas manufacturers of goods are accountable to their shareholders and employees, psychologists peddling their wares in education are and should be subject to public scrutiny. The public is here defined as follows:

(a)   the children who are recipients or targets of actions and interventions by psychologists;
(b)   their parents, who may or may not exercise choice about the applications of psychology to their children;
(c)   teachers who may use psychological principles and practices in their own work or who work alongside psychologists;
(d)   schools' governing bodies, which may employ psychologists in the future;
(e)   professional organizations concerned to maintain standards of professional competence;
(f)   society, which funds higher education and academic and professional training.

What is not being questioned here is the undoubted fact that educational psychologists in the main have striven to provide high-quality service. But these questions are pertinent: what constitutes quality and how can it be demonstrated, measured and maintained?

Put very simply, what services users and a wider public would want to know and have guarantees about is that:

[handwritten margin note: ed psychs are accountable to :]

(a)   educational psychologists do what they say they do;

(b)   what they say they do is open to inspection and verification: that their methods, their 'tools of the trade', are available and their procedures explained;

(c)   when they write about what they do in letters and reports, these are readily available to all concerned.

It is then expected of a particular profession or occupation to set and monitor its own standards (see Royal College of Nursing Health Visitor Standards, 1990). As far as the practice of educational psychology is concerned, a range of mechanisms for describing and tracking professional performance has been piloted and applied. Some of these, like the EPS Annual Report to Committee, have been standard in some LEAs for years; others, like appraisal schemes, are more recent and echo the moves within education to adopt teacher appraisal, now of course to become widespread and mandatory. Yet others, like performance indicators (Fitz-Gibbon, 1990), are emerging and are contentious (and see Chapter 8); unresolved and perhaps unresolvable issues are to do with the balance between an indicator (facts, descriptive data) and an outcome (the criterion of effectiveness being the number of referrals or formal assessments processed by a service in a given year). All these measures provide a system of quality checks and balances, as do codes of practice that encompass the ethical basis for professional conduct (a theme taken up within European perspectives in the final chapter).

There is, then, greater awareness of the need for guarantees of standards of performance and accountability of professional activity at all levels of the profession, as Table 1.1 illustrates. The activities denote a mix of traditional and recent applications.

These various measures serve a variety of different purposes for the educational psychology services concerned, but have been largely discrete measures. It is certainly compatible with views of educational psychology services as organizations, analogous to those in other services as well as to those in industry and commerce, to expect them now to develop strategies towards ensuring and maintaining quality, in other words 'total quality control' (Fox, 1991).

But would it be equally apposite for educational psychology services to go as far as adopting or adapting the British Standards Institution Quality Assurance Scheme known as BS 5750 (see 'References' under BSI)? The standard was issued in 1979 for

Table 1.1 *Guaranteeing Quality: Examples of Extant and Emerging Practice*

Source	Example
Association of Educational Psychologists	• Code of practice
British Psychological Society	• Register of chartered psychologists • Code of conduct
Training courses in the UK	• Review and accreditation (via BPS) • Course brochure
Educational Psychology Services	• Aims, objectives, policy • Appraisal scheme • Annual report • Brochures • Development plans • Performance indicators • Product portfolio • Mission statement • Quality circles

manufacturing industry initially, but has developed over the years into services and has recently been updated for professional work, including education and training. Its acceptability and use are now widespread in the international community. The standard specifies the procedures and criteria to ensure that products or services meet customers' requirements. Its procedures are certainly commercially focused, but a number of them would apply to any service; for example, developing quality systems, reviewing management responsibility, record keeping, conducting internal quality audits and so on.

At a seminar organized by the National Association of Principal Educational Psychologists in October 1990, which was conducted by a consultancy firm, this list of hypothetical benefits from introducing quality assurance systems in educational psychology services was postulated:

(a)   establishing a good quality standard and continuous improvement in efficiency of the service;
(b)   providing a sound basis for training and development of employees;
(c)   ensuring understanding by employees of the aims and methods of the service;
(d)   providing an excellent marketing and public relations tool;
(e)   potentially putting educational psychological services in the forefront of good quality management within local authorities;
(f)   taking a recommended first step in the introduction of total quality management.

THE RELATIONSHIP BETWEEN PSYCHOLOGY AND EDUCATION: A QUESTION OF ALLEGIANCE?

A number of 'psychologies' underpin and inform the contributions to this book, but because the contexts are mostly (but not in all cases) educational, it may not be an easy task to identify which aspects of applied psychology within education are derived from the ostensible major, primary discipline of psychology. Also, it is a concomitant part of growing professional experience that the original 'psychological' knowledge and understanding becomes refined or adapted or overlaid by perspectives and practices from allied branches (see Chapter 7), and that a feature of accruing specialist expertise is that the professional has to become selective about information and skill acquisition. Specialism in the early years/special needs area will call for quite specific sources of knowledge about theory and research in child development and early childhood education, as well as for core educational psychology knowledge, to cite just one example. Miller (1989) found that a number of educational psychologists he surveyed who use behavioural approaches saw the psychology that informed their interventions as deriving at least partly from other paradigms.

To what extent does or should it matter that practice is derived from a diversity of theory and research sources? Certainly it has been perceived by educational psychologists themselves as a dilemma. Bardon (in D'Amato and Dean, 1989) expresses the conflict thus: 'To be a psychologist and to be in schools is described as being a "border provincial" required to speak the language of both psychology and education while often regarded by each as belonging to the other' (p. 2). Furthermore, it may be the case that the diluted psychology taught to student teachers in training establishments trivializes hard-won psychological insights and findings from empirical work, and conveys or perpetuates the impression that psychology is a weak, derived discipline based largely on common sense. Also, in 'giving psychology away' lightly to intending or practising teachers, there is the danger of giving an impression that the findings are not only pat but cut and dried. As Francis observed (1985), 'it is widely acknowledged that in any scientific enterprise the findings are no more than tested hypotheses still open to further testing' (p. 175).

Jones and Sayer (1988) are sceptical about the impact of psychology and psychologists in schools and propose reformulations that will help to make school and children-applied psychology, pertinent to teaching, learning and theory, raise its credibility. Powell and Solity (1990) critically assess the applications of various types of psychology, most notably behavioural approaches, and their reformulations propose an encompassing model that embraces teachers and educational psychologists as equals in processes of reflection leading to joint action.

What might be a distinctive contribution of psychology in and to education is explored and challenged by Norwich (1988), who examines what is 'psychological' about 'psychological advice' (with reference to the formal assessment procedures which are part of the Education Act 1981) as opposed to 'educational advice'. This particular example has gained especial poignancy with the advent of the requirement under the Education Reform Act 1988 and Circular 22/89 that children's statements of need must be related to the National Curriculum. This requirement exposes the erstwhile and continuing practice on the part of at least some educational psychologists of relying on standardized assessment as their 'psychological advice'. While a significant number of educational psychologists have reappraised and are reappraising their assessment practice in the light of the National Curriculum (Mallon and Tee.1991), it remains the case that, from the outside, applications of psychology appear diverse, unarticulated and unquestioned.

Another source of unease in this whole area of the relationship of psychology to education is the dissonance between the status of academic educational psychology and that of applied or practitioner-based educational psychology. The simplistic stereotypes each 'side' has of the other include charges of irrelevance and remoteness (towards academically inspired, hypothesis-testing, empirical work) and irresponsibility (towards the 'loose' paradigms employed by practising educational psychology). A publication which epitomizes the communication gulf is the Claxton *et al.* pamphlet (1985).

Wittrock's proposed solution (Wittrock and Farley, 1989) to what has been an endemic issue is that 'Lasting improvements in practice will continue to come from advances in theory and models that are applied, evaluated and revised in empirical research conducted in realistic educational settings' (p. 75). In fact, educational psychologists would heartily endorse a blueprint based on this formulation. Indeed, those who gave evidence to the Summerfield Committee (1968) stressed that their qualifications and training should be used in these ways, and they bemoaned the fact that their other activities and externally imposed demands on their time precluded research time.

The situation remains much the same now, despite an increase in the amount of project-based work. For until employers (and who will they be in the future?) acknowledge and pay for the distinctive contribution educational psychologists can make in terms of Wittrock's formulation, and perceive that they can be key agents in 'altering the variables' (Bloom, 1979), the ambiguities of what is the right and proper allegiance towards psychology and/or education will remain.

TRAINING TO PRACTISE EDUCATIONAL PSYCHOLOGY

Theory and practice dimensions and the notion of allegiance are of course directly relevant to educational psychology training courses, whose organizers do not, with few exceptions (Gray and Lunt, 1990), write publicly about training issues. The ambiguity of the allegiance described above is further evinced by the fact that the fourteen such academically based training courses in the United Kingdom are pretty well divided equally between being located within psychology and education departments.

The nationally agreed Core Curriculum, last revised in 1990 and currently once more under revision, reflects these joint orientations but with a predominance towards psychology as the major parent discipline. The Core Curriculum contains these elements (headings which are of course further subdivided to give detail under each heading):

(a)   personal skills and communication;
(b)   collecting information and assessment;
(c)   intervention approaches;
(d)   disabling conditions and special educational needs;
(e)   professional practice;
(f)   research and evaluation;
(g)   issues in child development.

Equal opportunities perspectives are expected to inform each curriculum area.

The Core Curriculum statement acknowledges the particular strengths, interests, expertise and specialisms that each course has, and indeed over the years different courses have become associated with certain orientations and innovations. Within such a small profession, whose members numbered approximately fifteen hundred at the last count (carried out in 1990 by the Association of Educational Psychologists), transmission of information, and application of ideas and innovative practice often first tried out on the training courses by trainees and their tutors (who are always experienced educational psychologists), spread quickly. There is plenty of evidence of such cross-fertilization in the 'house' journals, and many trainee educational psychologists' dissertations provide evidence, too, of cooperative work. Also, within this framework of training course–educational psychology service collaboration, a notable development of the 1980s was the growth of professional development opportunities for practising educational psychologists. This has often led to significant curriculum and intervention initiatives, the production of inservice training materials, and new assessment and appraisal approaches.

Although this is not a book about the training of educational psychologists, the writers hope that its subject matter and the fact that a number of them are closely associated with this training will testify to the interaction between training and the field. Moreover, they hope to cast light on training course aims and goals and the fact that training courses always strive to provide a relevant, broad and balanced curriculum.

In recent years much has been achieved corporately, by course tutors, in overhauling assessment and supervision practice, but at the present time there are a number of major challenges for training courses to address if the profession is to continue to be provided with quality graduates. The necessity for courses to respond to the philosophy and provisions of the Education Reform Act 1988 and the Children Act 1989 is obvious enough, and these major pieces of legislation pervade this volume. But the possibility of the independence or privatization of the educational psychology services may also have a profound impact on training courses at an ideological level, which in turn will impact on issues of provision, resourcing and consumerism, and reverberate in fundamental social policy issues (Zigler *et al.*, 1983).

Another challenge to the profession, to which training courses will have to respond, is *NCVQS* the government requirement for the National Vocational Qualifications framework to encompass professional qualifications and training. Conceptualized into a number of hierarchical, sequential levels of increasing and demonstrable competencies, this government-initiated national scheme is intended to raise and harmonize standards of occupational and vocational training (see 'References' under NCVQ). At the time of writing, in 1991, it is highly likely that there will be major repercussions for the structure and organization of educational psychology courses if they have to adopt this system, with only too evident implications for practising educational psychologists themselves. During 1991 a standing committee appointed within the British Psychological Society has been set up with a brief to examine the applicability of the competencies framework for educational psychology. That the notion of compressing and organizing knowledge and skills into sequential units of learning is contentious, if not fraught with pitfalls, is attested in Kelly *et al.* (1990).

These developments have, too, to be considered in the encompassing nexus of the European single market, which is explored in the final chapter.

MODELS OF SERVICE DELIVERY: IN WHOSE BEST INTERESTS?   *accountability*

Most of the contributors to this book describe or anticipate a range of educational psychology practices that would endure irrespective of their sources of income or employers. Only four or five years ago such debates about future prospects in this vein would have seemed inconceivable. Yet Sutton (1981) foresaw temptations for practitioners and parents in having alternative or competing services, and in his discussion pre-empted a number of the conflicts and paradoxes now so exercising the profession:

> Those whose social consciences are offended by such private trading might reflect that the harsh economies of such a market-place could introduce a degree of direct accountability and reality-testing that is not apparent in the general run of public practice, and that the demands engendered might prove a useful spur for psychological practice as a whole. (p. 157)

The debate and the trends throw into stark relief the very basis of and justification for the existence of a service that has always been free for users. The individualized service that educational psychologists have traditionally offered to children, their families and teachers has lain at the core of the provision. Yet at a macro level educational psychologists acting within a service structure could offer intervention strategies designed to reach more people, and yet again are on record as having participated in preventive approaches. Portage is a supreme example of psychological participation in a preven- *PORTAGE* tive-intervention strategy that operates at all levels within a given community and at the same time empowers the parents whose children the scheme is designed to support.

That educational psychologists have engaged less in preventive psychological approaches (Felner *et al.*, 1983) or action research (Rapoport, 1987) than they would have wanted is due less to their inclinations than to public perceptions about and expectations of their role and function. Ever since the first school psychologists functioned in the United Kingdom the expectation was that they would be concerned with 'damage limitation', remedial and curative approaches to identified deviant and pathological conditions. That legacy, while diffused into a positive, benevolent conception of 'special educational needs', has never been shaken off successfully by educational psychologists themselves.

So we have reached a point in professional history, in the early 1990s, where the funding and employment patterns could go in a number of ways. There have always been a tiny handful of independent, consultancy-based educational psychology services in existence, and their numbers are now growing. We could envisage a range of models and, depending upon one's ideological viewpoint, each could be characterized as a 'good fit' or a 'worst scenario'.

The options appear to be those as set out along the continuum in Figure 1.1, which describes a gradation from a 'stay as you are', steady-state model of centrally funded educational psychology services to a free-floating, totally privatized agency model.

It is impossible to predict whether or not any or all these models could coexist, in part because the future of LEAs themselves is uncertain. The prospect of alternative and probably competing models has been greeted gloomily by some, cautiously by others and positively by a number of educational psychologists (Farrell, 1989). The inherent issues and dichotomies are addressed by Thorburn (1990), who considers that coexistence is possible and for some psychologists an expedient solution to problems of combining childcare with part-time employment.

There would need to be extensive, open professional and public debate about the many issues. But the key question for a profession which has such a pedigree of public service is the one posed above: 'in whose best interests'?

The traditional view of independent agencies is that their workers are and have to be motivated by at least breaking even financially, at best making a profit. So wariness about this model stems from a belief that such a service, unlike the centrally funded model, cannot operate altruistically with a client's best interests central to the enterprise.

Such dichotomies are self-evidently simplistic, even to those committed to public service ideologies. Perhaps we need to clarify the salient features of the two models at

Public service

- Retained by LEA on basis of 100 per cent funding

- Partial delegation: funded part by LEAs, part by schools and others buying in services

- Becomes an agency, on contract to LEAs/schools, and therefore free and accessible to parents

- Becomes an independent, private consultancy, selling services in a competitive market

- Dissolved: educational psychologists operate solo or in consortia

Privatized service

Figure 1.1 *Future directions in educational psychology services.*

the extremities of the continuum outlined in Figure 1.1. The lists presented below are hardly intended to be definitive or inclusive; rather they are offered as a stimulus, a contribution to the debate on future directions of service delivery. There is no particular order or sequence to the listed features.

The features of a public educational psychology service are:

(a)   It is free to the client/user.
(b)   It can offer a range of services.
(c)   It offers security to the employees.
(d)   It has little or no competition.
(e)   Its independence is not guaranteed (so there is a potential conflict of loyalties).
(f)   It has extensive knowledge of local provision and child settings.
(g)   It has ready access to other agencies.
(h)   It has coherence and continuity.

The features of a private educational psychology service are:

(a)   It is a fee-charging service.
(b)   It has independence.
(c)   It can offer a range of services, particularly in consultancy and training.
(d)   It is in competition with other services.
(e)   It does not guarantee job security.
(f)   It is not necessarily familiar with local provision and child settings.
(g)   It is a consumer-driven service.

The lists are offered as neutrally as is possible, with the potential overlay of value-laden terminology as reduced as I can make it. For it will be evident that:

(a)   there is overlap between the lists;
(b)   readers will interpret each feature as positive or negative depending on their existing values.

If the criterion of, say, a child's best interests were to be paramount, each feature (the parts) of each list (the sum) could be tested against that criterion.

Several writers in D'Amato and Dean (1989) look ahead in constructive and optimistic mood to the prospects of 'school psychologists' (the American term equivalent to the UK educational psychologist) moving in greater numbers into private practice, and indeed, diversifying into working in other settings (higher education, business, etc.) from the invaluable springboard of their school-based practice, which is seen to confer particular skills that can generalize to other settings.

INTERNATIONAL PERSPECTIVES ON THE PRACTICE OF EDUCATIONAL PSYCHOLOGY

At a time when the reality of a single European market is upon us (and see the final chapter) and when, largely thanks to mass and instant communication and travel opportunities, the world shrinks to the manageable dimensions of a global village, it becomes less of a luxury than a necessity to embrace the perspectives of other models of service delivery. Moreover, the expectations deriving from equal opportunities policies make it professionally and ethically imperative to acknowledge other practices.

Visits, exchanges, conferences and articles are of course the main means of finding out. But what I advocate goes beyond the simplicity of recommending these obvious fora. We need now to go further than taking anthropological and comparative stances towards exploring, and discover commonalities and differences in:

- child and family policies.
- public versus private provision.
- effective means of service delivery.
- education as a national priority.

so that, internationally and corporately, we can work to achieve the provision of effective child-focused services, especially educational psychology services (or their equivalent).

A longitudinal international perspective is available, as we have data from Wall's (1956) UNESCO survey we can build on. Another way of conceptualizing changes in psychological practice over time, within a comparative framework, is to adopt a stage approach, such as is outlined in Saigh and Oakland (1989) by those editors in Chapter 1. Within this global perspective they go on to identify a number of universal problem areas facing professional (school) psychologists, such as status and the inadequacy of technology and back-up services, and move on to anticipate future needs and trends. They foresee expansion and diversification of professional activities and responsibilities as hinted at earlier in this chapter, and justify their stance by asserting that 'This expanded focus is needed to bring about a better understanding of the cultural, social and political factors that strongly influence the delivery and acceptance of services' (p. 20).

For educational psychologists in the United Kingdom these findings are at one and the same time a reassurance and a challenge. Our vision of our own future can be influenced and guided by the one fact that, as educational psychology trainers and practitioners, we have more in common with others across the world than divides us.

REFERENCES

Amnesty International (n.d.) *The United Nations Convention on the Rights of the Child.* Amnesty International, 99–119 Rosebery Avenue, London EC1R 4RE.

Bloom, B. (1979) *Alterable Variables: The New Direction in Educational Research.* Edinburgh: The Scottish Council for Research in Education.

BSI (British Standards Institution) Quality Assurance Executive Guide (to BS 5750), PO Box 375, Milton Keynes, Bucks.

Cameron, J. and Sturge-Moore, L. (1990) *Ordinary, Everyday Families—A Human Rights Issue.* Under Fives Project, MENCAP London Division, 115 Golden Lane, London EC1Y 0TJ.

Chazan, M., Moore, T., Williams, P. and Wright, J. (1974) *The Practice of Educational Psychology.* Harlow: Longman.

Claxton, G., Swann, W., Salmon, P., Walkerdine, V., Jacobsen, B. and White, J. (1985) *Psychology and Schooling: What's the Matter?* Bedford Way Papers 25. London: Institute of Education, London University.

D'Amato, R. and Dean, R. (eds) (1989) *The School Psychologist in Nontraditional Settings.* London: Lawrence Erlbaum.

DECP (Division of Educational and Child Psychology) (1980) *Psychological Services for Children in England and Wales.* Occasional Papers, 4 (1 and 2).

Farrell, P. (1989) 'Educational Psychology Services: Crisis or Opportunity?', *The Psychologist*, 2 (6), 240–1.

Felner, R., Jason, L., Moritsugu, J. and Farber, S. (eds) (1983) *Preventive Psychology; Theory, Research and Practice*. Oxford: Pergamon.

Fitz-Gibbon, C. (ed.) (1990) *Performance Indicators*. BERA Dialogues, no. 2. Clevedon: Multi-lingual Matters.

Fox, M. (1991) 'The EPS—a quality service', *Educational Psychology in Practice*, 6 (4), 229–33.

Francis, H. (ed.) (1985) *Learning to Teach—Psychology in Teacher Training*. Lewes: The Falmer Press.

Freeman, A. and Topping, K. (1976) 'What do you expect of educational psychologists?', *Journal of the Association of Educational Psychologists*, 4 (3).

Gilham, B. (ed.) (1978) *Reconstructing Educational Psychology*. London: Croom Helm.

Gray, P. and Lunt, I. (eds) (1990) 'Training for Professional Practice', issue of *Educational and Child Psychology*, 7 (3).

Hanvey, C. and Russell, P. (1990) *Children with Special Needs*. Workbook 4, Working with Children and Young People, K254. Milton Keynes: Open University Press.

HMI Report (1990) *Educational Psychology Services in England, 1988–1989*. London: Department of Education and Science.

Jones, N. and Frederickson, N. (eds) (1990) *Refocusing Educational Psychology*. Lewes: The Falmer Press.

Jones, N. and Sayer, J. (eds) (1988) *Management and the Psychology of Schooling*. Lewes: The Falmer Press.

Kelly, D., Payne, C. and Warwick, J. (1990) *Making National Vocational Qualifications Work for Social Care: Can there be a Context-sensitive Approach to National Vocational Qualifications?* London: National Institute of Social Work.

Mallon, F. and Tee, G. (1991) 'Psychologists and the National Curriculum—identifying relevant skills', *Educational Psychology in Practice*, 16 (4), 187–91.

Miller, A. (1989) 'Paradigms lost: what theory informs educational psychologists in their use of behavioural approaches?', *Educational Psychology in Practice*, 5 (3), 143–8.

NCVQ (National Council for Vocational Qualifications) 222 Euston Road, London NW1 2BZ.

Norwich, B. (1988) 'Educational psychology services in LEAs: what future?', in Jones, N. and Sayer, J. (eds), *Management and the Psychology of Schooling*. Lewes, The Falmer Press, 107–18.

Powell, M. and Solity, J. (1990) *Teachers in Control: Cracking the Code*. London: Routledge.

Quicke, J. (1982) *The Cautious Expert*. Milton Keynes: Open University Press.

Rapoport, R. (1987) *New Interventions for Children and Youth: Action Research Approaches*. Cambridge: Cambridge University Press.

Reason, R. and Webster, A. (1990) 'Developing a product portfolio for psychological services', *Educational Psychology in Practice*, 6 (1), 4–13.

Rieser, R. and Mason, M. (1990) *Disability Equality in the Classroom: A Human Rights Issue*. Inner London Education Authority: contact 23 Walford Road, London N16 8EF.

Royal College of Nursing (1990) *Standards of Care for Health Visiting*, RCN, Harrow, Middlesex HA1 2AX.

Saigh, P. and Oakland, P. (eds) (1989) *International Perspectives on Psychology in the Schools*. London: Lawrence Erlbaum.

Summerfield, A. (Chair) (1968) *Psychologists in Education Services*. London: HMSO.

Sutton, A. (1981) 'Whose psychology? Some issues in the social control of psychological practice', in MacPherson, I. and Sutton, A. (eds), *Reconstructing Psychological Practice*. London: Croom Helm, 145–65.

Thorburn, L. (1990) 'LEA *v.* private practice: a false dichotomy', *Educational Psychology in Practice*, 6 (1), 19–26.

Wall, W. D. (1956) *Psychological Services for Schools*. New York: New York University Press for UNESCO.

Watts, P. (1990) 'Clarifying service aims', in *Developing Effective Services: In Response to the HMI Report*. Summary of study day on 26 September 1990, organized by West Midlands Branch of the AEP, Dudley LEA. Contact A. Facherty, EPS.

Wittrock, M. and Farley, F. (eds) (1989) *The Future of Educational Psychology*. London: Lawrence Erlbaum.

Wolfendale, S., Lunt, I. and Carroll, T. (eds) (1988) 'Educational psychologists working in multicultural communities: training and practice', *Educational and Child Psychology*, 5 (2).

Zigler, E., Kagan, S. and Klugman, E. (eds) (1983) *Children, Families and Government: Perspectives on American Social Policy*. Cambridge: Cambridge University Press.

Section I

Focus on Individuals

Chapter 2

Making a Difference for Children: The Educational Psychologist as Empowerer of Problem-Solving Alliances

Allan Sigston

ECONOMICS, ETHICS AND CASEWORK

Educational psychologists work within an increasingly financially devolved and accountable environment and as a consequence the profession is being presented with some crucial ethical dilemmas. The ideology of consumer forces shaping provision is firmly at the centre of the Education Reform Act 1988 and although it might be mitigated under various scenarios it seems unlikely that it will disappear. The concept of the consumer encompasses two normally assumed and thus unquestioned features: firstly, that the consumer is the beneficiary of the goods or services provided; secondly, that the consumer pays for the goods or services received. The prospect of schools paying for educational psychology services notionally on behalf of individual pupils raises thorny questions about whose interests the psychologist will be representing. If there is conflict between the needs of the paymaster and the needs of the child it seems inevitable that the former will carry undue weight.

It is argued here that there is an inherent tension in the caseworking relationships that educational psychologists have with schools. Quite properly, headteachers and governors must try to administer their schools so as to achieve a balance between limited resources and needs across the school as a whole. Individual children brought to the attention of educational psychologists are almost exclusively those that represent threats to this complex equilibrium by absorbing larger amounts of resources. It seems vital to acknowledge and respect these differences as one of the bases of an effective collaborative relationship, for schools are the most common medium in which educational psychologists seek to facilitate changes for children. It is equally apparent how compromised the position of the educational psychologist is if he or she is financially dependent on the school. As a consequence such moves sit uneasily alongside a fundamental tenet of the Children Act 1989, which places the needs of the child as paramount.

Where local education authorities (LEAs) employ educational psychologists without recourse to financial support from schools there is the potential for a free service to parents and children that avoids this obvious pitfall. If 'market forces' are to operate fairly in some alternative model then parents and children must be given at least equal weight to that of schools in determining the shape of educational psychology services.

The economics of service provision has focused attention usefully on the expectations of users and consumers of educational psychology services. These services are taking increasing account of these factors in offering their expertise. The issue for the 1990s seems to be how this can be achieved without subverting ethical goals that assert the primacy of children's needs.

THEORETICAL ISSUES IN CASEWORK

The discipline of psychology has seen its share of schisms: the early emphasis on the introspective study of mental events, Watson's redefinition of psychology as the science of behaviour, psychoanalytic and phenomenological theories. Contemporary psychologists might see themselves as humanistic, behaviouristic, social, analytical, phenomenological, cognitive or systemic, to name but a few. With each division the exponents have differentiated into further, more esoteric groups. For example, Mahoney and Lyddon (1988) report that there are at least twenty distinguishable cognitive therapies. Perhaps because psychology is still relatively young and has grown prolifically over the last century, there is little evidence of any of these schools of thought diminishing. Even a systematic attack on the poor predictive validity of Freudian analytical concepts within undergraduate courses has left them alive and well in the minds of therapists, literary critics, advertising executives and, indeed, the public at large. While opposing camps might argue about the validity of alternatives, those schools that continue to thrive must have certain merits that account for their continued viability as accounts of human affairs.

Like other professional applications of psychology, educational psychology includes practitioners that embrace all these viewpoints. Yet a consensus appears to have emerged (at least on pragmatic grounds) that educational psychologists can best assist in meeting the needs of individual children by indirect work, most usually through parents and teachers. This shift from direct contact with the client to assisting an intermediary consultee mirrors changes that have taken place in other branches of professional psychology, particularly mental health consultation (Caplan, 1970). The attractions of indirect client casework for most educational psychologists seem to be a mixture of pragmatism, based on assumptions of economy and efficiency, and a belief that those with greatest contact with the child are best placed to effect change.

INDIRECT CASEWORK: THE CENTRALITY OF THE CONSULTEE'S CONSTRUCTION OF THE PROBLEM

Intrinsic within the indirect approach are deep phenomenological issues. Many educational psychologists carrying out such consultations make the philosophical assumption of dualism. That is, they start from a presumption that there is an external, objective problem that the consultee directly senses; therefore it is possible within the consultation to 'get to the truth of the matter' and offer objectively correct solutions.

Alternatively, constructionist theorists, who include psychologists as diverse as Piaget, and Kelly (1955), would argue that the consultee seeks meaning in the child's behaviour by relating it to the consultee's own knowledge structures or belief systems. During the consultation it is encoded and communicated to the consultant, who in turn seeks meaning in the consultee's account. The process of seeking meaning, assimilating input into current structures or accommodating through the development of new ones becomes the basis of the consultation. However one might label these processes, the argument is apparent that up to and during the consultation the substance of discussion is undergoing profound transformations and the focus is not the child's behaviour but the consultee's interpretation of it.

Other branches of psychology lead to similar conclusions about the centrality of the consultee's cognitions. Stevens (1980) offers strong evidence on the extent to which racial stereotypes influence judgments of behaviour. She asked groups of US school psychologists, teachers and parents to rate identical behaviour enacted on film by visibly Anglo-American, Mexican-American and Afro-American children for positiveness and negativeness. Overall the behaviours of the Anglo-American child were rated most positively and least negatively, with the converse true for the Afro-American child. Another manipulation involving a concocted biography that indicated social class suggested a further main effect favouring middle over working class. Perhaps the only comfort for psychologists from this study was that their observations were the least biased. Despite the demands of such an experiment for socially desirable or at least more objective appraisal, the findings support the widely held view that stereotypes significantly influence our judgments of others.

Hargreaves, Hester and Mellor (1975) conducted a qualitative study of teachers' views of deviance in secondary schools. They describe three stages in the development of a stereotype; speculation, when teachers seek similarities between the pupil and other pupils they know or have known; elaboration, when incidents are sought to confirm speculations; stabilization, when teachers feel they know the pupil and are confident in making predictions about how he or she will behave. Like other interactionist theorists they propose that the setting of expectations in this way is instrumental in shaping the self-concept and behaviour of the person being stereotyped.

The burgeoning field of attribution theory has suggested that pupil behaviours that intrude on teachers' needs (such as 'disruptiveness') tend to be attributed with controllability and intentionality on the part of the pupil. Behaviours that are seen as interfering more with pupils' needs (such as social withdrawal) are more likely to be seen as resulting from causes outside of pupils' control. This in turn appears to shape the 'helping' intentions of teachers along a disciplinary–pastoral continuum (for instance, Brophy and Rohrkemper, 1981).

Whichever way one approaches the problem of indirect casework it is clear that consultees' accounts and subsequent behaviour are dependent on their subjective understanding of the context. In some situations educational psychologists may be happy to minimize its significance. For example, consider the case of a child of nine who is a virtual non-reader. If a parent or mainstream class teacher were to express concern, the child's disparate level of achievement from his or her peers would provide relatively objective evidence of the severity of the problem. There are tests of various kinds that could be used to verify this further. In this instance an educational psychologist might make a contribution at a 'technical' level; for instance, by recommending a teaching strategy. In comparison, if a teacher were to seek a consultation about the 'disruptive' behaviour of a child who had joined the class from overseas with little knowledge of

English or experience of schooling, there are a host of interpretive issues to consider for both the educational psychologist and the teacher.

Starting from a premise of the likely benefits of indirect casework, it is apparent that differing psychological theories lead us to similar conclusions about the importance of the consultee's subjective experience. This does not simply distort a 'real' problem but is as integral a part of the context as the observable behaviour of the child who is the subject of the consultation. This implies that the role of the educational psychologist must address the consultee's construction of the problem, and in many instances this will far outweigh the importance of any 'technical' contribution.

ONE MODEL OF CONSULTATION FOR EDUCATIONAL PSYCHOLOGISTS

Conoley and Conoley (1982) have elaborated Caplan's (1970) model of consultation for US schools psychologists' practice. Their concept of consultancy embraces the notion of indirect work with the qualities listed below:

(a)   Consultations are initiated by the consultee.
(b)   The consultee is free to accept or reject the service.
(c)   The service is confidential.
(d)   The consultation is seen as a collaboration of peers with complementary expertise.
(e)   Only work-related problems are dealt with.
(f)   There is an emphasis on primary prevention; that is, the prevention of difficulties arising in the first instance rather than remediation (Caplan, 1969).
(g)   The goals of the consultant are to: provide an objective viewpoint; extend the consultee's skills; extend the consultee's freedom of choice; increase the consultee's commitment to the consultee's choices.

Within this model the consultant is essentially a facilitator helping the consultee to reveal hitherto unrecognized options. There may be occasions when it would be appropriate for the consultant to offer expert knowledge but the emphasis is primarily on the consultee mobilizing his or her own resources and expertise.

There is no doubt that the model has many attractive features for educational psychologists. It can be argued that the beneficiaries of the service are the teachers in that it is aimed at working with their concerns. To this extent it would fit well with the idea of schools paying for educational psychology services. It recognizes the importance of the subjective experience of the consultee. It stresses the importance of the quality of the relationship between the educational psychologist and the consultee. The model is eclectic in that the consultant can draw on a wide range of theoretical frameworks. None the less, it is not difficult to identify troubling scenarios.

Suppose that an educational psychologist were consulted about a child showing severe self-injurious behaviours. It appears morally unsustainable to resolve the problem through allaying the anxiety that prompted the request for the consultation unless it is accompanied by an improvement in the child's predicament.

The issue is more starkly apparent in such an example, but it underlies all casework and illustrates one of the intrinsic difficulties of the educational psychologist's role. For in securing collaboration with a consultee the educational psychologist may encounter a problem of accountability in respect of the needs of the child (and see Chapter 5).

MANIFESTATIONS OF THE PROBLEM-SOLVING PARADIGM

At least superficially, the problem-solving paradigm seems to relate to the empirical approach to psychology. Although advocates represent diverse theoretical roots and the paradigm is evident in a variety of applied areas that include organizational change strategies (such as organization development: French and Bell, 1984), action research (for instance, Kemmis *et al.*, 1981) as well as client-centred work by educational psychologists. Proponents articulate the paradigm within their own frameworks, often with idiosyncratic vocabulary. It is argued here that all conform broadly to the following characteristics:

(a)   Frameworks consist of series of steps or phases that a consultant and consultee(s) work through.

(b)   While the numbers and labels of steps may vary they can be conceptually placed within three superordinate stages:
      Clarification is where a clearer articulation of consultees' concerns is sought;
      Intervention consists of the formulation and application of a set of actions designed to alleviate the problem(s).
      Evaluation involves assessing the efficacy of the intervention.

(c)   There are feedback loops whereby information collected may lead to returning the consultation to earlier stages.

Figure 2.1 describes a number of problem-solving frameworks illustrating these fundamental similarities.

Enthusiasts within educational psychology have tended to be most smitten by the content aspects of the problem-solving paradigm which are most often associated with *Behavioural* behavioural approaches. In the USA, Thomas and Walter (1973) specify fifteen steps in their model, including 'baseline of focal behaviour' (no. 5) and 'execution of the modification plan' (no. 10). While the terminology is somewhat softer, the eleven steps in the original Stratford and Cameron (1978) model still hint strongly at the authors' preferred framework; for example, 'Assist client to identify probable controlling conditions' (no. 5). *determining reinforcements...*

This can be contrasted with the process orientation of the paradigm used in organization development, initiated by Kurt Lewin. In this setting the paradigm is seen as useful in providing a focus for members of an organization, holding different perspectives on its functioning, to reach shared and more complete understanding. In this way responsibility for change remains with the organization's members and commitment to action is enhanced. The longer-term social and psychological consequences may often be more significant than the specific outcomes of the exercise.

It could be assumed that from both the content and process positions such frameworks would be fundamental to the purposeful resolution of problems and as such would form the basis of educational psychologists' practice, but the evidence would suggest otherwise.

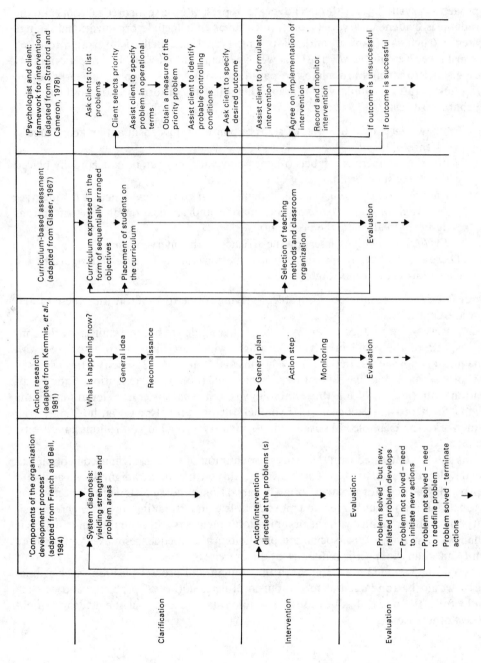

Figure 2.1 *Examples of the problem-solving paradigm.*

THE PROBLEM-SOLVING PARADIGM AND EDUCATIONAL PSYCHOLOGY PRACTICE

From Burt's employment as the first educational psychologist for the London County Council the profession's responsibilities have been closely tied to the allocation of special educational provision. The 1944 Education Act defined a number of categories of child who were believed to require forms of education that differed significantly from those made for the majority of 'normal' children. The need for local education authorities was for divining these special 'types' of child, who were thought to constitute approximately 2 per cent of the population. At first this was considered a health matter, and hence the province of doctors. Over time it came to be seen as more of a psycho-educational problem. It involved *The Discovery of Children Requiring Special Education and the Assessment of their Needs*, the title of a Department of Education and Science circular to local education authorities in 1975 that proved a watershed in the development of the profession.

Educational psychologists' pivotal position in respect of recommendations for entry to designated special schools led to a similar, and perhaps more influential, 'gate-keeping' role to a substratum of alternative units and special tuition arrangements that proliferated particularly during the 1970s.

The Warnock Report (DES, 1978), and its distantly related offspring the 1981 Education Act, enshrined the notion of provision based on the unique needs of individuals rather than categories of handicap. The Warnock Report asserted that all children had needs and that these are related to the child's context as well as to her or his abilities. It was suggested that as many as 20 per cent of pupils might be regarded as having special educational needs at some stage of their educational careers. This figure seems as scientifically precise as the length of the proverbial piece of string; Gipps, Goldstein and Gross (1985) provide an interesting historical analysis illuminating its dubious roots. The popular misinterpretation of 'Warnock' philosophy has led to a search not only for the 2 per cent, but also the remaining 18 per cent that are said to be residing in our mainstream schools. The point in respect of educational psychology practice is that the philosophical shifts that have taken place have, as yet, left functional aspects of the role virtually unaffected. This continues to be mainly concerned with defining those children considered to be 'worthy' of resources over and above what is 'normally' found in schools. As a result, in many LEAs the subtext of the majority of discussions between educational psychologists and school staff is about access to resources. The dynamic of this relationship tends toward referrers portraying problems as too difficult to resolve within the prevailing school context, rather than considering how interventions might be implemented to the benefit of the child. At best this role might be viewed as targeting limited resources on the most needy; at worst (in the case of special schooling) it may be seen as the disposal of more awkward or demanding pupils from the mainstream (Barton and Tomlinson, 1984).

While it may be possible to describe this role in more positive terms, most educational psychologists would agree that substantial amounts of casework time are allotted to dealing with resource or placement issues. Many educational psychologists would report it taking up most of their working week. There are reasons to suppose that this situation may deteriorate following the progressive implementation of the 'market-orientated' 1988 Education Reform Act (Gersch *et al.*, 1990). It is difficult to conceive of this work as being more than peripheral to the process of resolving problems.

Educational psychologists have made significant contributions at a national level on issues as diverse as parent involvement (for instance, Wolfendale, 1989), child involvement (for instance, Gersch and Cutting, 1985), pre-school intervention (for instance, Cameron, 1982), curriculum-based assessment (for instance, Thomas and Feiler, 1988), peer tutoring (for instance, Topping, 1988) and integration (for instance, Galloway and Goodwin, 1987). At the local level educational psychologists have done much to carry through these ideas in debate, inservice training and contributions to policy making. None the less an overall analysis suggests that educational psychologists spend much of their time trapped in a set of responsibilities and modes of working that are often unsatisfying and, at times, may undermine attempts to ameliorate difficulties for children and young people. Working within the problem-solving paradigm seems to offer educational psychologists an opportunity to break out of this cycle. Its intrinsic attractions include its clear purposefulness and accessibility to parents and young people. It is collaborative and cumulative rather than fragmented. It aligns with the post-Warnock tenets of special needs philosophy, through stressing individual needs in their context (rather than pathology) and what Bloom (1979) has termed 'alterable variables' that can engender change.

Perhaps the most compelling attribute of the problem-solving paradigm is its accountability. Accountability is apparent within cases where the contributing agents will each have agreed responsibilities. Accountability is also possible across cases in permitting an audit of the types of concern and action taken by educational psychologists, institutions or individuals working within them. This allows educational psychologists and co-workers to be more reflective about their practice and biases.

THE CONCEPT OF THE PROBLEM-SOLVING ALLIANCE

The problem-solving paradigm operationalized with teachers seems to have an inbuilt bias for action on behalf of the child which the consultation approach alone lacks. It could be criticized, however, for a restrictive view of needs and problems, given that these could be examined solely from the teacher's viewpoint. Some educational psychologists have sought to deal with this by dispensing with the idea of a single consultee in favour of a collective, including the person expressing the concern with others who have a special interest in the child's wellbeing. These could be regarded as members of a problem-solving alliance (adapted from Albert Kushlick's notion of a 'therapeutic alliance': see Sigston, 1987).

The most obvious members of the alliance in respect of school-based concerns are the child's teacher(s) and parents and the child himself or herself (to the extent to which he or she is able to participate). The membership of the alliance can change over time and people's contributions (including that of the educational psychologist) can wax and wane.

As the problem-solving alliance works through the stages of clarification, intervention and evaluation, the fora naturally prompt discussion of judgments made by participants as they grapple with achieving some shared meaning. For example, a teacher's concerns about a child's 'disruptiveness' would usually require considerable elucidation and explanation in the course of clarifying the difficulty with a parent, an educational psychologist and possibly the child herself or himself.

This mode of working seems to combine the advantages of working with those closest to the child, while valuing the subjective experiences of participants, within an accountable framework. In particular, the active involvement of all the members of the alliance encourages 'triangulation' on the needs and difficulties of the child (and thus a greater reassurance that it is these that have primacy), and solidarity about the goals of intervention. It may even hold out the promise of positive effects on relationships that will transcend the immediate situation.

A FRAMEWORK FOR THE 1990s

The following features extrapolated from the Caplan (1969)/Conoley and Conoley (1982) consultation model could outline the nature and ground rules of a generally available casework service to schools in the 1990s, based on the concept of the problem-solving alliance:

(a) Where a concern is expressed about a child in school the service offered consists of a series of consultations framed within the problem-solving paradigm.

(b) Consultations take place with an alliance of people comprising the person expressing the concern and others with a direct responsibility for the child's wellbeing.

(c) Members of the alliance are free to leave at any time. *'wax e wane' - natural development*

(d) The focus of the consultations is the child's needs and difficulties and not those of the members of the alliance (although the child may be a member).

(e) The primary purpose of the consultations is to highlight what can be done in the future rather than what has happened in the past.

(f) Individuals may set the boundaries of confidentiality of information contributed during the consultation except where child protection is a clear issue.

(g) Members of the alliance are seen as peers with complementary expertise.

(h) The goals of the educational psychologist are to empower the alliance through: providing an outside viewpoint; extending skills; extending the members' freedom of choice; increasing their commitment to decisions.

A service offered within these parameters seems to have the marketing advantage of being both clearly defined and self-evidently purposeful. At the same time it secures ethical objectives.

THE CONTRIBUTION OF PSYCHOLOGICAL EXPERTISE

The difficulties in successfully working within this approach should not be underestimated. The issues under discussion by the alliance are likely to be highly emotionally charged. Much, though not necessarily all, of the work of the educational psychologist pertains to working with groups. Facilitating such a group through the problem-solving process cannot be a simple matter of objective bargaining. It requires considerable skill in promoting the growth of high-quality relationships, dealing with disparate constructions of the problems and securing commitment to action.

It is proposed that consultations of this type can be considered usefully at three overlapping levels that are illuminated by different theoretical schools of psychology. The significance of each of the levels varies according to the nature of the concerns being worked with, but it is postulated that all three will be evident in consultations carried out by effective practitioners. The purpose of the resumé that follows is not to give an exhaustive review of relevant psychology but to signal some especially fruitful areas to draw upon.

Objective application of the problem-solving paradigm

This is the extent to which the educational psychologist moves through discrete stages of her or his particular preferred model of the problem-solving paradigm (that is, the direction of the process). It draws mainly upon the rationalist and empirical traditions within psychology, perhaps more than on a specific body of knowledge. The notions of generalizing from theory or past experience and of generating and testing hypotheses are crucial and integral aspects of undergraduate psychology courses.

Critical skills for the educational psychologist are agenda setting and record keeping.

Facilitation of the consultation

This is the forming of high-quality relationships within the problem-solving alliance and the usage of appropriate techniques to assist the members of the consultation in exploring options and committing themselves to goals, action and evaluation. Counselling psychology provides a rich resource on how this may be facilitated at an interpersonal level. While the basis of counselling as a psychotherapeutic relationship between a designated counsellor or therapist and client is not directly applicable, there are numerous parallels.

C- Rogers

The personal qualities of effective non-directive counsellors outlined by Carl Rogers and subsequently refined by others seem to provide a basis for establishing rapport (Rogers, 1977; Truax and Carkhuff, 1967; Tyler, 1969). Egan (1990) has described a model for counselling that conceives of the counsellor as a 'skilled helper'. His approach is a further example of the problem-solving paradigm, which includes 'Identifying and Clarifying Problem Situations and Unused Opportunities', 'Developing Preferred Scenarios' and 'Helping Clients Act'. Egan addresses superordinate skills of communication like listening, focusing and summarizing. He articulates also a number of substeps that include specific techniques. Much of this model appears to translate relatively easily into the context of the problem-solving alliance.

Group ψ

In facilitating the consultation the educational psychologist is faced with dilemmas about the appropriate choices of techniques and moments to use them. Models based on individual consultations are unlikely to be totally adequate for this purpose, given the greater complexity of group interactions. Among others, Schein (1987, 1988) has explored the interpersonal process of groups and how this relates to the tasks undertaken. His work has been primarily geared toward managers and consultants working in business environments, but the difficulties of communication, utilizing disparate viewpoints and motivating group members in carrying out purposeful tasks are akin to those of the problem-solving alliance. For similar reasons many educational psychologists may find inspiration in family therapy theory.

Within the problem-solving alliance it is possible to de-emphasize pathology in favour of desired goals. It is worth reflecting that the setting of achievable but challenging goals is considered to be a vital factor in team building and one of the most provenly effective motivators in work settings (Locke, Shaw, Saari and Latham,1981; Tubbs, 1986).

Dealing with blocks to the problem-solving process

This involves working with the consultee on impediments to action on behalf of the child who is ostensibly the subject of the consultation. This encompasses the largest set of psychological theories and thus presents the greatest amount of choice to the consultant. It is at this level that subjective and individualistic aspects of the consultee's (and the consultant's) perceptions are addressed, highlighting the relevance of the constructionist, analytical and social strands of psychology outlined at the beginning of this chapter.

For the practitioner the debate over the supremacy of one approach, to the exclusion of others, is sterile. The pertinent issue involves exploiting an explanatory framework that yields ways through the block. To an extent, the greater the range of frameworks available to the educational psychologist the more strategies can be generated. There is an analogy to applied theory in the natural sciences. For instance, in understanding and predicting the behaviour of light in differing situations it is useful to conceptualize it as rays or wave motions or energy. An attempt to craft a lens for someone's spectacles beginning from quantum mechanics theory would be ridiculously cumbersome. The number of models in psychology may be much greater but the principle of choice on the criterion of utility is the same. By matching theoretical options to observations it is possible to make discriminating choices of strategies.

Blocks to the problem-solving process also reside within the consultant. The concepts of supervision and co-consultation have been developed to help practitioners achieve new perspectives on and insights into the contexts within which they work (Stoltenberg, 1981; Holloway and Wampold, 1986). Indeed it can be argued that the problem-solving approach (embodying these three levels) can be used reflexively with psychologists to develop professional practice.

Within the three levels described, the breadth of theory in psychology seems to be more of an asset than a hindrance. In the absence of the problem-solving paradigm the inevitable emphasis is on the contradictions and incomplete applicability of different models to the situations in which educational psychologists work: a recipe for conflict. It is proposed that the problem-solving alliance allows educational psychologists to make choices within the body of psychology that are more assured of satisfactory outcomes for the child in question.

Argyris (1976) has described how managers appear to have 'espoused theories' that sharply contrast with their 'theories in use' as demonstrated by their actual behaviour *in situ*. Usually, this is interpreted pejoratively, with the 'espoused theory' being more consultative or considerate, but it is also possible that the 'theory in action' represents a better match to organizational circumstances. Anecdotally it is interesting to reflect on educational psychologists who are regarded by peers as especially effective. It is the supposition here that while their 'espoused theories' may reflect a close sense of affiliation with a particular strand of psychology, their 'theories in use' incorporate the above levels and draw upon a wider range of psychology, if only intuitively.

DEVELOPING THE PROBLEM-SOLVING ALLIANCE IN THE 1990s

In general the problem-solving paradigm has failed to make significant inroads into educational psychology practice. Explicit attempts to work within a problem-solving alliance are still rarer. The intention at this point is to examine the key factors that may influence its future application.

Systemic factors that maintain current practice

Given that LEAs have to provide education for all while their constituent institutions do not share the same responsibility, educational psychologists, or something similar, would need to have been invented if they did not already exist. For someone must act as the buffer between bidders and providers, and it appears untenable to have this role invested in a group that does not have *prima facie* qualifications or that is clearly partisan. While problem-solving approaches may be at the heart of the profession's aspirations, as described earlier, issues of resource allocation are at the centre of its existence. This predicament seems basically true of the roles of educational psychologists (or their equivalents) in other parts of the world.

The mechanics of the Education Reform Act 1988 primarily concern the distribution of resources across public sector education and their movement with 'consumer' pressures. There continues to be no obligation on institutions to attempt to meet all the needs that may arise out of an initial allocation of resources, and therefore the dilemmas of allocating additional resources remain. Even if the obligation could be passed to schools a need for brokerage between their subdivisions would still arise.

In other words, while legislative changes may profoundly affect the culture of education, employing bodies and the like, the fundamental difficulties of allocating resources on which the profession has been built will remain. In some senses this might be seen as a message of hope, but it also highlights the difficulties of extricating the profession from variants of current casework practice. For as was argued earlier, this introduces a potential hidden agenda into every consultation, which is concerned, principally, with securing additional or alternative resources rather than promoting the resolution of problems.

Assuming the continued existence of services based within LEAs, there is a great deal that educational psychologists could offer to help to achieve more equitable and effective distribution of resources. The problem for educational psychologists is how they might make this contribution without subverting their casework aims. Inevitably solutions must be placed within local conditions, but they would seem to require two elements. One concerns the development of means of resourcing institutions as a whole in ways that are progressively more sensitive to children's and young people's needs. The other is linking the resourcing of 'exceptional' bids to problem-solving action rather more than to the child's supposed psychopathology.

Initial and post-experience training of educational psychologists

Within the UK initial training in educational psychology has been closely linked to institutions with distinctive philosophies about the application of psychology to education. While there may be an increasing consensus across courses about the use of indirect consultation, the problem-solving paradigm has tended to feature more on courses stressing behavioural methods of intervention, which has served to compound the myth of association between the two.

The preceding analysis suggests that the diversity of approaches represented by the courses could be a strength to the profession overall, given a shared view of the centrality of the problem-solving alliance. It suggests further that all courses could usefully reappraise the less represented aspects of psychology that contribute to the three levels at which the consultant is working. Given the history of educational psychology training, a reorientation of the profession in the way advocated would give rise to training needs for practising educational psychologists.

The expectations of schools

The unspoken understanding of educational psychologists as validators of resource bids has been a recurrent theme in this chapter. For many schools a move toward the problem-solving paradigm would clash with role expectations. There would be a choice of whether schools should be expected to accommodate themselves to such a change or an explicit renegotiation of role should take place. The latter seems less likely to cause feelings of disorientation and frustration. Personal experience of working within problem-solving alliances suggests that it assists cooperation and mitigates some of the adversarial aspects of interactions between educational psychologists and schools.

The situation for parents would be very different. Many of them come with stereotypic notions of psychologists, associating them with psychiatrists and severe forms of mental ill health. For them membership of a problem-solving alliance is likely to seem less threatening and more manifestly purposeful.

CONCLUDING COMMENTS

In summary, couching educational psychology casework practice within the problem-solving alliance increases its purposefulness and accountability in respect of children's needs. It can only fulfil this promise if the complexities of the consultancy relationship are acknowledged. Most fundamentally this implies an acceptance on the part of the educational psychologist of the centrality of subjective constructions of problems.

To work successfully within problem-solving alliances, educational psychologists need not only to move through the stages of the problem-solving paradigm, but also to use crucial skills to facilitate the consultation and work with blocks to the process. This implies the relevance of a far wider range of psychological theory than has hitherto been associated with the approach within the profession.

The challenge of a change of practice in this direction brings with it a set of issues to be addressed by the profession. Among these are: educational psychologists' contributions to the equitable allocation of resources to meet needs in schools, the expectations of schools and professional training.

It is proposed that the approach described here can help educational psychologists to have a far more significant effect on the range of opportunities open to the most vulnerable and needy children and young people who have traditionally constituted our main client group. In so doing it may also achieve some of the unrealized potential of psychology in education.

REFERENCES

Argyris, C. (1976) 'Leadership, learning and changing the status quo', *Organizational Dynamics*, Winter, 29–43.

Barton, L. and Tomlinson, S. (eds) (1984) *Special Education and Social Interests*. London: Croom Helm.

Bloom, B. (1979) *Alterable Variables: The New Direction in Educational Research*. Edinburgh: The Scottish Council for Research in Education.

Brophy, J. E. and Rohrkemper, M. M. (1981) 'The influence of problem ownership on teachers' perceptions of and strategies for coping with problem students', *Journal of Educational Psychology*, **73** (3), 295–311.

Cameron, R. J. (ed.) (1982) *Working Together: Portage in the UK*. Windsor: NFER-Nelson.

Caplan, G. (1969) *An Approach to Community Mental Health*. London: Tavistock Publications.

Caplan, G. (1970) *The Theory and Practice of Mental Health Consultation*. London: Tavistock Publications.

Conoley, J. C. and Conoley, C. W. (1982) *School Consultation: A Guide to Practice and Training*. New York: Pergamon.

DES (1978) *Special Needs in Education*. (Warnock Report). London: HMSO.

Dessent, T. (1987) *Making the Ordinary School Special*. Lewes: The Falmer Press.

Egan, G. (1990) *The Skilled Helper* (fourth edition). Monterey, CA: Brooks-Cole.

French, W. L. and Bell, C. H. (1984) *Organization Development: Behavioural Science Interventions for Behavioural Improvement* (third edition). Englewood Cliffs, NJ: Prentice-Hall.

Galloway, D. and Goodwin, C. (1987) *The Education of Disturbing Children: Pupils with Learning and Adjustment Difficulties*. London: Longman.

Gersch, I. and Cutting, M. C. (1985) 'The child's report', *Educational Psychology in Practice*, **1** (2), 63–9.

Gersch, I., McCarthy, M., Sigston, A. and Townley, D. (1990) 'Taking an educational psychology service into the 1990s', *Educational Psychology in Practice*, **6** (3), 123–31.

Gipps, C., Goldstein, H. and Gross, H. (1985) 'Twenty per cent with special needs: another legacy from Cyril Burt?', *Remedial Education* (now called *Support for Learning*), **20**, 72–5.

Glaser, R. (1967) 'Adapting the elementary school curriculum to individual performance', reprinted in Hooper, R. (ed.) (1977) *The Curriculum: Context, Design and Development*. Edinburgh: Oliver & Boyd (for the Open University).

Hargreaves, D., Hester, S. K. and Mellor, F. J. (1975) *Deviance in Classrooms*. London: Routledge & Kegan Paul.

Holloway, E. and Wampold, B. (1986) 'The relation between conceptual level and counselling related tasks: a meta analysis', *Journal of Counselling Psychology*, **30**, 227–34.

Kelly, G. (1955) *The Psychology of Personal Constructs*. New York: W. W. Norton.

Kemmis, S. *et al.* (1981) *The Action Research Planner.* Deakin University, Geelong, Victoria, Australia 3217.

Locke, E.A., Shaw, K.N., Saari, L.M. and Latham, G.P. (1981) 'Goal setting and task performance: 1969-1980', *Psychological Bulletin*, **90**, 125-52.

Mahoney, M.J. and Lyddon, W.J. (1988) 'Recent developments in cognitive approaches to counselling and psychotherapy', *The Counseling Psychologist*, **16** (2), 190-234.

Rogers, C.R. (1977) *On Becoming a Person: A Therapist's View of Psychotherapy.* London: Constable.

Schein, E. (1987) *Process Consultation* (vol. II). Reading, MA: Addison-Wesley.

Schein, E. (1988) *Process Consultation* (vol. I). Reading, MA: Addison-Wesley.

Sigston, A. (1987) 'Meeting the needs of young people with severe learning and behaviour difficulties', *Association for Child Psychology and Psychiatry Newsletter*, **9** (2), 23-5.

Stevens, G. (1980) 'Bias in attributions of positive and negative behaviour in children by school psychologists, parents and teachers', *Perceptual and Motor Skills*, **50**, 1283-90.

Stoltenberg, C. (1981) 'Approaching supervision from the developmental perspective: the counselor complexity model', *Journal of Counselling Psychology*, **28**, 59-65.

Stratford, R.J. and Cameron, R.J. (1978) 'Target practice: preparing accountable educational psychologists', *Occasional Papers of the Division of Educational and Child Psychology* (British Psychological Society), **11** (1).

Thomas, E.J. and Walter, C.L. (1973) 'Guidelines for behavioral practice in the open community agency', *Behavior Research and Therapy*, **11**, 193-205.

Thomas, G. and Feiler, A. (1988) *Planning for Special Needs: A Whole School Approach.* Oxford: Basil Blackwell.

Topping, K. (1988) *The Peer Tutoring Handbook.* London: Croom Helm.

Truax, C.B. and Carkhuff, R.R. (1967) *Toward Effective Counselling and Psychotherapy: Training and Practice.* London: Aldine.

Tubbs, M.E. (1986) 'Goal setting: a meta-analytic examination of the empirical evidence', *Journal of Applied Psychology*, **71** (3), 474-83.

Tyler, L.E. (1969) *The Work of the Counselor.* New York: Appleton-Century-Crofts.

Wolfendale, S. (ed.) (1989) *Parental Involvement: Developing Networks between School, Home and Community.* London: Cassell Educational.

Chapter 3

Educational Psychologists and 'The Case for Individual Casework'

Tony Dessent

In this chapter I intend to make the case for the educational psychologist's involvement in individual casework. Making such a case feels somewhat at odds with much of what I have argued for and attempted to develop as a practising educational psychologist over the past fifteen years. First then some personal/historical context.

As an EP I received my initial training in the mid-seventies. It was an exciting time of rethinking and 're-constructing' (Gillham, 1978). It was a time when the profession was beginning to gird its loins and drag itself out of, as I saw it, the sterile treadmill of individual casework, psychometrics and the professional suffocation of child guidance. At the beginning of my career I felt part of a process which was attempting to extend the educational psychologist's role into new and developing areas. The words on our lips (often repeated with ritual significance at every local and national gathering) were 'prevention', 'INSET', 'consultative', 'role', 'project work', 'giving psychology away' and the rarely understood notion of 'systems work'. Like many other similar minded EPs of the time, I found in practice that the expectations 'out there'—in the schools, in the headteacher's office, in the classrooms and the education offices—were somewhat at odds with my notions of what the modern, post-reconstruction EP was all about. I can well remember attending a conference where an education officer, having listened to a few EPs talking about the importance of their role in INSET and LEA policy development, commented (at least half seriously) that he thought there might be time for this on a Sunday afternoon after the essential statutory and individual casework had been completed! So, there were some insistent views out there (and there still are) which reinforced the notion that individual casework was the proper (perhaps the only) focus of an EP's work. Views and attitudes, as I saw it at the time (and still do), which needed to be changed and altered.

Why then should an educational psychologist like myself, trained and raised in those reforming days, now be focusing upon the case for educational psychologists to work at the individual level? Is it the process of age, experience and the inevitable drift towards more conservative views and values? Has the reforming zeal of the 1970s ebbed and waned? I would like to think not.

Let me begin by putting forward at the outset some beliefs and principles which I held then and which continue to be important to me in guiding my own work:

(a)   Educational psychologists (and the LEAs which employ them) should develop policies and working practices which *actively reduce the need for individual casework approaches*.

(b)   Direct individual casework should be limited, as far as possible, to those pupils and students who have the most exceptional, unpredictable and even unique needs.

(c)   Educational psychologists need to develop, extend and broaden their role further within LEAs and within local authority services in general. Such extensions of role would encompass responsibilities and duties well beyond both the traditional and current child/special needs focus.

(d)   As part of this process of broadening and extending roles, traditional and historical barriers between educational psychologists and other professional groups, such as officers, advisers and inspectors, should progressively be reduced. (Moreover, I believe this would be a good thing for educational psychologists and a good thing for educational psychology.)

(e)   Within and alongside these sets of beliefs, however, I have another. This is a belief that the individual casework role is an important one; that it places educational psychologists in a unique and privileged position *vis-à-vis* schools as institutions and the educational environment and community outside of schools. This role should continue and EP casework skills should be further developed and refined.

My task in this chapter will be to unpack some of these beliefs and principles and, in particular, to examine the arguments for and against individual casework. In the process, I will attempt to address a number of questions:

(a)   Why have educational psychologists both historically (and currently) been under pressure to work mainly at the individual level?

(b)   Why should their role be widened?

(c)   What is the rationale for the educational psychologist's individual casework role and how does it interact with other roles?

(d)   What implications arise for educational psychologists in the future within the context of the 1988 Education Reform Act?

THE PRESSURE FOR INDIVIDUAL CASEWORK

Job advertisements for educational psychologists make interesting reading these days. Principal educational psychologists, motivated either by a natural desire to make their own psychology service sound like heaven on earth or by a genuine recruitment difficulty (or both), ensure that their job advertisements promise a lot. INSET, project work, consultative work and policy involvement are often writ large. Few advertisements tell the whole truth in this respect.

> We require an educational psychologist to spend all of the working week (and more) dealing with an enormous and insurmountable individual case load of statutory and non-statutory work. Much of your work will be of a crisis-oriented, fire-fighting nature. The demands for individual casework placed upon you will be essentially unmeetable. This is a challenging post and only candidates with endurance, a sound heart (and a feeble mind) need apply.

Many educational psychologists entering a service for the first time might be forgiven for thinking that an advertisement of this kind does in fact reflect more accurately the day-to-day work expected of them.

The pressure for individual casework comes from a number of sources. Some of these are obvious and others are perhaps more subtle.

Special education and the educational psychologist's statutory functions

I can recall some years ago presenting, at a national gathering of educational psychologists, an overhead transparency showing an uncompleted sentence: 'If I went on strike tomorrow the LEA would have to find somebody else to. . .?' A significant number of individuals within the audience produced responses which indicated that EP functions were at root about their role within the field of special education. Most answers mentioned EPs' statutory assessment role, their involvement in segregated placements and their link to the statementing process. This is in no way surprising if we look at the history of the profession. I have made the point elsewhere (Dessent, 1988) that the strong historical links which the profession of educational psychology has had with those assessment processes leading to special educational placement has made them central figures in 'defining specialness' or 'individual exceptionality'.

Cyril Burt described his priority as 'how to ascertain educationally sub-normal pupils using psychological tests and other scientific procedures' (Burt, 1957). Post-Burt, educational psychologists have progressively developed their psychometric box of tricks to identify, ascertain, categorize and recommend placements for those pupils having significant special educational needs. Thus, pre-Warnock and pre-1981 Act, educational psychologists were essentially involved in the business of defining what was to count as a significant special educational need. These were pupils usually *en route* to special schools or special units of some kind.

Since the 1981 Act, the focus of our work has to some extent changed. Educational psychologists have added to their role of 'defining specialness' a further role—that of 'defining resource-worthiness'. Our current approach to resourcing pupils with special needs requires the existence of professional groups, such as educational psychologists, to define those individual pupils who require, merit or deserve special or additional resourcing. Arguably, the work which educational psychologists carry out in this area constitutes the main reason for their employment by local education authorities (LEAs). In effect, the education service has evolved a special education means test for deciding which pupils have special educational needs requiring, in the words of the current legislation, 'resources additional to those normally available in ordinary schools' (DES, 1983). While teachers and administrators as well as medical and paramedical staff all contribute to this process of defining resource-worthiness, it is educational psychologists who are regarded as having a primary role in this respect.

Thus the defining and gate-keeping role which educational psychologists have historically played has evolved and broadened. We have moved from a focus upon defining a candidate for segregation to defining specialness and exceptionality and more recently to defining resource-worthiness. The names may have changed but the function has not. What has remained constant is the need, in-built within any social system or organization which is selective in some way, for definers and gate-keepers.

EPs have with varying degrees of 'professional willingness' fulfilled this role. While the special education system continues to require these functions, the pressures on educational psychologists for individual casework will continue largely unabated. As far as individual work is concerned it will continue to be business as usual and we can expect no sign of any recession!

I have described elsewhere (Dessent, 1987, 1988) some possible ways forward in terms of addressing these issues. In particular, I have drawn attention to possible new approaches to resourcing special educational needs in ordinary schools. I remain convinced that reducing these particular pressures for individual casework is certainly possible. However, it requires a root-and-branch approach to policy and provision for children with special needs within LEAs. Only when this occurs (and educational psychologists have a role to play in making it happen) will it be possible for educational psychologists to make a more rational, a more prescribed and a more effective approach to individual casework. Educational psychologists will then be able to move beyond the role of resource definers and begin to become a resource themselves.

Boundary and territory pressures

Educational psychologists are familiar with demarcation disputes with other professional groups. Bill Gillham, writing in 1978 about some of the 'directions of change' which were emerging at that time, made the following comment:

> Very broadly speaking educational psychologists are becoming less clinical and more educational which means there are problems of adjustment to other professional groups, such as educational advisers, who sometimes feel that psychologists are invading their territory by taking an interest in school organisation and curriculum reform, instead of confining their attention to individual 'cases'. There can be no more simple index of the drift of change than these demarcation disputes: ten years ago the role conflict would have been with medical officers and child psychiatrists. (p. 16)

Perhaps, as a consequence of the 1988 Act and some of the restructuring which has occurred within LEAs, some of these territorial issues have decreased. For example, a number of LEAs are incorporating their psychological service into their advisory and inspectorial structures. However, my own impression is that there still exists within many LEAs some unease in this respect. Boundary and territorial issues arise with special needs advisory teachers and inspectors/advisers. The battlegrounds in terms of professional territory often revolve around EP involvement in INSET, in policy and provision for children with special needs and more recently in curriculum approaches in areas such as reading. The furore created by the Martin Turner (1990) reading standards 'exposé' was fuelled to a large extent by the now familiar conflict between the 'structure-loving' fraternity within psychology services and the field of special education on the one hand, and the real books/primary ethos brigade, which is more frequently found among advisers and inspectors, on the other.

In many LEAs educational psychology services have made significant progress in terms of broadening their traditional role. However, territorial issues are still, I believe, creating significant pressure on many EPs to maintain the focus of their work on assessment/diagnostic work at the level of the individual child.

Internal pressures

The profession of educational psychology has itself worked to maintain and increase the pressure for psychologists to operate at the individual casework level. In this respect the profession has displayed its own insecurities and its own lack of self-confidence as a professional group. These internal pressures are revealed in a number of ways. There has, for instance, been a great deal of rhetoric in the profession about 'giving psychology away' (Miller, 1969). This wish to give psychology away has, however, always fallen short of a commitment to give some aspects of psychometric assessment away. Why do some ability and personality tests remain closed and therefore effectively barred from use by teachers and others? Why have educational psychologists made few, if any, attempts to work with their LEAs to establish patterns of resourcing for children with special needs, which reduce the need for educational psychologists to be involved in statutory and non-statutory resource-defining activities? Within both these examples, I sense a profession which still needs to cling on to the area of individual work for few if any good professional reasons. The reasons are more likely, to my mind, to relate to professional protectionism. While the profession of educational psychology itself remains uncertain about its potential contribution outside of the individual casework arena its message to the outside world—its 'mission statement'—will remain confused and confusing.

Few educational psychologists would argue against the notion that the profession should work towards increasing the skills and confidence of teachers and other direct contract staff in order that they themselves are able adequately to assess and meet the needs of 'exceptional' children. The corollary—that educational psychologists should progressively reduce the need for their own direct involvement in individual casework—can be controversial: for a profession which sees its future 'security of tenure' as being based upon demands for individual casework it can be very controversial indeed. Some educational psychologists may feel that the profession cannot afford to be too successful at giving psychology away. Where would it all lead if we really were more successful at skills transmission approaches, at developing new resourcing and support approaches which reduce the need for gate-keepers and resource definers? Some would fear that educational psychologists would have worked themselves out of a job. I believe that confronting, understanding and working with the paradoxical aim of 'doing ourselves out of a job' is fundamental to the future work of educational psychologists.

Public stereotypes

Ask the man or woman on the street about his or her picture of a psychologist and the response is relatively easy to predict. The 'trick cyclist' stereotype, which makes no distinction between psychiatry, psychotherapy and psychology, predominates. We are all familiar with the stereotype which exists in the public mind of the psychologist as mind-reader, analyst and therapist—an image in education which is reinforced for parents by the need to 'refer' a child who is struggling educationally to this remote, specialist expert. Thus, the individual casework role of educational psychologists is reinforced by these dominant public stereotypes of educational psychologists as clinicians. Progressively altering this image and stereotype is of some importance for the future of educational psychology. Educational psychologists do need to gain a higher public and media profile in terms of their contribution to educational research, to learning processes and to curriculum and policy issues. As education progressively moves to the top of the political agenda in the UK during the 1990s, new opportunities in this area will arise. The need for objective data as well as methodologically sound and informative research which is grounded in practical school and LEA concerns will increase. Educational psychologists could gain a public profile which would enable a broader image to develop of what educational psychology is or could be about. The notion of the EPs contribution to developing a 'psychology of schooling' (see Jones and Sayer, 1988) needs to impact as much upon the public imagination as it does upon headteachers and the educational fraternity.

THE CASE AGAINST INDIVIDUAL CASEWORK

This is not the place for a comprehensive exposition on the rationale for educational psychologists to have a wider role than the traditional focus upon individual casework. A plethora of books and journal articles exists in this respect, each extolling the potential contribution which psychologists could make to an ever-increasing number of areas including in-service training, systems work, project work and research and development activities. My intention in this section is to highlight not just the 'received wisdom' but also the 'hidden agenda' behind the rationale for EPs to play a broader role.

The received wisdom

The received wisdom begins of course with Burt. It is easy to forget that Burt's original post as Great Britain's first educational psychologist with London County Council in 1913 was indeed a very wide-ranging one. His appointment involved half of his time being devoted to psychological research. Burt (1964) maintained that the work of an educational psychologist was essentially that of a scientific investigator and researcher. Burt was not unique in this respect. I recall, on arrival in my first post as an educational psychologist in the mid-seventies, discovering in the filing cabinet of my office a fascinating historical document. It was a booklet dated 1947. It had been written by an educational psychologist whose services had been bought in and commissioned by the education authority of that time (shades of LMS!). The report involved a wide-ranging survey and study of the incidence levels of pupils with educational difficulties within a large geographical area. It was combined with a set of recommendations concerning the necessary provision (within special schools) to meet the identified needs. The power and influence of the report had been considerable.

In this example, as in the case of Burt's original post, the importance of work which is at a different level, or at least several stages removed, from the individual clinical role is the salient feature. Many educational psychologists (and I would be one of them) would argue that working in this way—at the level of *organizations*, at the level of *policy* and working essentially through *others* to affect change at the individual level—is where educational psychology can be most effective. The rationale for these beliefs lies essentially within our developing theoretical and conceptual understanding of special educational needs and of the social and environmental influences that determine pupil behaviour within educational contexts. We now know four things with increasing certainty.

Special educational needs are relative

Special educational needs arise from the interactions between pupil characteristics, schools, teachers, parents, the community and the professionals who are involved. Klaus Wedell (1983) comments, 'the problems of the handicapped are the result of the interaction between the nature of their deficiencies and the nature of their environment. The needs of the handicapped are, therefore, seen to be relative both to the deficiencies "within" the child and the deficiencies of the "environment".' Wedell's (1981) succinct and useful definition of special educational needs illustrates well the relativistic nature of special educational needs. He comments, 'the term "special educational need" refers to the gap between a child's level of behaviour and achievement and what is required of him'.

Pupil behaviour is the result of complex interactions between the pupil and the environment

Faupel (1990) describes this as the ecological approach. He notes that 'Understanding problem behaviour will not be found by focusing on the child, nor by focusing on the school but in the study and analysis of the *interactions between them.*'

Schools make a difference

The evidence that schools indeed make a difference to both pupil behaviour and performance has been steadily accumulating in recent years within the literature on school effectiveness (for instance, Rutter *et al.*, 1979; Reynolds, 1985; Mortimore *et al.*, 1988). This evidence further pushes us away from a sole reliance upon 'within child' variables in understanding pupil behaviour and performance.

Individual casework rarely produces long-term effects

Most educational psychologists recognize that no matter how skilful and sensitive their work at the individual casework level, their efforts will be insignificant in comparison with developments which impinge upon organizations and systems and which operate at the policy level. At its best, effective individual casework may have some transitory, generalizable effects within *one* institution. At worst it compounds the organizational and institutional problems and becomes 'part of the problem rather than part of the solution'.

The hidden agenda

If the conceptual and empirical arguments against individual work are not enough, there is a whole hidden agenda within educational psychology which reinforces the case against individual casework.

It is undoable

Educational psychologists are never likely to be able to meet the volume of demands which could be placed upon them for individual casework so long as psychological services remain both 'open' and 'free'. Most services have to develop 'referral deflection' devices in order to cope with potentially infinite demands. Lengthy bureaucratic processes of referral and contract visiting are identical organizational devices for deflecting and minimizing the potentially unmeetable demands which could be placed upon services. We justify lengthy referral forms by commenting on the necessity for schools to provide high-quality information prior to referral. We justify contract visiting on the grounds of its supposed preventive merits. Both are, at root, about controlling unmeetable demands.

It is difficult work

My own experience of working as an educational psychologist at a wide variety of levels leads me to conclude that effective individual casework is often the most stressful and difficult part of the role. Within their casework role educational psychologists are usually needing to engage with complex personal, ethical, economic and sometimes political issues. Individual casework often has strong emotions and feelings lurking somewhere in the background. The strong emotions rarely belong to the pupil. More often they belong to the headteacher, the teacher, the parent, the social worker etc.

Poor links with psychology as a discipline

Ironically, many educational psychologists might view with some cynicism the extent to which their casework involves anything which seems to relate to their background discipline of psychology. This is particularly the case for those psychologists who have abandoned psychometrics and who have gone on to find limited mileage in the application of behavioural approaches and the rag-bag of associated packages which has been tagged the 'cargo culture'. Educational psychologists in this situation find themselves operating at the individual level in much the same way as a specialist teacher and with little clarity about the distinctive contribution they are making as psychologists.

It is low-status work

Inspecting, advising, consulting, supporting, monitoring and reporting are certainly the high-status activities of the 1990s within LEA advisory and support services. Those who work at the individual level come way down the pecking order. In this respect educational psychology services have, relative to advisory and inspection services, lost some status in recent years by having the individual pupil as their principal focus as opposed to the institution or the whole school. This difference in status has been very concretely reinforced by increasing disparities in pay scales between advisers and inspectors on the one hand and educational psychologists on the other.

The case against individual casework is therefore a powerful one. At both a theoretical/conceptual level and at a very personal and pragmatic level, the forces working against individual casework are considerable. These forces have historically and incrementally led the profession away from a prime focus on changing the individual, and towards a focus on institutional and systems change. The profession has moved through a series of stages:

stage 1: sort the child out (for example, child guidance/treatment and therapy/ psychometrics and diagnosis)
stage 2: sort the teacher out (for example, INSET/behavioural methods/precision teaching/intervention packages and the 'cargo culture')
stage 3: sort the parents out (for example, Portage/paired reading)
stage 4: sort the LEA out (for example, systems work/advisory role/policy involvement)

THE CASE FOR INDIVIDUAL CASEWORK

Let us begin with an anecdotal story. Imagine the scene: a senior education officer has called a meeting involving a wide range of LEA representatives (administrators, inspectors, advisory teachers, educational psychologists). The meeting has been called to discuss LEA policy and provision for children with emotional and behavioural difficulties. A tap on the office door—enter a secretary with a telephone message scribbled on a memo pad: 'Vincent Smith, age 7, has been excluded from Dreamy Dale Primary School—please ring the headteacher urgently.' The memo is passed to the primary inspector, to the special needs inspector and then to the education officer chairing the meeting. The education officer reads the memo and then scans the array of professional expertise and advisory support within the room. The education officer's eyes fasten eventually on the educational psychologist and the memo finds its way into the psychologist's hands. End of story.

A familiar scenario, perhaps. A wide range of LEA officers, advisory and support staff will feel they have a legitimate contribution to make to policy and provision decisions relating to children with special educational needs. However, when it comes to an *individual child*, few of these individuals are likely to have, or want to have, a direct involvement. Of course the reasons which lie behind Vincent Smith's exclusion could be many and various—family difficulties? disturbed pupil behaviour? Maybe. Perhaps we might also find the following of equal significance:

(a)   classroom management skills;
(b)   headteacher management skills;
(c)   pastoral care and discipline policy;
(d)   teacher stress;
(e)   relationships between the school and parents;
(f)   teacher/headteacher competence levels;
(g)   teacher/school INSET needs;
(h)   LEA exclusions policy;
(i)   school special needs policy;
(j)   LEA special needs policy.

The point I am making here is that the action at the level of the *individual child* provides all of the important evidence about the *system* within which education takes place. What happens to 'Vincent Smith', and to the individual child with special needs, is the acid test or litmus paper of the education system. It is this evidence which is more powerful and more informative than any number of judgments made on the basis of school inspections, of consultative visits, of discussion with teachers and indeed of ordinary classroom observations. It is relatively rare for inspectors, advisers and administrators to gain detailed knowledge of the kind gathered by educational psychologists of how the system is working for the individual child. Gaining access to information at this level (at the level of the individual child, the individual child's parent, the individual child's classroom teacher), and being able to *use* the information gained to influence future policy and provision, places the educational psychologist in a unique, privileged and enormously powerful position.

I know of no stronger justification and argument for the individual casework role than this. Its power, however, lies in the *connection* being made between individual casework and policy and provision decisions. For many educational psychologists this connection is either fragile or non-existent. For others, making the connection is not seen, by themselves or by other people, to be part of their role. In my view educational psychologists need to maximize the potential which exists for *connecting the individual and the system*. This connection is vital whether the system is the school or more broadly the LEA. In this respect educational psychologists need to operate not only as the eyes and ears of the LEA but also as part of its brain.

The case for individual casework is predicated on this connection between the individual and the system. The rationale for individual casework lies also in some further, specific, professional advantages which educational psychologists enjoy and are able to bring to bear on their work.

'Objectivity' and breadth

Educational psychologists have the potential as a group to bring to their individual casework role a form of objectivity and impartiality which results from their broad-based, generic role within LEAs. There will be other workers who operate at the individual casework level who have greater specialized knowledge about specific areas of disability and need. Educational psychologists cannot, and should not, seek to compete with specialist teachers in this respect. The strength of educational psychologists, which is not typically shared by specialist teachers, lies in their broad-based approach to assessment and intervention across the full range of disabilities and special needs. This broad, generic base enables educational psychologists to develop a degree of objectivity and impartiality.

Specialization within the field of special needs brings with it many advantages in terms of expertise and knowledge. It also brings a number of disadvantages in terms of the LEA's overall role in planning and making provision for special needs. 'Disability specialists' will typically, and understandably, push hard in terms of advocacy for resources for their particular group. Advocacy of this kind can significantly distort an LEA's overall pattern of provision and resourcing. Specialization also typically brings with it an emphasis upon demarcating the *differences* and difficulties of the pupils within the specialized group of concern. For example, there is a natural tendency for specialist teachers of the sensory impaired to emphasize the differences between hearing impaired pupils and other pupils (with or without special needs). In reality there are great similarities between the needs of different disability groups in terms of 'educational treatment'; for instance, between children with hearing difficulties and children with communication difficulties. These similarities need to be addressed in terms of overall LEA provision. Specialization too can bring with it a sometimes unhelpful and inflexible dogma in terms of pedagogy and approaches to learning. The auralism/signing debate within the field of hearing impairment might be an example.

Educational psychologists have a role to play with *all* pupils with special educational needs. They are usually the one professional group within LEAs that has a direct casework responsibility for pupils with exceptional needs across all areas of difficulty and all age groups. EPs are of course not free themselves of some of the possible disadvantages of specialization. They too have their prejudices and preferred approaches. I am reminded here of those EPs who reportedly respond to all individual referrals (regardless of their nature) by recommending a precision teaching package. However, as a professional group they have the potential to provide a broad perspective on disabilities and needs. They are more likely to resist and counterbalance unfair advocacy from any particular pressure group within specialized areas. They are more likely to be able to look at both pupil differences and pupil similarities across the full range of special needs. This broad base enables them as a professional group to take a balanced approach to particular dogmas in terms of pedagogy and learning approaches. Educational psychologists are in the unique position within the LEA structure of having detailed, daily, direct client contact across the full range of needs and disabilities. As such they are in a position to offer balanced and impartial advice to their employing LEAs and to the parents and the teachers of the children concerned.

The breadth of the educational psychologist's individual casework involvement confers other positive advantages. I am thinking here particularly of psychologists' assessment approaches. Educational psychologists will typically be concerned in terms of effective assessment practices to provide a comprehensive appraisal of a child's total learning context. Of particular importance will be the inclusion of some assessment of the child's personal, social and emotional functioning. Psychologists' assessments are also likely to take account of the child's behaviour and development within the community context, and importantly of parental needs and perspectives. The intensive involvement of educational psychologists in this latter area over the past decade or so (for example, portage, paired reading, parental involvement projects) provides clear evidence of the benefits of the breadth of psychological assessment approaches. Educational psychologists have led the way in terms of identifying not only the needs of parents of children with special needs but also the potential for parents to intervene and to support their children's learning. Many practising educational psychologists place a very high premium on their direct work with parents. In this respect they are one of the few professional groups working directly with parents which is in a position to enable both the LEA and schools to be responsive to the needs of parents and to working effectively in partnership with them.

The ability to recognize relativities and exceptionality

In their individual casework role educational psychologists have privileged access to a wide range of information concerning both individual needs and the responses made by schools and parents to those needs. They are an agency which, within the structure of LEAs, is well placed to comment upon the degree to which pupil needs and the needs of schools (particularly in their response to special needs) might be regarded as exceptional. The educational psychologist is a professional who often works across schools of widely differing types. These schools will be responding to different client groups in different catchment areas. Special educational needs are defined by context. 'Exceptionality' within one school can be the norm in another. Educational psychologists can see these relativities more clearly than any individual school. They are also in a position to make constructive use of the diversity of approaches which schools and parents adopt in responding to the individual needs of their children. In working with one teacher or parent who has an 'intractable' or difficult problem to solve, the educational psychologist may well be aware of another teacher or parent who has effectively managed the same difficulty elsewhere.

The 'educational voice' within the multidisciplinary world of disability and special needs

If educational psychologists did not exist, the educational system would need to develop a professional group of a similar kind to replace them. Such a group would need to represent an educational perspective and be well versed in the concepts of child development and special needs. This is a vital but often overlooked perspective on the educational psychologist's role. The world of disability and special needs has historically been dominated by clinical and medical concepts and by intervention and treatment approaches derived from the world of medicine. The development of the educational psychology profession was partly a response to this historical domination by the medical profession in what are essentially educational issues and concerns. Educational psychologists provide an interface between the education system and a number of medical and paramedical groups which have a legitimate involvement with children with special educational needs. Part of the educational psychologist's role in respect of these groups is to reframe, and sometimes professionally challenge, medical perspectives concerning a child's needs. If the consultant psychiatrist maintains that child X is 'clinically maladjusted' and needs a specialist therapeutic environment, how will an education department evaluate and act in terms of this assessment? Similarly, what happens if the speech therapist assesses a child as being 'dyspraxic' and requiring placement in a specialized setting for dyspraxic pupils? In both of these situations an education department will require a well-trained professional, equipped in terms of knowledge and understanding to judge the educational implications of non-educational assessments.

I have attempted in this section to look at some of the particular advantages and strengths of the educational psychologist's individual casework role. I would argue that while the overall aim of educational psychologists would be to work towards the 'safe delegation' of the majority of their individual work to others (teachers in particular), there will continue to be an important individual role for educational psychologists. This will be particularly the case in respect of a small number of individual pupils with exceptional (and probably life-long) needs. With these pupils and families there is still much to learn and much to do. We have only begun to scratch the surface in terms of intervention and management approaches with our most severely disabled pupils. Monumental strides have been made in our approaches to profound and multiply learning disabled children. However, problematic areas such as self-injurious behaviour and the management of areas of sexual development and personal hygiene are as yet poorly researched. Improvements in microtechnology are likely to influence the communication potential of disabled pupils massively, so long as they can be effectively harnessed by educationalists. Our understandings of the needs of parents and families as they respond to disability and the special needs of children is still in its infancy. We are beginning to comprehend the range of *conflicts* and needs which underlie parental responses to disability and handicap. Examples from my own experience of working with families would include:

(a) the needs of parents to expect normality versus the needs of parents to make their child special;
(b) the need to blame others versus the need to blame themselves;
(c) the fear that they as parents have not done enough/tried enough/pushed enough versus the concern that they are expecting too much;
(d) the need to devote themselves entirely to the child versus the need to share responsibility for the child;
(e) the need to be a teacher of the child versus the need to leave teaching to others;
(f) the need to think about the future versus the need to avoid thinking about the future.

Extending our understanding of these conflicts and needs and developing provisions and responses which are sensitive to them must be a major goal for education and a range of other services in the future.

   The educational psychologist's individual role will need to develop progressively in these areas in order for educational psychologists to extend their ability to be an effective resource. This will only be possible within an LEA framework which makes the connection between the educational psychologist's individual casework role and the LEA's policy and system for meeting all individual needs.

IMPLICATIONS FOR THE FUTURE

At the time of writing this chapter many educational psychologists will have a nervous and uncertain eye on the massive structural and organizational changes which are currently impacting upon the education system. As the latest DES circular on local management passes into our in-trays, concerns and anxieties about the future shape of educational psychology services must be reaching a new high. At a time when there is much talk of the marketing of services, of delegating services to schools and of support services being placed on a 'buy-in/agency basis', the nature of the work which educational psychologists will carry out in the future takes on a new meaning. There are understandable fears that educational psychologists will come under increasing pressure to work *exclusively at the individual level*. This is related to widespread anxieties concerning pressures from schools, from parents and others to increase the volume of statutory assessment work as schools respond to both the National Curriculum and the local management of schools. Children who struggle to meet the expectations of nationally assessed levels of attainment and children who are expensive to educate within a limited delegated budget will, it is feared, not be wanted or valued by schools. If, in this situation, the survival of educational psychology services is dependent upon psychologists delivering a service which schools value and desire, the implications for the EP's future work seem clear. Are we about to see the end of educational psychology services as we know them? Is this 'worst case scenario' inevitable?

I think not, although the answer will depend crucially upon the political context of individual LEAs and upon particular LEA policy frameworks. Of particular importance will be the policy framework in existence within the field of special educational needs. It will also depend upon both LEAs and psychological services being clear about the perennial question of who is the client. We can no longer afford to fudge our responses to this question. The major client group for educational psychologists has been and is always likely to be the LEA. It is the LEA that employs educational psychologists (I know of no school within the maintained system within Great Britain which pays directly for the salary of an educational psychologist). The LEA employs educational psychologists in order to provide advice to the authority, to schools, to parents and to other agencies on the needs of children, particularly those with special educational needs. While it is certainly the job of educational psychologists to provide support to teachers and schools it is not the primary job of educational psychologists to provide a *consumer-based service to schools*. It is sometimes the job of educational psychologists to challenge and to act as 'critical friends' to schools. Educational psychologists play a role as a representative of the LEA to look at needs which are wider than the interests of any one school. The role and work of educational psychologists should be an integral part of an LEA's policy and approaches to children with special needs and to its policy and approach to professional and curriculum development.

In the post-1988 Act era there is a concern that the power and influence of LEAs themselves will be seen to decrease. With it the need for central services which represent aspects of an LEA's policy aspirations might similarly decline. There can be little doubt that this situation is likely to occur in many areas of LEA provision. However, the field of special education is unlike many curricular and policy areas. Special education is a policy and provision area which cannot be managed by delegation to the individual school. Nor is it likely to be effectively managed at a national/central level. The management and organization of provision for children with special needs is likely to continue to be crucially dependent upon policy at the LEA level (or at a similar localized level of management).

The implications of the current changes for educational psychologists are likely to vary across LEA boundaries. However, it seems probable that there will be a continuing need for a group of professionals who are working at the interface between individual pupils (their parents and schools) and policy and provision at an LEA level. The future shape and form of this professional group could alter dramatically in the near future. Educational psychology services which are currently distinct and discrete could become integrated within a broader LEA support and advisory structure.

Whatever the future holds for educational psychologists (and LEA support services in general) we can be certain of one thing: there will continue to be children who have highly individual educational needs. Their needs will continue to challenge the best of our teachers and the best of our schools. Understanding the needs of these pupils, their parents and their teachers—responding to them, learning from them and making the connections between their needs and the future response of the educational system—will be a continuing professional challenge. Educational psychologists are likely to continue to be around to confront this challenge.

REFERENCES

Burt, C. (1957) *The Causes and Treatment of Backwardness* (fourth edition). London: University of London Press.

Burt, C. (1964) 'The school psychological service: its history and development', Address to the First Annual Conference of the Association of Educational Psychologists.

DES (Department of Education and Science) (1983) 'Assessments and Statements of Special Educational Needs', Circular 1/83. London: DES.

Dessent, T. (1987) *Making the Ordinary School Special*. Lewes: The Falmer Press.

Dessent, T. (1988) 'Educational psychologist and the resource issue', in Jones, N. and Sayer, J. (eds) *Management and the Psychology of Schooling*. Lewes: The Falmer Press.

Faupel, A. W. (1990) 'A model response to emotional and behavioural development in schools', *Educational Psychology in Practice*, 5 (4), 172–82.

Gillham, W. E. C. (1978) *Reconstructing Educational Psychology*. London: Croom Helm.

Jones, N. and Sayer, J. (eds) (1988) *Management and The Psychology of Schooling*. Lewes: The Falmer Press.

Miller, G. A. (1969) 'Psychology as a means of promoting human welfare', *American Psychologist*, 24, 1063–75.

Mortimore, P., Sammons, P., Stoll, L., Lewis, D. and Ecob, R. (1988) *School Matters: The Junior Years*. Wells: Open Books.

Reynolds, D. (1985) *Studying School Effectiveness*. Lewes: The Falmer Press.

Rutter, M., Maughan, B., Mortimore, P., Ouston, J. and Smith, A. (1979) *Fifteen Thousand Hours: Secondary Schools and their Effects on Pupils*. London: Open Books.

Turner, M. (1990) *Sponsored Reading Failure*. Warlingham: IPSET.

Wedell, K. (1981) 'Concepts of special educational needs', *Education Today*, 31 (1), 3–9.

Wedell, K. (1983) 'Some developments in the concepts and practice of special education', *New Horizons Journal of Education* (Hong Kong Teachers Association), 24, 99–108.

Chapter 4

Ecological Interventions

Gary Thomas

ecol'ogy, *n.* a study of plants, or of animals, or of peoples and institutions, in relation to environment. [Gr. *oikos*, house, *logos*, discourse.] (*Chambers English Dictionary*)

An *ecological* approach might at first glance seem a strange way to describe the work of educational psychologists. The word 'ecological' is usually used to describe the relationships of the living world rather than the activities of groups of professionals. The use of the word might also suffer the charge of being simply fashionable—inducing a meaningless association with an issue which is currently in vogue.

On reflection, though, the term seems a particularly apposite way of describing a particular kind of psychological approach. Moreover, as a term it turns out to have a distinguished pedigree in educational and psychological literature. The use of the term in education certainly antedates the current preoccupation with all things environmental.

In its 'green' sense ecology refers to the relationships between living things in the environments that they inhabit. It is the study of the complex interrelationships that take place in those environments. A 'given' in this study is that the lives of individuals who inhabit these environments are inextricably intertwined with the nature and quality of those environments. Changes in any small aspect of the environment will have knock-on effects which will affect the lives of the organisms that populate it. Further, there will be an equilibrium in this environment, or ecosystem, and this equilibrium will be maintained.

Without labouring the 'green' analogy, it is clear how such a model is applicable in the human sciences and in applied psychology. Psychological endeavour has traditionally been essentially individual centred. This orientation permeates the applied field, where interventions often take place in something of a vacuum, with scant consideration of the physical and social environments within which individuals learn and behave. The ecological metaphor enables an understanding that things are not that simple. Behaviours may emerge in an environment that are a consequence of conditions outside the narrow ambit of the individual. Changing one or two features of this system may have unanticipated consequences, or may have no effect at all.

THINKING ECOLOGICALLY: A REORIENTATION

A year or so ago I received a call for papers for a conference. The blurb began: 'Educational psychologists are first and foremost psychologists.' Though the statement was seemingly innocuous (straying between the benign and the banal), something else I had read at about the same time led me to wonder whether the best interests of children (or, less importantly, the best interests of educational psychology) are served by adherence to such an idea:

> [Psychologists'] advice has had very little impact on the practice of teaching . . . Some [reasons for this] arise out of the manner in which those who have studied teaching and learning have *oversimplified the lives of classroom participants*. (Desforges *et al.*, 1985: my italics)

This found resonance. My belief in the contribution of traditional psychological method to my work as an educational psychologist has slowly been chipped away, both by what I have seen happening in real life—the classrooms I have gone into, the children, teachers and parents I have talked with—and by my reading. A passage from Barrett (1978), in which he warns of the hegemony of ideology, summarizes the way I had become beguiled by the elegance of certain kinds of psychological theory:

> The greater and more spectacular the theory, the more likely it is to foster our indolent disposition to oversimplify: to twist all the ordinary matters of experience to fit them into the new framework, and if they do not, to lop them off. (p. 149)

When I read this I recognized grudgingly that this is what I as an educational psychologist had been doing. Every time parents or teachers or children had opened their mouths, every time I made a classroom observation, I was compressing what was said or done into my own theoretical mould. These theoretical moulds, from wherever they derive, are the Procrustean bed of the educational psychologist; there is the danger that in compacting, trimming and generally forcing the worlds with which we work into our own moulds we distort and misperceive those worlds. While an ecological approach does not remove this tendency entirely, it at least seeks a wider set of explanatory features for children's behaviour; it seeks to contextualize them.

A number of commentators have remarked on the weaknesses of the traditional experimental paradigm in psychology to account for, to interpret or to explicate the behaviour of individuals or groups as part of the wider ecosystem. As I have noted elsewhere (Thomas, 1985), this paradigm, rooted in 'individual method', is one with which psychologists have a natural affinity. Within such a paradigm the influence of the wider environment is conscientiously ignored. Not only is it ignored; it is actively eliminated, studiously 'controlled for'. This may be valid in the laboratory. But for educational psychologists, eschewing the importance and effects of wider systems in the lives of individuals clearly has grave shortcomings.

Not only in educational psychology has the legacy of Wundt and Skinner constrained the emergence of alternative methods of thinking about the problems we confront; Secord (1986) asserts that the 'individual and inward polarities' (p. 150) of social psychology have stunted the growth of ecological psychology in that field also. The hegemony of experimental psychology and methodological behaviourism have inhibited the assimilation of new ideas to the psychological enterprise generally. But in education it is the dominance of behavioural psychology which has done most to limit the respectability of more contextually sensitive ways of viewing the worlds with which we work.

I pick on behavioural psychology because it is perhaps the clearest example of its genre, and of the idea that 'pure' can unproblematically inform 'applied'. It has seemed so methodologically self-confident, so sure of the value of its contribution to real-world problems. It proudly boasted its scientific, empirico-inductive foundations (for instance, Bijou, 1970) in such a way that alternatives were made to seem less than adequate. In fact, its proponents sometimes seemed to believe that they had the monopoly on methodological rigour and scientific method. Further, there appeared to be the assumption among some—even in the 1970s and 1980s—that behavioural psychology had been drawn from the white heat of contemporary psychological discourse.

My contention is that, on the contrary, behavioural method is currently looking distinctly yellow at the edges. It is inadequate to cope with the increasingly complex problems with which educational psychologists are confronted. In this it is not alone. It is unreasonable to expect that the methods and findings of 'pure' psychology should slide effortlessly into the messy real world where variables can be neither controlled nor eliminated.

METHODOLOGICAL FOUNDATIONS OF APPLIED PSYCHOLOGY

Anyone who questioned the solid-as-a-rock foundations of experimental or behavioural psychology at the time I was doing my first degree was regarded as soft in the head; criticism was usually of the 'Isn't it all rather dehumanizing?' variety. Those questions were easy to counter.

But a set of neglected, or ignored, questions about appropriate methodology were tougher—and people have been asking them for some time. Koch (1964), for instance, summarizes an important methodological question about current psychological discourse and the way that it has rooted itself in a limited kind of legitimate data, namely that prescribed by the logical positivists:

> In every period of our history we [psychologists] have looked to external sources in the scholarly culture—especially natural science and the philosophy of science—for our sense of direction. And typically we have embraced policies long out of date in those very sources . . . Psychology is thus in the unenviable position of standing on philosophical foundations which began to be vacated by philosophy almost as soon as the former had borrowed them. (pp. 4–5)

In other words, the assumptions of logical positivism about the legitimacy of particular kinds of data for scientific study are no longer valid.

There is a certain hubris which leads those who are wedded to the traditional, narrowly focusing experimental paradigm to proceed as though those who resist are either hopelessly romantic or unscientific. Or they assume evangelically that resistors simply have not seen the light. But Egan (1984) summarizes the arguments for a modern (that is, post-Popperian) reinterpretation of what constitutes 'scientific' thus: 'Science is not a method. Doing science is not a matter of "applying" or "using" a method, but of using the proper methods to answer particular questions about particular phenomena' (p. 132).

It is, then, valid to look elsewhere for an appropriate foundation and superstructure for our applied psychology—to look for the 'proper methods' for answering the questions in which we as educational psychologists are interested. Barker (1968) makes the point well. He highlights the legitimacy of alternative forms of enquiry and analysis by invoking an example of alternative, but equally valid, explanations for the same event. He asks us to imagine the movement of a train of wheat across the Kansas plains. How is this movement to be explained? An economist will explain it in one way, while an engineer will explain it in another. 'Both the laws of economics and the laws of engineering are true; both operate in predictable ways on the train' (p. 12). The usefulness of the analysis for the situation in which it is framed will depend on the model used to make the analysis and the tools it provides for making that analysis.

EDUCATIONAL PSYCHOLOGY AS APPLIED PSYCHOLOGY?

Educational psychologists are steeped in the view of themselves as applied scientists. Taking an ecological view demands a broader perspective. It demands, first and foremost, a reappraisal of what constitutes *science*, and whether science in the human field can be *applied* in the ways that we have assumed.

Associated with the traditional paradigm is the notion that pure science should 'feed' applied science, that there is some sort of continuum between the pure world and the applied world which allows such feeding to take place. My contention is that it is illegitimate to make such an assumption. There are discontinuities between these two worlds which demand that an alternative set of methodologies is adopted to tackle the problems of the real world.

The notion that the transmission of ideas should necessarily be from the pure field to the applied field is perhaps responsible for the fact that applied psychology turns into so many dead ends. The assumption that this traffic should automatically be one way is not justified. The fact that the assumption *is* at the root of so much in applied psychological practice leads to what Hargreaves (1978) calls the 'unwarranted' use of techniques based on psychological notions:

> After . . . original ideas and instruments are developed by psychologists there follows a phase in which over-zealous educational psychologists make somewhat premature applications of, and exaggerated claims for, these ideas and instruments and use them in ways that are not strictly warranted. (p. 5)

I would go further. There is no necessary continuity between the world of pure psychology and that of the educational psychologist. The expectation that this *should* be the case leads to forms of intervention that are often inappropriate.

Naughton (1981) makes the point well in distinguishing between science, technology and 'craft knowledge'. He asserts that the notion that there is a one-way traffic of ideas from science to technology is refuted by the actual history of science, which shows the process of continual interaction between the two. He says that technology (applied psychology in our case) involves the application of kinds of knowledge other than the purely scientific. Many technologies flourished long before scientific theories could have informed them. Thus, it is misleading to call our technologies, our methods of working with and changing real-world problems, 'applied science'. They are 'craft knowledge'. Lee (1988) concurs about the validity of craft knowledge or 'craft psychology', as she calls it, noting that 'the critical issue is whether the strategy will work under the actual work requirements of daily life' (p. 146).

Naughton goes further in saying that our aim should not be to establish all-encompassing theories. Rather, he quotes Checkland (1972) and Popper (1945) in saying that our orientation ought to be toward 'piecemeal social engineering'. In playing down the importance of theory in understanding people-based problems, Checkland finds not only Popper for company: Kuhn (1970), for example, notes that even in 'harder' fields than psychology, scientific advance is now seen not so much as resting on the testing of theory, but rather in a 'series of non-cumulative developments'. Likewise, Quinton (in Magee, 1982) suggests that we should be looking to 'the piecemeal dissipation of confusion' rather than the construction of all-explaining theory.

Toffler (1985) asserts something very similar. He suggests that the study of people and their relationships within institutions and organizations are marked by what he calls '*ad hocery*'. The successful use of such *ad hocery* presages, if Toffler is correct, the demise of the kind of tidy-mindedness which gives rise to a requirement for theory and hypothesis in the study of real-world problems.

These notions—of piecemeal dissipation of confusion, of *ad hocery*, of craft knowledge and of piecemeal social engineering—although from different ideological stables, are congruent in one important respect. Central to these notions is the belief that problem solving—particularly of the kind engaged in by educational psychologists—requires a different kind of understanding of the world from the one that 'applied science' has traditionally offered. Educational psychologists require strategies which start from the problem in context. Strategies which are forced by a formulation of the problem constructed out of a body of experimental knowledge are less likely to be helpful. Figure 4.1 compares these differences.

It is in the use of *craft psychology* that heuristics such as systems thinking or ecological psychology assist. They enable an organization of real-world problems, with the ultimate goal being effective action to improve the situation—not understanding for understanding's sake. Stevens (1985) concurs in suggesting that the success of applied psychology pivots on its ability to free itself from the traditional concern of psychology, which is to explain and predict. He goes on to assert that the primary goal of the teacher and the educational psychologist is problem solving rather than explanation.

Ecological thinking can, then, be thought of as a reorientation rather than a theory, a methodology or an approach. Taking as its starting point the indivisibility of the larger wholes which individuals inhabit, it seeks ways of assigning significance to these; of appropriating and using these wider situations in finding solutions to the problems individuals experience. It can do this in a variety of ways, which I examine in the following section.

ECOLOGICAL MODELS

Popkewitz (1984) says that we use our chosen methodological traditions, or paradigms, as *lenses* through which we see the world. It is a nice metaphor, into which all kinds of psychological model can immediately be seen to fit. Traditional psychological method, for instance, is like a convex lens, enabling the user to focus in great detail on small

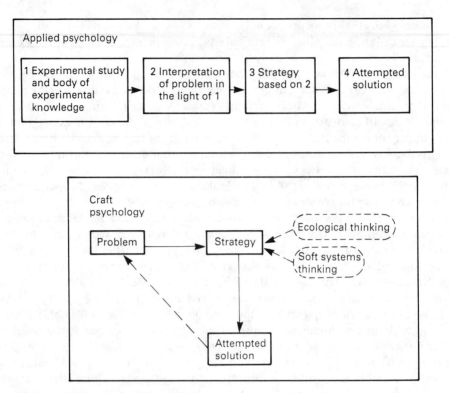

Figure 4.1   *Applied psychology versus craft psychology.*

features of the target. Such a close-up, as I have tried to indicate, has its weaknesses in applied psychology.

By contrast, an ecological model is like a wide-angle lens, enabling an examination of the wider situation which surrounds the target, and encouraging—in the case of the educational psychologist—activity in that wider situation. The metaphor also enables a distinction to be made between an ecological approach and an eclectic approach. The eclectic lens is rather like a gnarled and bubbled glass which the viewer moves from side to side and up and down, hoping at last to get an adequate view of the target. The muddled rag-bag of techniques and methodologies which goes under the banner 'eclectic' is no substitute for a consistent set of principles for viewing the world.

In essence, an ecological view enables a recognition that children live in a variety of contexts, each one impinging upon the other. Any attempt to oversimplify the richness of the ways in which these contexts interplay is bound to have shortcomings. An ecological view says that it is impossible to disentangle the functioning of a constellation of phenomena simultaneously interrelating in the classroom. Viewed in this way, classrooms, and indeed all the environments that children inhabit, are ecosystems— complex and organic. Such a view contrasts with the view of classrooms as modules whose inert workings are, through controlled manipulation, open to inspection and analysis—the legacy that the tradition of psychology has made to education.

Although it is Barker (1968) who has generally been credited with introducing the notion of ecological psychology, Doyle (1977) did much to introduce the idea to education. He suggested that the ways teachers and children behave in classrooms reflect the cumulative effects of an ongoing process—a continuous process of adaptation to the environment and reappraisal of its demands. He suggested, in the context of teacher education, that it would be more profitable to examine the structure of the classroom environment in preference to skills-based training of teachers. He suggests that the latter, if it has any effect at all, is short-lived.

Bronfenbrenner's ecology of human development

Bronfenbrenner (1979) has perhaps contributed most systematically to furthering the ways in which the ecological approach can be used. He says that laboratory studies sacrifice too much to gain experimental control and analytic rigour; they lead to 'the science of strange behaviour of children in strange situations with strange adults for the briefest possible periods of time'. Although this is said in the context of developmental psychology, its immediate relevance to educational psychology is clear: he believes we need to observe behaviour in natural settings while children are interacting with familiar adults over prolonged periods of time.

Kounin (1967) makes much the same point. He points out the value of ecological, naturalistic observation in which many coexisting events are studied. We have, he says, to make sure that important variables are not overlooked for unimportant ones simply because the latter fit our conceptual schemata or are more easily measurable.

Bronfenbrenner offers a conceptual framework for analysing the layers of the environment that have a formative influence on the child. He emphasizes the importance not only of the child's interactions with adults and other children, but also the influences of the larger environment—the parents' work and the family's community. Culture and society are viewed by Bronfenbrenner as a set of 'instructions' for how settings are made. He sees ecological environments as being composed of micro-, meso-, exo- and macrosystems. The nested nature of these is shown in Figure 4.2.

A microsystem is a pattern of activities, roles and interpersonal relations of an individual in a given setting. A mesosystem is a system of microsystems. An exosystem is a

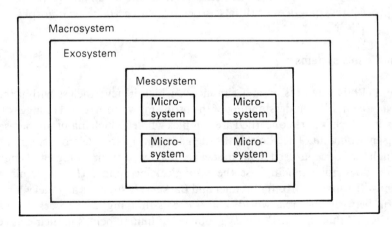

Figure 4.2 *Bronfenbrenner's model of systemic influences.*

setting where the individual is not involved but where events occur that affect or are affected by the individual's setting. A macrosystem comprises the belief systems or ideology that structure other, lower systems.

Bronfenbrenner also suggests that ecological methodology, in the context of the discussion above, is more scientific than its alternatives, that it is 'more elegant and constitutes "harder" science—than the best possible contrived experiment addressed to the same research question' (p. 36). He suggests that psychologists should aim to analyse systematically the nature of the existing accommodation between the person and the milieu.

Barker's ecological psychology

Barker's (1968) attempts to define attributes of behaviour settings share features with those of Bronfenbrenner. He suggests that behaviour settings have both static and dynamic attributes. On the static side, the setting consists of one or more standing patterns of behaviour-and-milieu, the latter comprising elements such as house, classroom, a windy day. On the dynamic side, the setting comprises the interpersonal relationships among people and groups. Science, Barker says, attempts to keep apart the static and the dynamic, the physical and the behavioural. But their *interaction* is the *focus* of his attention; he gives the name *synomorphs* to the settings in which these interactions occur.

Barker clearly intended his model to be useful in the real world rather than the laboratory. By taking as a starting point the integration of behaviour and environment, he intends to be able to predict real-world events and solve real-world problems. Unfortunately, the Byzantine complexity of his model and the impenetrability of his language render his aims unmeetable. (One wonders, for instance, whether anyone who says that behaviour settings consist of 'behaviour-and-circumjacent-synomorphic-milieu entities' [Barker, 1968, p. 20] can be taken seriously.) This is a pity, since his central thesis is as powerful as it is important for educational psychology. Amidst Barker's complex analysis is a continual reiteration of the influence of the physical environment and its interaction with a range of other influences such as the ideologies of the participants, and the procedures, practices or rituals associated with certain 'synomorphs'.

Checkland's soft systems

Checkland (1981) attempts greater simplicity, which is nevertheless within the framework of a more holistic understanding of the problems we confront. He suggests that the matters with which we are concerned are complex wholes which maintain themselves in a changing environment. They do this through adaptation and control action.

Although the concepts used in his model are borrowed from biology and engineering, Checkland does not explicitly use the ecological metaphor. However, his aims are congruent with those of Bronfenbrenner and Barker. He suggests a model which draws a distinction between the 'real world' and 'systems thinking' and forces an analysis of both. He asserts that the 'soft', messy problems of human beings in their everyday lives are not amenable to the methods of the 'hard' systems tradition.[1] He suggests that hard systems tradition can handle *natural* (that is, biological) systems and *designed* systems (such as bicycles, computers, mathematics) but cannot cope in situations dominated by human perceptions. He calls the latter *human activity systems*. His soft systems method suggests the following sequence of events and processes.

First, a statement is made of the situation in which there is perceived to be a problem; each social situation is taken to be an *interacting* system of roles, norms and values. Second, an analysis is made of the problem. This involves drawing (literally) a 'rich picture' of the situation, in which the relationship of structure and process are noted.' At this stage *themes* are extracted and these themes represent statements about the situation which the analyst regards as puzzling, problematic, interesting or significant. This analysis has so far been at the real-world level. But at the third stage we descend into soft systems thinking. Here, the analyst identifies systems operating in the situation and their function in that situation. It is here that an analogy with the ecosystem is clearest. The aim is to identify from the 'rich picture' the *functions* of behaviours and sets of behaviours within the situation. Checkland gives the name 'relevant systems' to these. From these relevant systems a 'root definition' is arrived at, which essentially describes the analyst's view of the problem situation on the basis of the posited relevant systems. The fourth stage involves the construction of 'conceptual models' of the systems isolated in stage 3. The final stages involve a journey back into the 'real world' and a comparison of these models with what exists in the real world. Figure 4.3 summarizes this process.

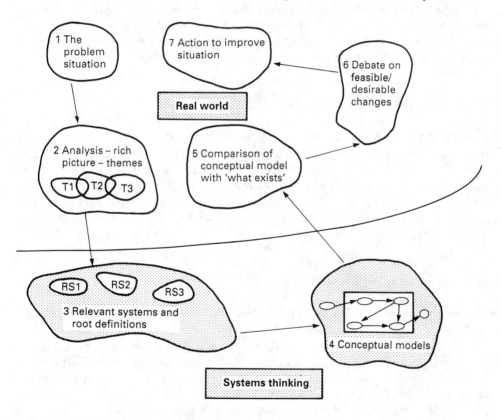

Figure 4.3   *Naughton's (1981) version of the soft systems methodology.*

Shared features of the models

These ecological approaches share much with each other. They also share a great deal with other ways of trying to contextualize the problems which children or teachers may experience. Symbolic interactionism, structuralism and phenomenological psychology all, in their different ways, share the goal of locating these problems in a wider frame. Educational psychologists will, though, quite legitimately seek ways of operationalizing the ideas from each of these models. Techniques for doing this have to be usable. While some frameworks—perhaps interactionism can be taken as an example—provide no structure within which strategies can be framed, others (Barker's model being a good example) prescribe structure of such complexity that they are unlikely to be employed by the busy educational psychologist.

An ecological perspective provides a framework without prescribing a narrow set of procedures. It is important to stress that there is no single way of taking an ecological approach. Although there are those who would seek to set down a new set of paradigmatic boundaries for the approach (such as Jasnoski, 1984), an ecological approach is best viewed as metatheoretical (see Ekehammar, 1974; Willems, 1977; Turvey and Carello, 1981).

Perhaps more than this, it could be said that the aim of an ecological approach is to puncture the paradigmatic skins of other approaches, to force a reappraisal of the traditions, habits and methods with which these interface with the subjects with which they are concerned. In Bronfenbrenner's terms, it enables one to view the wider ecosystems which individuals inhabit, and it enables a view to be taken of the 'instructions' which these provide for the individuals who inhabit them.

AN ECOLOGICAL VIEW IN PRACTICE

Ecological approaches reach from the 'rigorously naturalistic' methods of Doyle to those whose methods are rooted in positivism. As an example of the latter, Krantz and Risley (1977) note that an ecological focus in behavioural method is at least as successful as contingency management, while possessing few of the familiar sequelae of the latter: ecological variation can take place without large expenditure, without cost to the teacher and regardless of the theoretical orientation espoused by the school, as made clear by Rogers-Warren and Warren (1977).

With behaviour management

Let me give an instance which springs from this last example. An educational psychologist is called in by a school to look at a child who is being disruptive. A common (but, I accept, by no means universal) way of approaching this will be to make an analysis which involves observation to elicit the consequences for the child's disruption. The attempt will then be to manoeuvre those consequences in such a way that they are contingent upon alternative behaviours. The essence of the method is in consequence management. Wheldall (1988) makes the point well; he says that behavioural methods currently employed in British schools are often typically characterized by 'crude consequence management strategies which are both intrusive and also less likely to bring about generalisation of learned behaviour to control by the natural environment' (p. 172).

From an ecological vantage point it is possible to see that the behaviourally derived strategy adopted in my example neglects important elements of its own model. By focusing on consequences, it minimizes the significance of antecedents and setting conditions for the child's behaviour. These provide the 'instructions' or the template for all that takes place within. The organization of the lesson, the nature of the curriculum, the physical structure of the classroom and its 'geography' will all affect the ways in which children behave and learn. These factors are at least as important as the specific consequences of the behaviour.

Further, these factors are sometimes more easily changed in negotiation with a teacher than are specific consequences for behaviour. Focusing on the latter involves some quite substantial analysis and monitoring. Focusing on features in the wider environment (the antecedents of the behavioural model, or the exosystem of Bronfenbrenner's) can take place comparatively easily. For example, Wheldall *et al.* (1981) and Bennett and Blundell (1983) show how simply rearranging the seating arrangements in a class can have significant effects on the engagement of the children therein. Similarly Lucas and Thomas (1990) show how rethinking the classroom geography can prevent problems arising.

Willems (1977) suggests that eco-friendly alterations can be made to behavioural observation. He suggests increasing the number of behaviour categories observed; increasing the number of children observed; observing other dimensions of the behaviour (for example, was the behaviour done with someone else? who instigated it?).

Staying with the same behavioural example, a review of class management research indicates how stubbornly we can stick with a particular way of viewing and analysing classroom behaviour. We can hold to such methodology despite evidence, both from our own senses and from research, that something else—more complex and more subtle—is happening in a particular situation. More and more research is showing that the beguilingly simple contingencies that were once assumed to be associated with children's behaviour are in fact oversimple. Brophy (1981), for example, concludes his substantial overview of the use of teacher praise with the warning that 'the data suggest qualifications on our enthusiasm in recommending praise to teachers (who, in any case, seem to be intuitively aware of its limitations)' (p. 27). He suggests that when praise is intended as reinforcement, it frequently takes on some other function. The important point that Brophy makes as far as an ecological approach is concerned is that the *meaning* of praise is determined not by the enthusiasm or number of decibels with which it is emitted, but rather by the *context* in which it occurs.

It is worth digressing for a moment to reflect on the significance of Brophy's work. Human activity systems (in Checkland's terms, above) are governed by language. New worlds are created when language is used, yet in the unthinking application of behavioural psychology, this simple fact is skirted around. Through language, new meanings and understandings are constructed which render invalid the simple contingencies asserted by the application of the methods of natural sciences to human behaviour. Wittgenstein came to view human discourse as set within a series of language 'games', in which the rules of the game were constantly being reformulated by the participants; one has to understand the *context* and the *rules* of each game—its ecology, if you like—

before being able to illuminate the meanings therein. Quinton (in Magee, 1982) sums it up thus:

> Wittgenstein's theory of action seems to imply that there can be no social and human sciences which use methods parallel to those of the natural sciences. Instead, the study of man and society has to be interpretative in character . . . the form of social life being studied is, one might say, language-impregnated. (p. 92)

Kounin (1970), on the basis of videotaped observations of the classroom, came to conclusions similar to those of Brophy about the significance, or otherwise, of specific, decontextualized behaviours. He said that the success of teachers' classroom management was not dependent on clarity, firmness or intensity of 'desist effort'; nor did it matter 'whether she focuses on the misbehaviour, or on the legal activity or both; nor whether she treats the child positively, negatively or neutrally' (p. 70). These decontextualized teacher behaviours, Kounin found, were relatively unimportant elements of a teacher's management strategy.

More important than these ways of approaching individuals for the success of class management were, according to Kounin, some complex strategies which enabled the teacher simultaneously to manage varied aspects of class activity: in effect, ways of managing the ecosystem of the classroom. These strategies included 'withitness' and 'overlapping'; that is, the ability to maintain smoothness in activity flow by, for instance, dealing with misbehaviour while not interrupting the flow of learning activity; initiating and maintaining 'flow'—keeping the session moving along smoothly without, for instance, 'overdwelling' on a particular behaviour or learning point; maintaining group focus by keeping the children alert to the presence of the teacher and accountable for their work.

By deliberately taking a wider purview, and by using methods of analysis in keeping with that wider view, he is able to arrive at a model which has more general utility than others which stem from a more focused perspective.

A simple, readable account of the contribution of ecological thinking to educational problems, and in particular to the question of classroom behaviour, is given in Apter and Conoley (1984).

With learning difficulties

In children's learning, as well as in the question of their classroom behaviour, one has the choice of either focusing *narrowly* on the topic to be learned and the methods to be employed in instruction, or of *enlarging* the situation to see how learning might be improved. The former carries with it ever more specialized and professionalized methods of teaching, which do not meld easily with the exigencies of classroom life. Indeed, there is little evidence for their success, and proponents of some of the more specialized methods of teaching have now revised their opinions of these in the light of experience of their use.

For example, Bloom (1984), one of the high priests of the objectives movement, with his 'mastery learning', now directs his attention not so much to the minutiae of instructional procedure as to the general context of the learning situation. Focusing narrowly on instructional procedures is impossible for the teacher in a busy class. Even if she had the time to learn the procedures for their use, she would be unlikely to be able to implement them.

Instead, Bloom now suggests concentrating more on features of the class such as 'student support systems', similar to peer tutoring. These, he says, together with other cooperative learning efforts, are almost as effective as mastery learning procedures. (It is important to remember that the success of mastery learning procedures was established not in 'real' classrooms, but in one-to-one tutorials.) He goes on to say that changing teachers' methods of teaching should no longer form the focus of our concerns. Rather, this concern should be towards helping teachers become more aware of ways in which they can teach a cross-section of children, towards children's learning styles, towards the curriculum and towards home environmental supports. His endorsement for an ecological approach is tacit, but the framework he now proposes fits neatly into Bronfenbrenner's model.

The point, I think, is that the system adopted directs the adopter to a particular way of working. Adopting a narrowly focused approach neglects the realities of the classroom. Not only this, but it also narrows our view of what education is about; Bloom (1984) laments that after a million sales of his *Taxonomy of Educational Objectives*, which has been so influential in American schooling, 'our instructional materials, our classroom teaching methods, and our testing methods rarely rise above the lowest level of the taxonomy: knowledge' (p. 14). Ainscow and Tweddle (1989), in an honest reappraisal of the use of objectives in the UK, come to similar conclusions.

By taking an ecological view, by seeing how systems relate and interrelate, by seeing what support systems exist within and outside the classroom, planning for children's learning can become simpler and more effective. If we adopt this approach as systematically as we planned the use of objectives at the beginning of the 1980s, it will not only become simpler to facilitate children's learning, but that learning will also become more natural.

By enlarging rather than narrowing the focus, ways of helping children are brought into view which are easier to implement. By adjusting comparatively easily influenced features of the classroom, changes which will be beneficial to *all* children may be effected. Furthermore, these methods are likely to be more successful, for a variety of reasons. Others concur with Bloom that there is little ground for believing that effort expended in instructional design has any payoff which is superior to simpler ways of helping. There are plenty of studies (for instance, Tizard *et al.*, 1982; Jackson and Hannon, 1981) to show that children can make extraordinary progress when having help from their parents, whatever the technique used to help them:

> Of much greater practical significance is the fact that teachers and parents working in collaboration did improve the academic performance of the children *without the parents being given any special training in the techniques of tutoring*. (Tizard *et al.*, 1982, p. 13: emphasis added)

Of course, what is common to the success of a range of successful approaches—approaches as different as parental involvement, direct instruction and instrumental enrichment—is enthusiasm, and amount and intensity of help. Evidence in support of this assertion is provided by DeVault *et al.* (1977) in a re-evaluation of the various Project Follow-Through curricula. It seems that given a few broadly defined parameters within which any reasonably sensitive adult works with children (such as enthusiasm, patience, the ability and willingness to give encouragement), such help can hardly fail to be successful. If this is the case, then effort will more profitably be spent in *analysing environments* with the aim of maximizing such help (perhaps, for instance, through parental involvement, as in the above example) than in refining instruction.

It is interesting to note that an ecological perspective may only be arrived at after we have realized that the avenue down which our predilections for traditional psychological methodology have led us is a cul-de-sac. The EDY project (McBrien and Foxen, 1981) aimed to help teachers and other classroom personnel to use operant techniques with children with severe learning difficulty. It was soon appreciated that the methods which were being used in the package involved a lot of work with individual children, and that this created problems for the classroom teacher. Without special attention to the problem it is difficult to reconcile the need for such intensive individual help with the need to keep the larger body of children in a class engaged (the 'But what am I supposed to do with the other thirty?' problem). EDY—eventually—resolved the problem by employing 'room management', a technique geared around the organization of the classroom, which is aimed at enabling the provision of extra individual teaching sessions while facilitating group engagement.

Whole-school approaches

A whole-school approach to meeting special educational needs has become a popular idea (see Thomas and Feiler, 1988). In it we can see the recognition of the fact that interventions with individuals will not be as effective in the long term as a properly coordinated policy. Such a policy will incorporate statements about attitudes held collectively within the school, as well as specific strategies and procedural guidelines (see Roaf, 1988). Bronfenbrenner's model provides a valuable framework within which to work when considering how such a policy might take shape. Special needs may be seen to be exaggerated or diminished by the ideology, procedures, curriculum, layout and everyday classroom arrangements within the school. The focus on special educational needs has, in Bronfenbrenner's terms, taken place traditionally at the microsystem level. But an ecological perspective—a whole-school approach—forces an examination of the wider systems involved. At the macrosystem level, the school may choose to include statements about its ideology as a school: its stance on rights, needs and opportunities. At the exosystem level it may consider the influence of the curriculum or the nature of the management structure within the school. A properly devised whole-school approach provides an exemplar of an ecological perspective.

'Settings-based' classroom applications

I have suggested above that Barker's model, while providing an important framework, becomes too complex to be of practical use. However, if the notion of behaviour settings is distilled out of his work, the significance of these settings in shaping the behaviour of those within becomes clear. If this is done in relation to classroom analysis, a number of avenues become visible, and in the following paragraphs I give some examples of ways in which classroom settings have been analysed and altered with the objective of improving the ways in which children's learning needs are met.

Weinstein (1979), in a major review of classroom environment research, cites a particularly interesting case study comparing two classrooms that were similar in all but physical layout. In classroom A, desks were arranged so that only two or three children could work together; areas for different activities were set apart by barriers such as bookcases. Areas for quiet study and areas for activities were also set apart; the teacher's desk was in the corner so that she was unable to direct activities from it and had to move around the room a great deal. By contrast, in classroom B large groups of children (up to twelve) were supposed to be working together (despite the individualized curriculum), areas for different activities were not clearly designated and the teacher's desk was centrally located—enabling her to direct activity from her seat. In classroom A conversation was quieter, and the children were more engaged, with longer attention spans than those in classroom B.

There is evidence that children prefer non-traditionally organized classrooms (that is, not organized in the traditional Plowden format with groups). Pfluger and Zola (1974), for instance, found that children preferred a large space in the centre of the room, with furniture along the walls. Children may even prefer being in formal rows rather than being in groups (see Bennett and Blundell, 1983; Wheldall *et al.*, 1981). The physical arrangement of the classroom is clearly noticed by the children, and is important to them. Likewise, Lucas and Thomas (1990) suggest that a change in the layout of the ubiquitous groups-based British primary classroom (inspired by Plowden) is welcomed by children; it also has clear organizational benefits.

Contrary to the findings of Bennett and Blundell, and Wheldall *et al.* (above), Rosenfield, Lambert and Black (1985) found that students seated in circles were significantly more engaged than those in rows. Those who were in groups were more engaged than those in rows but less than those in circles. Rows produced a greater number of 'withdrawal responses' than either of the other two table configurations. The difference in finding between Wheldall *et al.* and Bennett and Blundell on the one side, and Rosenfield *et al.* on the other, is testimony to the case that behaviours are situationally determined. The situation may have been wider and the context richer than any of these researchers imagined, with factors in these wider situations responsible for differences in the findings.

There is evidence (for example, Delefes and Jackson, 1972) that an 'action zone' exists in many classrooms: most of the teacher's interactions occur with children at the front and in the middle of the class (this is even in classrooms which in theory have no front). Research shows (Saur *et al.*, 1984) that if an action zone exists, then hearing impaired children who happen to be sitting at the periphery of the class are doubly disadvantaged. Not only children with sensory disabilities will be handicapped by the action zone: withdrawn children, or the 'intermittent workers' of the ORACLE study (Galton *et al.*, 1980) might also be doubly disadvantaged by the existence of such a zone. There is clearly scope here for thinking about the geography of the classroom, the movement of the teacher around the classroom and the placement of certain children within the class if those children's needs are to be met appropriately.

Linked with the classroom geography are the tasks we are expecting children to do. Johnson *et al.* (1983) have shown that merely putting children into integrated settings and expecting them to integrate is not enough. Indeed, moving special children to ordinary classrooms may have effects very different from those we expected. Johnson *et al.* show that 'special' pupils may be viewed in negative ways whether they are in mainstream classes or not. Physical proximity carries with it the possibility of making things worse rather than better. The success of integration schemes seems to depend a lot on how teaching is organized and how interaction among pupils is structured. It depends, in Barker's terms, on how comprehensively we consider the interaction of a range of physical and human systems in the classroom.

Gould (1976) has taken further the analysis of space within schools by making an analysis of territories and their boundaries, and by looking at different categories of space, such as personal space, group space and public space. I have used these ideas (Thomas, 1991) in attempting to look in more detail at some of the difficulties experienced by support teachers in moving into the 'territories' of their colleagues. Such an ecological examination may help in defining tasks and areas for work in shared classrooms and may be useful in suggesting operational strategies for the personnel involved.

The importance of the physical nature of settings was recognized by the Elton Committee (HMSO, 1989; see also Hutton, 1990). Research commissioned by the committee showed that of the constellation of features which might be linked with discipline in schools, it was settings-based features (such as the provision of soft floor coverings) which showed the clearest and most positive associations. Rather than suggesting an approach which focuses narrowly on behaviour management, the committee recommends a range of strategies, many of which involve attention to settings. The attention to such a broad range of features essentially amounts to a whole-school approach—an ecological approach—to discipline.

AN ECOLOGICAL PERSPECTIVE AND THE NOTION OF 'NEED'

By using an ecological 'lens' it becomes possible to see a number of ways in which the classroom environment, and the environment of the school as a whole, can be analysed and changed in such a way that benefits will accrue to the children therein. As I have tried to indicate, a number of models help to explicate these environments and the systems which operate within them. These models have the great advantage of being essentially problem solving in nature.

Moreover, using the ecological lens makes for an approach which is more in keeping with recent thinking on special needs. Traditional approaches may have done much to discourage uptake of Warnock's ideas on decategorization. Despite the best efforts of Warnock and the 1981 Act to do away with labels and categories, there manifestly remains (perhaps because of what attribution theorists would call 'fundamental attribution error') a predilection among education professionals for locating problems in individuals. The tenacity with which we adhere to such a focus is evidenced in a new generation of categories: MLD (moderate learning difficulties) instead of ESN(M); SLD (severe learning difficulties) instead of ESN(S); EBD (emotional and behaviour difficulties) instead of maladjusted. And there is now the super-category, SEN. The new thinking was supposed to have been about specifying what children's needs actually were, rather than simply using labels. The new perspective demands that we identify needs—not children. It demands that having identified those needs we aim to meet them through the provision of appropriate resources. Traditional approaches, however, encourage an individual-centred focus. An ecological orientation, on the other hand, encourages a view of the child's learning milieu, and the features of that milieu which can be changed in such a way that needs are met.

One of the most interesting findings of recent research (see Tann, 1988; Wheldall, 1988) is that in the mainstream class this matching of setting to needs does not generally occur. Special education has been even less successful, primarily because of the traditions and methodologies which have driven it. Traditionally in special education—perhaps because of its close allegiance with applied psychology—the attempt has usually been to meet special needs through the provision of new or different methods of assessment or teaching, usually to a pre-specified group of children in a setting removed from other children.

An ecological perspective enables a reappraisal of the ways in which needs are met. By explicitly focusing on the environment—the setting—in which children learn it melds more easily with a modern view of meeting needs.

Changing the ecosystem of the school or classroom is an unfamiliar way of meeting needs, yet it is far more in tune with post-Warnock thinking than more traditional methods. It does not necessarily involve the identification of specific children, nor does it involve the construction and execution of complex teaching or remedial programmes.

CONCLUSION

I have argued not simply for the legitimacy of an ecological perspective, but for its appropriateness for educational psychologists. The traditional notion of educational psychologists as applied scientists encourages particular styles of work which are unlikely to stimulate an examination of the wider situation—of the settings within which children, teachers and parents behave and interrelate. I have suggested that educational psychology is better seen as a developing framework of craft knowledge rather than as applied science. If this is the case, then strategies such as those provided by Bronfenbrenner, Barker and Checkland are available as ways of using this knowledge appropriately and systematically. Their ideas—about focusing on, analysing and changing behaviour and learning settings—are relatively new to psychology and their methods present unfamiliar challenges. As yet there are few examples of an explicitly ecological perspective or methodology in educational research or in the practice of educational psychology.

However, where behaviour settings have formed the focus for analysis of classroom and school situations, powerful insights are given on the ways in which children learn and behave in these settings. Where a broader view is taken, that view may lead to the formulation of both ameliorative and preventive approaches to the problems confronted by children and teachers in schools. Through its search for the broader determinants for behaviour, such an approach lends itself naturally to a more integrated, coordinated strategy—as, for example, in the devising of whole-school approaches to special educational needs. It is both legitimate and necessary for educational psychologists to be involved in such processes.

There are, then, good grounds for claiming that a wider perspective, encompassing an examination of, for example, school policy, curriculum and physical environment, all 'count' as coming within the proper ambit of *psychology*, and thus the remit of psychologists. Some educational psychologists have begun to fear that their attention to matters such as these will incur the displeasure of advisory and inspectorial colleagues, who may perceive a trespass on their domain. In my own experience such concern is very largely unwarranted. In any case, as I have attempted to show, there are incontrovertible arguments for the case that a contextually sensitive psychology is an appropriate model for educational psychologists to be employing, and these arguments need to be made.

NOTES

(1) However, during the 1980s the 'hard' tradition was the guiding force in nearly all systems-based interventions initiated by educational psychologists.
(2) This bears similarities to Barker's notion of 'synomorph', in which static and dynamic elements interrelate.

REFERENCES

Ainscow, M. and Tweddle, D. (1989). *Encouraging Classroom Success*. London: Fulton.

Apter, S. J. and Conoley, J. C. (1984). *Childhood Behaviour Disorders and Emotional Disturbance*. Englewood Cliffs, NJ: Prentice-Hall.

Barker, R. G. (1968). *Ecological Psychology*. Stanford: Stanford University Press.

Barrett, W. (1978). *The Illusion of Technique*. New York: Anchor-Doubleday.

Bennett, N. and Blundell, D. (1983). 'Quantity and quality of work in rows and classroom groups', *Educational Psychology*, **3** (2), 93–105.

Bijou, S. W. (1970). 'What psychology has to offer education—now', *Journal of Applied Behaviour Analysis*, **3**, 65–71.

Bloom, B. S. (1984). 'The search for methods of group instruction as effective as one to one tutoring', *Educational Leadership*, May, 4–17.

Bronfenbrenner, U. (1979). *The Ecology of Human Development*. Cambridge, MA: Harvard University Press.

Brophy, J. (1981). 'Teacher praise: a functional analysis', *Review of Educational Research*, **51** (1), 5–32.

Checkland, P. B. (1972). 'Towards a systems based methodology for real-world problem solving', *Journal of Systems Engineering*, **3** (2), 87–116.

Checkland, P. (1981). *Systems Thinking, Systems Practice*. Chichester: John Wiley.

Delefes, P. and Jackson, B. (1972). 'Teacher pupil interaction as a function of location in the classroom', *Psychology in the Schools*, **9**, 119–23.

Desforges, C., Bennett, N., Cockburn, A. and Wilkinson, B. (1985). 'Understanding the quality of pupil learning experiences', in Entwistle, N. (ed.) *New Directions in Educational Psychology 1. Learning and Teaching*. Lewes: The Falmer Press.

DeVault, M. L., Harnischfeger, A. and Wiley, D. E. (1977). *Curricula, Personnel Resources and Grouping Strategies*. St Ann, MO: ML-GROUP for Policy Studies in Education, Central Midwestern Regional Lab.

Doyle, W. (1977). 'The uses of non-verbal behaviours: toward an ecological view of classrooms', *Merrill-Palmer Quarterly*, **23** (3), 179–92.

Egan, K. (1984) *Education and Psychology*. London: Methuen.

Ekehammar, B. (1974). 'Interactionism in personality from a historical perspective', *Psychological Bulletin*, **81**, 1026–48.

Galton, M. J., Simon, B. and Croll, P. (1980). *Inside the Primary Classroom*. London: Routledge & Kegan Paul.

Gould, R. (1976). 'The ecology of educational settings', *Educational Administration Bulletin*, **4** (2), 14–26.

Hargreaves, D. H. (1978). 'The proper study of educational psychology', *Association of Educational Psychologists' Journal*, **4** (9), 3–8.

HMSO (1989). *Discipline in Schools*. (The Elton Report). London: HMSO.

Hutton, T. (1990). *The Elton Report: A Study Pack*. Oxford: Oxford Polytechnic School of Education.

Jackson, A. and Hannon, P. (1981). *The Belfield Reading Project*. Rochdale: Belfield Community Council.

Jasnoski, M. L. (1984). 'The ecosystemic perspective in clinical assessment and intervention', in O'Connor, W. A. and Lubin, B. (eds) *Ecological Approaches to Clinical and Community Psychology*. NY: John Wiley.

Johnson, D. W., Johnson, R. T. and Maruyama, G. (1983). 'Independence and interpersonal attraction among heterogeneous and homogeneous individuals: a theoretical formulation and a meta-analysis of the research', *Review of Educational Research*, **53** (1), 5-54.

Koch, S. (1964). 'Psychology and emerging conceptions of knowledge as unitary', in Wann, T. W. (ed.) *Behaviourism and Phenomenology*. Chicago: University of Chicago Press.

Kounin, J. S. (1967) 'An analysis of teachers' managerial techniques', *Psychology in the Schools*, **4**, 221-7.

Kounin, J.S. (1970). *Discipline and Group Management in Classrooms*. New York: Holt, Rinehart & Winston.

Krantz, P. J. and Risley, T. R. (1977) 'Behavioural ecology in the classroom', in O'Leary, K. D. and O'Leary, S. G. (eds) *Classroom Management: The Successful Use of Behaviour Modification*. (second edition) NY: Pergamon.

Kuhn, T. (1970) *The Structure of Scientific Revolutions*. (second edition) Chicago: University of Chicago Press.

Lee, V. L. (1988). *Beyond Behaviorism*. Hillsdale, NJ: Lawrence Erlbaum.

Lucas, D. and Thomas, G. (1990). 'The geography of classroom learning', *British Journal of Special Education*, **17** (1), 31-4.

McBrien, J. A. and Foxen, T. H. (1981) *The EDY In-service Course for Mental Handicap Practitioners*. Manchester: Manchester University Press.

Magee, B. (1982) *Men of Ideas*. Oxford: Oxford University Press.

Naughton, J. (1981). 'Theory and practice in systems research', *Journal of Applied Systems Analysis*, **8**, 61-70.

Pfluger, L. W. and Zola, J. M. (1974) 'A room planned by children', in Coates, G. J. (ed.) *Alternative Learning Environments*. Stroudsberg, PA: Dowden, Hutchinson & Ross.

Popkewitz, T. S. (1984). *Paradigm and Ideology in Educational Research*. Lewes: The Falmer Press.

Popper, K. R. (1945). *The Open Society and its Enemies*. London: Routledge.

Roaf, C. (1988). 'The concept of a whole-school approach to special needs', in Robinson, O. and Thomas, G. (eds) *Tackling Learning Difficulties—A Whole School Approach*. London: Hodder and Stoughton.

Rogers-Warren, A. and Warren, S. F. (eds) (1977). *Ecological Perspectives in Behaviour Analysis*. Baltimore: University Park Press.

Rosenfield, P., Lambert, N. M. and Black, A. (1985). 'Desk arrangement effects on pupil classroom behaviour', *Journal of Educational Psychology*, **77** (1), 101-8.

Saur, R. E., Popp, M. J. and Isaacs, M. (1984). 'Action zone theory and the hearing impaired student in the mainstreamed classroom', *Journal of Classroom Interaction*, **19** (2), 21-5.

Secord, P. F., (1986). 'Social psychology as a science', in Margolis, J., Manicas, P. T., Harre, R. and Secord, P. F. (eds) *Psychology: Designing the Discipline*. Oxford: Basil Blackwell.

Stevens, L. M. (1985). 'Teacher training and changing patterns of provision'. Paper presented to the International Congress on Special Education, July 1985, University of Nottingham.

Tann, S. (1988). 'Grouping and the integrated classroom', in Thomas, G. and Feiler, A. (eds) *Planning for Special Needs*. Oxford: Basil Blackwell.

Thomas, G. (1985). 'What psychology had to offer education—then', *Bulletin of the British Psychological Society*, **38**, 322-6.

Thomas, G. (1991). 'The new classroom teams: their nature, dynamics and difficulties'. Unpublished PhD thesis. Oxford Polytechnic.

Thomas, G. and Feiler, A. (eds) (1988). *Planning for Special Needs*. Oxford: Basil Blackwell.

Tizard, J., Schofield, W. N. and Hewison, J. (1982). 'Collaboration between teachers and parents in assisting children's reading', *British Journal of Educational Psychology*, **52**, 1–15.

Toffler, A. (1985) *The Adaptive Corporation*. Aldershot: Gower.

Turvey, M. T. and Carello, C. (1981). 'Cognition: the view from ecological realism', *Cognition*, **10**, 313–21.

Weinstein, C. S. (1979). 'The physical environment of the school: a review of the research', *Review of Educational Research*, **49** (4), 577–610.

Wheldall, K. (1988). 'The forgotten A in behaviour analysis: the importance of ecological variables in classroom management with particular reference to seating arrangements', in Thomas, G. and Feiler, A. (eds) *Planning for Special Needs*. Oxford: Basil Blackwell.

Wheldall, K., Morris, M., Vaughan, P. and Ng, Y. Y. (1981). 'Rows v. tables: an example of the use of behavioural ecology in two classes of eleven-year-old children', *Educational Psychology*, **1** (2), 171–84.

Willems, E. P. (1977). 'Behavioural technology and behavioural ecology', in Rogers-Warren, A. and Warren, S. F. (eds) *Ecological Perspectives in Behaviour Analysis*. Baltimore: University Park Press.

Section II

Focus on Organizations

Chapter 5

The Educational Psychologist as Consultant

Alan Labram

INTRODUCTION

Consultation has become a burgeoning area of activity over the last few years. The consultant is generally perceived as an objective, highly skilled specialist, and a glance at any business telephone directory will reveal the plethora of consultation services available in the fields of business, science and technology. Within the education sector individuals, local education authorities (LEAs) and indeed governments have all been willing to resort to consultancy agencies, often private firms, seeking enlightenment over issues of the moment—usually at no little expense. The results, where public, have been variable, ranging from being pertinent and useful to irrelevant and impractical. Perhaps this is not so surprising. Some analyses of the consultation process suggest that unless potential consultees know exactly what they are looking for, the experience is likely to be a disappointing one. In truth, it is easier to ascertain that all is not well within an organization than it is to identify the cause of the problem. How then can a prospective consultee decide whether consultation is likely to prove helpful?

The idea of this chapter is to explore consultancy in a number of different forms with the aim of assessing their relevance to the work of the educational psychologist. Both the present and possible future range of consultancy skills will be considered with an eye to the role of the EP within an education system gearing up to face the demands of the next century.

Following a decade of almost unprecedented change and upheaval within education, it is perhaps not surprising that the influential although comparatively small number of professionals within educational psychology should see their role change and adapt in response. During the late 1970s, educational psychologists were operating in a way that had been largely unchanged for many years. A survey carried out by Topping (1978) found that nearly all the children seen by educational psychologists in his area were assessed outside the classroom and half of the classteachers were unaware of what the EP did with the child. In a follow-up of nineteen referrals Topping found that all advice given by the EP was specific to the referred child. Daly (1981) has suggested that one of the limitations of this child-centred approach is that it takes no account of teachers who

71

express a willingness to receive more general advice, and does not attempt to obtain institutional change. In the same article, Daly reports the findings of a small but interesting survey into the perceived effectiveness of a range of different activities carried out by a sample of EPs. While consultations with various professionals about children they had seen individually were perceived as generally helpful, consultations with professionals about children not seen individually were high on the list of least effective practices.

Why should this be so? Is it that the EPs did not have the skills to act as consultants outside the individual referral, or did the consultees expect too much? Possibly the style of consultation was inappropriate or possibly what took place was not consultation at all. Exactly what constitutes a consultation is a very important question.

Sayer (1988) provides a useful guide. Consultancy is not advice, he argues, since those appointed by LEAs as 'advisors' are in a particular role of advising the employer (that is, the LEA) or are present in schools as representatives of the LEA. Even without the official title, many educational psychologists regard the giving of advice as something to be used sparingly since the essentially one-way nature of the exercise is contrary to the collaborative approach to the work which is now seen as most effective. Even more clearly, consultancy is not inspection. Inspectors, both national and local, do not by and large go into schools at their request, to help tackle particular problems in a collaborative exercise. Finally, although sharing some of its features, Sayer argues consultancy is not counselling since the essentially personal and confidential nature of counselling is in contrast to the organizational and communal features of consultancy.

CONSULTANCY—FOR WHAT PROBLEMS?

Broadly speaking, the kinds of problem which consultants are asked to help resolve require one of two categories of involvement. The first of these can be termed the technical involvement. To be effective in this role, the consultant will need to draw upon expert knowledge and skills in order to help resolve specific problems. Such an approach relies upon careful and accurate diagnosis so that the appropriate technical expertise is forthcoming, and clear and understandable communication to the client is given in order for successful implementation to be effected. The important point about this role is that the consultant supplies the solution.

The kinds of problem for which technical consultation is seen as appropriate are 'task' in nature. The introduction of a school system of record keeping for children with special educational needs or training teachers to use a particular diagnostic reading assessment would be examples. Aubrey (1990) argues that even in these situations the consultant must be aware of the relationship between technology and management and the complex nature of the social and psychological dimensions of organizational change, in order to be an effective change agent. She prefers the term 'resource' consultant to describe this kind of involvement. Whatever terminology is used, what is evident is that such consultancy provides a service in a situation where the clients cannot by themselves reach a solution.

If we look at the day-to-day work of the 'patch' educational psychologist, it is clear that much of what goes on in school-based sessions is consultancy of just this kind. EPs are in a unique position in their LEAs in that they are often best placed to have at their fingertips knowledge of and information about types of special resource, the implementation of LEA policies borough- or county-wide, personnel within the LEA hierarchy, LEA procedures, knowledge about relevant non-LEA provisions for children (such as child guidance clinics, dyslexia clinics, parental support groups and voluntary agencies) and how to gain access to these. It is unremarkable therefore that EPs are often used to supply advice and information. Indeed it is not an exaggeration to say that much of what EPs provide in traditional consultation sessions is a reductionist use of their knowledge and skills. This is not to say it is unimportant. To regard it as 'consultation' in the highest sense may be overstating the case.

A second category of consultancy may be termed 'process' consultancy. The process consultant takes as axiomatic the possibilities and advantages of members of organizations themselves diagnosing problems, arriving at possible solutions, implementing and evaluating these. The consultant's role here is to help the organization acknowledge and mobilize its own resources in order to arrive at solutions to the problem. This approach will be considered in more detail later in the chapter.

SPECIFIC SKILLS

It is evident that any consultancy will go through a number of key identifiable stages or phases and at each of these the consultant will need to draw upon different skills and be aware of different sensitivities. Although many authors have written about the phases of consultancy, what follows draws largely upon the thinking of Lynton Gray of the Polytechnic of East London. The first stage might be termed 'marketing'. In other words, how is it that a potential client is aware of the existence of the consultant and that he or she might possess the skills necessary to conduct a successful consultation? Educational psychologists possess a range of skills and expertise but they are not always the best at publicizing these. This seems a paradox since EPs often complain that many of their skills, acquired during a period of required training unmatched in terms of length among other education personnel, are untapped.

Once there is an agreement between consultant and client, they enter an initial phase where a number of 'entry skills' can be identified. Perhaps the first of these is to decide just who is the client. This is of course a perennial debating topic for EPs and the issues are well rehearsed. The next issue is to decide what the problem is. Once again, EPs are all too familiar with this issue. EPs are routinely presented with complaints about children in their regular casework and the wary EP will know that the complaint is not necessarily the same as the problem. So too with any consultancy: an initial task is to identify the real problem. As part of this initial phase the drawing up of a formal contract is highly desirable. Details will include the timescale over which the consultancy will be conducted. This is useful from both points of view. The client does not want the consultancy to drag on interminably, since problems change as do personnel over time. The consultant too does not want to be put in the position of either having to complete the task in an impossibly short time or of having the client making contact to try and prolong the involvement. Also relevant here is the cost. While state schools are not used to being charged precise sums of money for this kind of work, the introduction of local management of schools (LMS) as part of the Education Reform Act 1988 means that schools may well be in a position to buy in this expertise from outside, and if their LEA does not retain the educational psychology service as a centrally funded resource, they will have to.

Finally, the end point of the consultancy also needs to be agreed, not just in terms of time but also in terms of the exact nature of the outcome. Thus a report may well be the final act. Often, however, a formal report is not the most appropriate form of communication. A presentation may well be an alternative.

It can be argued that at the entry phase the effective consultant will negotiate the brief very carefully while the ineffective one will tend to accept the client's analysis and problem definition.

Once the entry phase has been negotiated there comes a phase of building relationships. At this point consultants need to address the question of whether they speak the language of the host institution. LEA psychologists with their extensive experience would clearly be at an advantage when working in schools, as compared with an outside consultant. As part of this an awareness of the internal hierarchy and the real power structure within the institution is essential. Access to all the relevant personnel is vital. At this critical phase the successful consultant will convey an impression of confidence, matched by impartiality and a rigid adherence to agreed dates and times.

Key skills will include interpersonal skills of a high calibre, including taking time to listen actively to what the client group is saying, and being able to put any aggression or resistance to use as part of the problem analysis. Taking time is important since any inflexibility here will be perceived as impatience on the part of the consultant. Ineffective consultancy will be characterized at this phase by nervousness and lack of confidence on the part of the consultant, as well as by over-criticism, impatience and the offering of 'instant' solutions, together with a resentment of aggression or resistance on the part of the client.

The next identifiable phase is one of diagnosis. At this point the consultant will need to be aware of the boundaries of the problem and know where to stop. Strategies for staying on task will need to be developed, as will those for remaining objective and resisting the temptation to adopt the role of therapist for members of the client group. Success at this point may well rest on being able to summarize accurately while avoiding imparting personal views.

The next key stage is that of influencing the organization or at least key sectors within it. It is essential here to recognize the key sectors in terms of authority and/or power, as a result of a careful analysis. As a result, the selection of an appropriate intervention strategy and its implementation can be effected.

Table 5.1 *Phases of a Typical Consultancy*

Phase	Strategy/skills	Required outcome
Marketing	Promotion	Agreement in principle by potential consultee
Initial phase	Negotiation	Agreed contract
Building relationships	Interpersonal	Trust and credibility
Diagnosis	Action research	Identification of problem and causes
Influencing	Selection of appropriate strategy	Successful implementation of strategy
Transition and withdrawal	Building independence Evaluation	Client has skills and competencies as originally agreed

The final phases are those of transition and withdrawal. Essential here is an ability to switch responsibility back to the client and to extricate oneself and avoid creating dependency. Appraisal and evaluation are essential and need to be rigorous. Any appraisal would include questions such as whether the EP is leaving the clients with the skills and competencies originally agreed. The successful intervention will have left the clients with a series of positive steps upon which to build independence.

CONSULTANCY SKILLS, PRESENT AND POTENTIAL

It is evident that psychologists in general and EPs in particular already possess much of the knowledge necessary for successful operation as a consultant of the 'technical' or 'resource' variety. It is debatable, however, whether they possess the expertise necessary to operate as a 'process' consultant. EP training courses in the United Kingdom are, by and large, of one year's duration and course tutors are constantly in the position of having to decide what to leave out in order for some timely addition to be included. Much of the course content, particularly the placement experience, is understandably geared towards the assessment of the individual child, at least during the early part of the course. The acquisition of much of the technical expertise is undertaken at this point and remains very much a fixture. Most courses will include 'systems' or 'whole-school' approaches to a greater or lesser degree, but a useful exercise might be to look at those skills which EPs have or might acquire which could be used as part of a consultancy portfolio. Such an exercise was conducted by a group of experienced EPs in 1990, the results of which I report here.[1] An initial brainstorm of key issues within schools which EPs might help them develop produced twenty-five items. Of these the group, using a simple voting system, identified eleven where EPs have existing skills, nine where EPs have skills in embryo and five where EPs lack the skills completely. The results are reported in Table 5.2.

Table 5.2 *Checklist of School-based Educational Psychology Consultancy*

Areas of existing skill	Areas of skill in embryo	No existing skill
Managing meetings	Staff selection	Appraisal
Behaviour management policies	Conflict management	Staff motivation
Interpersonal skills	Decision making	Marketing school image
SEN resource deployment	Stress management	School ethos
INSET planning	Action research	Non-teaching staff
Time management	Record keeping	
Working with parents and governors	Information gathering and interpretation	
Assessment policies	Staff development	
The pastoral curriculum	The National Curriculum content and method	
Negotiating skills		
Classroom organization		

An impressionistic analysis of these different areas reveals that they can be grouped under four broad headings, namely marketing, curriculum, resources and personnel. This last area contains most of the areas of skill, either existing or developing, and appears to be the key area of strength, with curriculum as a subsidiary. In contrast, few of the areas fall under the resource or marketing headings.

Since EPs may not wish to make a bid for involvement in these areas, this may not be significant. What is crucial, however, is that EPs develop the integral skills essential for successful consultation as outlined in Table 5.1. This would require not only the inclusion of these skills in initial training courses but the provision of professional development programmes for experienced EPs, together with sufficient time and funding.

In short, the result of this exercise points towards EPs regarding themselves as having a number of areas of existing expertise which could be promoted in developing a consultancy service. Neatly summarized as 'promoting people potential', they are a springboard from which EPs might begin to operate in a broader consultative manner and which would give the basis for any marketing strategy.

ETHICS AND CONDUCT

Consultancy raises a number of ethical issues, some of which will be familiar to EPs (and see Chapter 12). Perhaps the most important is that of confidentiality. Any consultee group as a whole and the individual members of that group need assurances that the consultant will observe the strictest confidence, both in communications outside the consultee group about the consultation and within the group about individual members' representations. A totally independent consultant may find this easier than an LEA EP. The overwhelming majority of EPs are employed by LEAs and schools may remain unconvinced that EPs can preserve confidentiality while the EPS is funded as a discretionary exception to the delegated education budget. It may well be appropriate and necessary for the prospective EP consultant to include, as part of the initial negotiations, the degree to which they are able to preserve confidentiality while at the same time remaining within the parameters of their job description with the LEA.

It is perfectly possible for consultee and consultant to come to an agreement specifying what might be revealed to third parties and under what circumstances, as part of the initial contract (Bromley, 1981) since confidentiality should not imply secrecy or collusion. Snell (1988) is unequivocal in regarding the level of confidentiality between consultee and consultant as being subject to contractual agreement, regardless of sponsoring organization.

Impartiality and neutrality are also ethical considerations which the potential consultee will require assurances on. The integrity of the consultant should be evident, but may well prove difficult to preserve if the nature of the topic under consultation is at variance with an EP's professional views. It would be difficult, for example, for an EP strongly committed to the principle of the integration of children with special educational needs within mainstream schools to remain an impartial consultant if the brief were to find ways of identifying SEN children with a view to transferring them to segregated educational provision.

Impartial consultation would be equally difficult in a situation where an EP had a vested interest. Situations might well arise where the consultee group, knowingly or otherwise, use an EP consultant in order to achieve particular ends. The existence of covert agendas is a real danger, not only to the consultant but also to members of the group itself—for instance, staff appraisal. This is another area where the LEA-employed consultant may appear to be at a disadvantage. EPs, however, are well used to filtering out ready-made solutions to problems in their casework, such as referrals to the EPS in order to gain extra staffing.

Snell (1988) sees honesty regarding intentions and expectations about what will happen as being the relevant principles here. They should, once again, form part of the advance information about a consultancy to the group members, while the EP reassures them that they retain the right to withdraw, should unforeseen circumstances lead to tension. It is an obvious feature of process consultation that the outcomes are indeterminate. Accordingly such get-out clauses may be necessary.

Within the United Kingdom, chartered educational psychologists have a strict code of conduct which provides an ethical base for practice. In order to provide a practical framework within which to work, I offer the following points as a basic checklist for practice in a school:

(a)   EPs should not assume they have skills in all areas of consultancy.

(b)   Senior staff should be aware of and give their backing to any consultancy initiative. They should know its purposes and scope and assume responsibility for informing colleagues, either personally or otherwise.

(c)   Schools have a long history and are always in a process of change. Consultants enter a dynamic institution and should not dismiss previous and ongoing development.

(d)   The terms of entry, scope of the problem to be addressed, personnel involved, timing and duration of visits and the intended outcome should be negotiated and formalized in a written contract. This should also include a statement about the nature of the confidentiality which will be observed.

(e)   All personnel who are affected by the issue under consultation should be invited to be involved.

(f)   Consultation sessions should always be arranged in advance.

(g)   Consultation time should not be wasted gathering information which can be found elsewhere.

(h)   At the end of every consultation exercise, a written report should be available which includes any recommendations for action.

(i)   Consultants should provide answers at the end of the exercise only, and only then if it was initially agreed.

MODELS OF CONSULTANCY

There are many forms of consultancy, each with its own strengths and weaknesses, areas of application and underpinning theory. Many of these models have developed outside the education sector but may help to inform EP practice. In this section it is intended to look at three such models which appear to have particular relevance.

Mental health consultation

Caplan (1970) describes a situation which is all too familiar to the 'patch' EP. The problem was that of having a potential client population of 16,000 children when he was working in an Israeli child guidance centre. For the small number of psychologists involved, dealing with large numbers of referred children at an individual level was an impossible task. Instead, Caplan initiated a scheme of consultation with those adults who had daily responsibility for the children. He identified and described four types of likely consultation while accepting that they are not as clear cut in practice. Caplan makes a distinction between the consultant (the psychologist), the consultee (the teacher) and the client (the child). In this respect Caplan echoes the work of Tharp and Wetzel (1969), who also made this distinction when writing about their 'triadic consultation model'.

In the first two of his four categories, Caplan distinguishes between client-centred and consultee-centred case consultation. In the first category, a traditional medical approach, the consultee asks the consultant for expert opinion and advice. This is then acted upon faithfully. In this way the intention is that not only may that particular case be resolved but it will act as an exemplar for future similar cases. The second category involves not so much the details of a particular case as the consultees' lack of skill in implementing specialist knowledge, lack of self-confidence and the effects of subjective emotional factors on their objectivity.

Caplan's third category, 'programme-centred administration consultation', describes how a consultant may help in the administration of a programme using expert knowledge of the system in order to facilitate its implementation, through the consultee. His last category, 'consultee-centred administration consultation', highlights how individuals might, through consultation, gain a better understanding of their own personal problems in attempting to develop a programme within an organization.

This consultation model clearly addresses issues concerning the consultee's personal involvement in the problems of the client. Thus it does not regard the consultee as an uninvolved conduit through which the remedies of the consultant may be administered in order to cure the client's ailments. Rather, the consultee is accepted as being both part of the problem and part of the solution. The model is fundamentally psychodynamic in theoretical approach. When adopted with teachers as consultees, for example, it would concentrate on the feelings generated within the teacher by a child displaying behaviour that was difficult to manage as much as on the behaviour itself. In this therapeutic approach to consultation, the professional objectivity of the consultee assumes less importance.

Figg and Stoker (1990) report the implementation of a mental health approach to consultation by a group of EPs. In the first part of their study they relate how EPs made themselves available to primary school teaching staff from their patch of schools. The sessions were held on a regular weekly basis at the local teachers' centre. Problems defined by the teacher were discussed with the EP, with the emphasis on the processes that appeared to be operating. The teacher and EP explored these and a range of options were determined, from which the teacher would choose a course of action.

Within the secondary sector, the arrangements were somewhat different. A school support team including professionals from within the comprehensive schools, social services and educational psychology service was assembled, with the aim of reducing the incidence of disruptive behaviour within the schools that the teachers represented. This secondary school phase of the project was two years in the planning. The authors report that once underway, it has been successfully operating over a number of years despite changes of staff. It is argued that this team approach to consultation has a key advantage over an individual approach, namely that all the other members of the group retain a level of objectivity which the teacher bringing the problem does not have. In this way they are able to act as co-consultants.

Considering the evaluation of the project, the authors report the effects of this consultancy approach in terms of the relationship between teachers and psychologists, citing the disappearance of referral forms and changes in the process of interaction over problem solving between the two groups as examples. Critics of the model have noted the blurring of the distinction between consultation and psychotherapy as well as the lack of any rigorous evaluation regarding the impact on clients, in this case the school pupils.

The problem-solving model

An approach to individual work with clients based on behavioural principles is no longer as state-of-the-art as it once was. Leach and Raybould (1977), writing explicitly about work in schools, detailed a practical yet experimentally sound approach to the behavioural analysis and modification of both learning and behaviour difficulties. Many EPs have routinely used this kind of approach in their daily work with individually referred children. However, it is clear that although teachers and parents are the main agents of change, their lack of expertise still requires the EP to offer a direct service to the client in most instances. Perhaps the best known and most successful exception to this rule is with the Portage approach to service delivery, where parents and primary carers are taught the skills necessary for them to affect directly their children's learning.

It is possible to adopt a consultation approach based upon the same behavioural principles but offering the EP a less direct role, and as a consequence involvement with a greater number of clients. Halfacre and Welch (1973) offered a step-by-step approach to behavioural consultation which fits neatly into the four main stages of the problem-solving model.

1 Problem identification

The essential elements here are that the consultant works collaboratively with the teacher or parent to pinpoint current areas of concern and express these in performance terms. Since a number of concerns may be evident, ranking these in priority order is necessary. It is essential for the consultant to establish rapport with the consultee at this stage. Key factors are respecting the view of the consultees, meeting them on their own ground and ensuring that any action that is forthcoming will be implemented where the problem is occurring.

Difficulties at this stage may derive from choice of target behaviour. Alternatives are to choose a low-level but easily modifiable behaviour or a high-profile behaviour that is hard to change. Additionally, consultees may find it difficult to express concerns in performance terms at first and may need help in gathering more information.

2 Problem analysis

Specific measurement criteria need to be agreed upon and their rationale clarified. Regular contact with the teacher or parent while collecting baseline information is important, to maintain motivation and ensure that changes in consultee behaviour do not invalidate the data. Once the results are assembled, a plan of action is decided with details of how it is to be implemented and what the criteria of success will be.

Difficulties at this stage may include deciding whether historical, intrapersonal and organizational variables should be included in the plan. Contextual variables and teacher expectations have a fundamental effect on pupil behaviour, but these may be absent from the problem analysis unless the consultant is familiar with the school environment.

3 Plan implementation

If all the key personnel have been involved at the earlier stages and have lent the plan their support, implementation will stand a much greater chance of success. In a school setting it is vital that all the parties that might have an interest are kept informed, even if they will not be directly involved in the plan implementation. The backing of senior staff is vital.

4 Evaluation

Target behaviours are remonitored and a comparison made with the baseline measurements. It is essential that the consultant still maintains contact with the consultee and that previously set criteria of success are addressed. At this stage the plan may require modification in the light of this information and any practical considerations.

The problem-solving approach to consultation focuses clearly on current problems which can be expressed in performance terms, identified by the consultee. Environmental variables are paramount and, crucially, evaluation and modification are key elements. The role of the consultant is to teach the consultees the skills and give them the expertise in order to effect change in the client. The consultee retains responsibility for the areas of concern, not the consultant.

The approach has a number of difficulties and possible drawbacks and may meet with some resistance. Many teachers express complaints about children because they feel it is not their province to teach children with pronounced learning or behavioural difficulties. They may not want the responsibility for these children. Other teachers demand access to extra specialist resources, which this system does not provide. Still others complain because the children are about to transfer to another class, teacher or school. Their concern is for what might happen in the future. This approach cannot address those very real concerns. In extreme cases, teachers expect such children to be removed, and this clearly denies that option.

Process consultation

During the period after the Second World War there emerged from the United States a new breed of industrial psychologist, interested in applying ideas derived from social psychology, management training, leadership theory and the psychology of group dynamics to the analysis of organizational behaviour. From the body of knowledge thus accumulated it became possible to identify those features which were characteristic of successful organizations, and to develop ways of planning and implementing organization-wide programmes to promote development. Peters and Waterman (1982) explored the management strategies that characterized America's most successful companies as part of a project on organizational effectiveness. One of the key factors they identified was regarding people as the most important resources within an organization. They found that relatively unsuccessful companies stressed the importance of managers and customers but neglected the people in the middle; that is, the non-managerial personnel. The scenario is not so far removed from that in schools, where teachers often feel they are caught in between the policy makers and the consumers, shouldering the responsibility for implementation.

One of the key activities featuring in a programme of organization development is that of process consultation (PC). This approach contains a number of underlying assumptions about the role of the consultant, the nature of help and the consultee. They are summarized in Schein (1988). Briefly, the consultee is accepted as well intentioned and seeking to improve things but lacking knowledge about problem diagnosis, how to go about changing things and the kind of help to seek in order to do this. It is difficult for individuals to effect change within organizations. Unless there is understanding of the problem and participation in the intervention planning by the consultee, both ability and willingness to implement the solution will be lacking. Furthermore, learning to repeat the exercise should similar problems arise in the future will not take place. The PC approach views the organization as imperfect but having the potential to be more effective providing it is able to identify and manage its own strengths and weaknesses.

The PC consultant cannot, in the time available, learn enough about the organizational culture to suggest reliable new courses of action. Such solutions are likely to fail through inappropriateness or through resistance by the members of the organization. Joint planning by the consultant and consultee is therefore essential. The final decisions, however, must remain with the consultee. The essential function of PC is to pass on skills of problem diagnosis, intervention planning and implementation to the consultee.

Schein (1988) outlines some of the major process issues that PC consultants must be familiar with. They include the following.

Communication processes

Schein emphasizes that modes of communication within organizations are as important as their content. The PC consultant will gather data on who communicates with whom and when. Some members of the organization may form informal sub-groups, which can have a variety of implications for the organization's functioning. Style of communication is also important, not only because of what it might reveal about the sender but because of its effect on the receiver. A more complex issue entails levels of communication. The PC consultant must be familiar with the existence of metacommunications and their implications.

Group cohesion

The PC consultant will need to be aware of issues concerning the functioning of groups, such as the individual's identity in that group, who has power control and influence in the group and whether the needs and goals of the group include those of the individual members.

Group problem solving

Groups vary in the methods they use to arrive at conclusions, ranging from decisions by default, through rule by a minority and rule by the majority to consensus and unanimity. The PC consultant will help the group recognize its own method and decide whether it is appropriate.

Leadership

There is an enormous relevant literature on this topic, including seminal publications by Lewin, Lippitt and White (1939), Fiedler (1967) and McGregor (1960). Style of leadership within the organization, in particular the source of power and influence from which it is derived, is significant. So too are the value system, security and confidence of the leader.

Tannenbaum and Schmidt (1958) identify the three most significant sets of forces as being those within the leader, within subordinates and within the situation itself. Hughes (1987) has written specifically about leadership roles in educational institutions, highlighting the ambiguity between the roles of leading professional and chief executive which managers experience.

Appraisal and feedback

Schein points out that appraisal is a common enough feature of life within business organizations. Within schools in the United Kingdom it is a reality from now on. Schein argues that the four key steps to appraisal are as follows:

(a) observation of the subject at work;
(b) evolution of a standard criterion;
(c) comparison of the observed behaviour with the standard via a system of measurement;
(d) assessment of any difference between (b) and (c).

Schein goes on to assert that appraisal is often a pale imitation of this, with snap judgments and poor-quality feedback being common. The PC consultant would have skills in the appraisal areas.

Intergroup processes

Schein argues that these are among the least studied dimensions within organizations. Although numerous sub-groups always exist, they may form along various lines, such as geographical, formal and social. The consequences of intergroup competition are negative in effect. There are a variety of techniques available to the PC consultant to identify these and if necessary plan an intervention.

In summary, the PC consultant should be 'an expert on how to help an organisation to learn without being an expert on the actual management problems that the organisation is trying to solve' (Schein, 1988). In short, the PC consultant passes on skills and knowledge to members of the organization that will help them diagnose their own problems and develop their own interventions.

CONSULTATION AND THE FUTURE OF EDUCATIONAL PSYCHOLOGY

There can be few EPs who have not recently contemplated the future of the profession with some unease. It is ironic that those for whom engendering change in others is bread and butter should find the prospect of change within their own profession so daunting. This is not to say, however, that EPs find themselves without relevant skills or the desire to change. The problem is knowing what the situation will demand of EPs in the next decade, in the light of seemingly endless developments within education and associated legislation. As Reason and Webster (1990) have pointed out, there is information overload and a sense of having to prepare for a situation that is at best unclear and at worst total chaos. These authors attempted to draw lessons from industry and put forward the idea of a 'product portfolio' for educational psychology services. They give examples of product portfolios for two different psychological services, the first seeking wide client contact and indirect service delivery, the second seeking a narrow range of in-depth, long-term contracts. In both of these examples consultancy figures as a 'mature product', which is how they describe work of an ongoing, steady kind for which there is a continuing market.

Too often, however, the consultation offered by EPs is of the kind in the 'narrow' portfolio described in Reason and Webster's article; that is, consultancy resulting from individual assessment. In order to widen the EP brief, consultancy relating to organizational change and management will have to become part of the services offered by EPs. This is no longer a matter of choice, since the criticisms often levelled at EPs tend to be variations of the following:

The EP does not have the time to see all the pupils experiencing difficulties.
By the time an EP is involved, the problem has become so serious that the EP's involvement is crisis intervention.
Children with less severe difficulties never get to the top of the EP's list.
Pupils in the lowest socio-economic groups have the greatest number of problems but have the least chance of EP involvement.
The EP does not help the school become more effective in dealing with its own problems.

How then might this situation be remedied? It can be argued that an EP wishing to develop as a consultant should have three clear aims: to help teachers develop general skills for dealing with the problems they face in schools; to develop strategies collaboratively with teachers for dealing with individual pupils; and finally to work towards the primary prevention of problems within the school. Many EPs have tried to develop their own service delivery along lines which address these issues by abandoning the traditional referral-driven system, which is the antithesis of the above. They have done this by adopting a time management system of regular school visits with joint identification of key areas of concern.

Consultation of the non-technical variety requires collaboration between EPs and teachers and has a number of implications. There is joint responsibility for the problems of all pupils between professionals. There is also shared accountability for problem resolution. Pooling expertise enables a greater variety and diversity of interventions to be generated. Because of the greater chance of success, and the positive side effects such as group morale and enhanced skills, the approach merits greater expenditure of time and resources.

CONCLUSIONS

In this chapter I have argued that consultancy should be a key area of involvement for EPs in the future, working with a variety of client groups such as parents and governors (for instance, Wolfendale *et al.*, 1990) but particularly teachers. EPs have a number of skills to offer as technical consultants, but if they are to develop beyond this, further skills such as those required for PC will be needed. There are a number of factors which might militate against this happening, not the least of which is personal diffidence or style. There are four broad issues that EPs will need to be clear on:

(a)   methodological problems such as negotiating access, the sequence of events and the techniques of PC;
(b)   theoretical issues such as what model of consultation is appropriate;
(c)   structural issues such as the limitations imposed by clients;
(d)   political issues such as who the client is, who owns the outcomes and deskilling those with managerial responsibility.

It is my contention that EPs have the basis for offering the full range of consultation services while acknowledging potential barriers. These include the facts that at the present time most EPs are LEA employees, and that the patch system may militate against it, with the possible problem of consultancy and casework 'polluting' each other. The possibility of at least two varieties of EP working within the same authority is not far fetched. If educational psychology services do follow the route of developing product portfolios, it is highly likely that specialist EPs would deliver different aspects. The days of the generic EP may well be numbered.

An alternative notion, the educational psychology practice, may have potential. A group of highly skilled psychologists offering between them a range of services may be the vision of the future. Within such a structure it would be possible for individuals or teams to specialize in consultancy in all its forms as part of a product portfolio. Schools will almost certainly develop a mentality of the market place with the advent of LMS. Support agencies will be required to offer a cost-effective service, and within EPSs consultancy may well become essential.

NOTES

(1) I am indebted to the 1989/91 group of EPs on the MSc Education Management course at the Polytechnic of East London for permission to use this data.

REFERENCES

Aubrey, C. (ed.) (1990) *Consultancy in the United Kingdom: Its Role and Contribution to Educational Change*. London: The Falmer Press.

Bromley, E. (1981) 'Confidentiality', *Bulletin of the British Psychological Society*, **38**, 41–3.

Caplan, G. (1970) *The Theory and Practice of Mental Health Consultation*. New York: Basic Books.

Daly, B. (1981) 'Towards accountable practices by educational psychologists', *Association of Educational Psychologists Journal*, **5**, 4–11.

Fiedler, F.A. (1967) *A Theory of Leadership Effectiveness*. New York: McGraw-Hill.

Figg, J. and Stoker, R. (1990) 'Mental health consultation in education: theory and practice', in Aubrey, C. (ed.) *Consultancy in the United Kingdom: Its Role and Contribution to Educational Change*. London: The Falmer Press.

Halfacre, J. and Welch, F. (1973) 'Teacher consultation model: an operant approach', *Psychology in the Schools*, **10**, 494–7.

Hughes, M. (1987) 'Leadership in professionally staffed organisations', in Hughes, M., Ribbins, P. and Thomas, H. (eds) *Managing Education. The System and the Institution*. London: Cassell.

Leach, D.J. and Raybould, E.C. (1977) *Learning and Behaviour Difficulties in School*. London: Open Books.

Lewin, K., Lippitt, R. and White, R.K. (1939) 'Patterns of aggressive behaviour in experimentally created "Social Climates"', *Journal of Social Psychology*, **10**, 271–99.

McGregor, D. (1960) *The Human Side of Enterprise*. New York: McGraw-Hill.

Peters, T.J. and Waterman, R.H. (1982) *In Search of Excellence*. New York: Harper & Row.

Reason, R. and Webster, A. (1990) 'Developing a product portfolio for psychological services', *Educational Psychology in Practice*, **6**, 4–12.

Sayer, J. (1988) 'Identifying the issues', in Gray, H.L. (ed.) *Management Consultancy in Schools*. London: Cassell.

Schein, E.H. (1988) *Process Consultation*, vol. 1 (second edition). Reading, MA: Addison-Wesley.

Snell, R. (1988) 'The ethics of consultation in education', in Gray, H.L. (ed.) *Management Consultancy in Schools*. London: Cassell.

Tannenbaum, R. and Schmidt, W.H. (1958) 'How to choose a leadership pattern', *Harvard Business Review*, **36**, 95–101.

Tharp, R.G. and Wetzel, R. (1969) *Behaviour Modification in the Natural Environment*. New York: Academic Press.

Topping, K.J. (1978) 'Consumer confusion and professional conflict in educational psychology', *Bulletin of the British Psychological Society*, **31**, 265–7.

Wolfendale, S., Harskamp, A., Labram, A. and Millward, I. (1990) 'Governors and special educational needs: a collaborative inservice training programme', *Educational and Child Psychology*, **7**, 46–53.

Chapter 6

Human Resource Development: Issues Facing Educational Psychology Services in Times of Changing Needs

Marianne McCarthy

INTRODUCTION

In this chapter the central theme that will be developed is that of human resource development as a means of achieving organizational goals and effecting change. This perspective will be considered in relation to the management of educational psychology services themselves and also as part of a service's portfolio of knowledge, skills and techniques. The following structure will be used to organize the key issues:

(a)   a rationale for the central importance of human resource development as a management strategy for achieving organizational development and effectiveness in an unstable environment;

(b)   a description of the essential elements of human resource development in the context of individual needs and organizational needs, which are embedded in the wider social and economic environment;

(c)   a description of some ways of approaching professional development within EPSs;

(d)   an examination of the ways educational psychologists can facilitate staff development within schools and in the wider network of the LEA if there is clarity of purpose and circumstance;

(e)   a consideration of the challenges facing educational psychology services in the 1990s from a human resource development perspective.

PRODUCTIVITY THROUGH PEOPLE

One of the eight attributes of excellence listed by Peters and Waterman (1982) in their investigation of successful American companies was the principle of 'productivity through people', the notion that the people within the organization are a major resource and that their development plays a central part in achieving organizational success. This concept has particular pertinence to EPSs since their 'product' in every sense is delivered through the educational psychologists themselves.

A central task for any manager is the planning of how resources should be used (a) in maintaining the service, and (b) in promoting development and change. In deciding how much time and resources managers of services should devote to the training and development of their staff, an examination of some of the expenditure on such developments in many large organizations would help by establishing its value. The following quotes are documented in *Managing People* (Open Business School, 1987, pp. 3–5):

> High performance businesses are twice as likely to train, and train twice as many employees as low performance businesses, and . . . high performance businesses have increased their training by 25 per cent over the past five years, with low performers reducing their training by 20 per cent. (Manpower Services Commission, 1985)

> IBM's philosophy is largely contained in three simple beliefs.
> I want to begin with what I think is the most important: our respect for the individual. This is a simple concept, but in IBM it occupies a major portion of management time. We devote more effort to it than anything else. (Thomas J. Watson, 1963)

> We are concerned with the pace at which change is happening. There is a need for constantly changing behaviour patterns. Training is seen as a change agent. Therefore it *has* to be more than the production of programmes aimed at maintaining the past. Any training programme we do is concerned with measurably improving standards of performance. We have a strategic view of the role of training in its ability to directly influence business activity. (Dennis Evans, Training Manager, Unipart International)

The perspective on training and staff development as an agent of change is a particularly relevant concept when considering the rapidly changing context of the 1990s for EPSs. Training and staff development could be viewed as an investment for the future where environmental, organizational and individual needs are brought together successfully to achieve an effective service delivery. This bringing together of three different but interrelated perspectives is a complex and difficult management task. As Schein (1978) points out, 'an effective Human Resource Planning and Development System must explicitly link its organisational planning to its human resource planning.'

ESSENTIAL ELEMENTS OF HUMAN RESOURCE DEVELOPMENT

The individual, environmental and organizational mix

The development of individuals within the organization is the central theme of this chapter. However, the importance of locating this perspective within a framework which acknowledges the many and complex variables that will impinge on such development cannot be underestimated. Some key factors are depicted in Figure 6.1 (adapted from Handy, 1985). Here the organization and its form, the system and structures it sets up, and the style of leadership adopted will be highly influential in the training, development and actions of its staff. The physical, technological and economic environment will continue to interact, facilitating or inhibiting development in an ongoing exchange. Individual aspirations, roles and functions both at home and work, feelings of job satisfaction, experience, age and motivations will all come into the arena. It is evident that all these variables will interact with one another in contributing to organizational

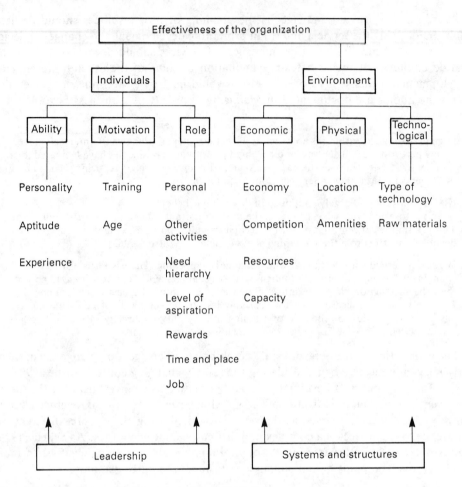

Figure 6.1   *Some factors affecting organizational effectiveness.*
Adapted from Handy (1985)

effectiveness. Each variable in itself has been the subject of considerable research. An understanding of the processes of learning, the role of the learner and the contexts in which learning takes place are crucial elements.

Factors affecting learning

It is important to consider issues relating to how people learn if as a manager you want to develop the knowledge, skills and understanding of your staff. In this area educational psychologists should be central resources since it is clearly an area of psychological knowledge and expertise. Theories of how children learn and what motivates them have been highly influential in the teaching and learning process. There is also some evidence that educational psychologists have extended their sphere of influence in developing skills and research into how adults learn most effectively (Cline *et al.*, 1990). The recent HMI report (Department of Education and Science, 1990) noted their success in such developments. Unfortunately there seem to be few examples where such expertise is used in a planned and systematic way for the development of individual educational psychologists and services, with some notable exceptions (Frederickson, 1988; Miller *et al.*, 1988).

There is no universally accepted theory of how people learn (Knowles, 1973; Boydell, 1976), but as Smith (1983) suggests, the effects of learning can be documented and also the different ways people approach learning tasks and activities. Some generally accepted observations about optimum conditions for adult learning are highly relevant for managers. These include the following characteristics, listed in the Open University module 'The Effective Manager' (Open Business School, 1987):

> Adults must *want* to learn . . . . [and] will only want to learn something if they see the need for it.
> They learn best by doing. They can learn by listening and watching, but they are likely to learn more effectively if they actively *do* something. Skills can only be learned by doing.
> They will resist or reject new learning which does not fit easily with what they know already from experience.
> They learn best in an informal environment.
> They want guidance not grading. They need feedback to tell them how well they are doing, but they fear other people knowing if they are doing badly. (pp. 64, 65)

An additional aspect to learning identified by Smith (1983) is important: 'Learning involves change, something is added or taken away. "Unlearning" is often involved, especially in adulthood . . . Fear, anxiety, and resistance often accompany and inhibit change.'

This notion of resistance to change is a particularly powerful concept when considering adult learning. There is a 'cost' to participating in such a learning process, which may involve changing established practices and promote feelings of inadequacy. Resistance may occur in order for individuals to maintain their own integrity or that of the system they are operating within. Also the personal histories that are brought to bear are highly influential—change attempts that have been unsuccessful, socialization processes which help establish and maintain a particular view of the world—and previous training experience and participation in present work setting are all relevant. In addressing the optimum conditions for effective learning, managers must also be aware of the aspirations of their staff—what motivates them to work and where they see their careers developing. The notion of 'career anchor' developed by Schein (1978) is useful.

Career anchors

The idea of career anchor focuses on an individual's 'occupational self-concept'. It has three components:

(a) self-perceived talents and abilities;
(b) self-perceived motives and needs;
(c) self-perceived attitudes and values.

Each of the three components is developed from actual work experience:

> The career anchor functions in the person's work life as a way of organising experience, identifying one's area of contribution in the long run, generating criteria for kinds of work settings in which one wants to function, and identifying patterns of ambition and criteria for success by which one will measure oneself. (Schein, 1978, p. 127)

Schein identifies five career anchors:

(a)   technical/functional competence;
(b)   managerial competence;
(c)   security and stability;
(d)   creativity;
(e)   autonomy and independence.

The attributes linked to each are different and, it is suggested, people with each of these anchors need to be managed differently, since they have fundamentally different aspirations for their career paths:

> The career anchor is a *learned* part of the self-image, which combines self-perceived motives, values and talents. What one learns is not only a function of what one brings to the work situation, but also reflects the opportunities provided and the feedback obtained. (Schein, 1978, p. 171)

In summary, to set up successful learning opportunities, managers need to take into account the career stages and career anchors of individuals in order to ensure relevance and promote motivation. They also need to consider what systems or structures need to be in place in the organization in order to reinforce and develop such learning.

PROFESSIONAL DEVELOPMENT WITHIN EDUCATIONAL PSYCHOLOGY SERVICES

As a prerequisite to matching an individual's training and development needs to those needs identified in the service, certain organizational structures need to be in place:

(a)   clear aims and objectives for the service, which are well documented and regularly reviewed;
(b)   mechanisms for deciding upon service priorities and needs, both short term and long term, which are well understood by service members;
(c)   effective recruitment and selection procedures;
(d)   written job descriptions detailing main responsibilities and activities;
(e)   a coherent time allocation policy;
(f)   a structure for induction to the service;
(g)   a framework for identifying, providing and monitoring training;
(h)   an appraisal process where individual needs can be identified and ways of meeting them negotiated.

It is hard to imagine how a realistic staff development programme could work within a service that has not defined its overall aims or built structures to review its functioning and development. What follows is a description of three powerful development techniques which can either facilitate or inhibit service functioning depending on how well they are integrated into service policy and practice.

Induction

Induction and staff development are part of the same learning process. The importance of establishing confidence in the learning environment of work at the outset cannot be overestimated for the new psychologist. The idea of the new recruit being in a period of transition is a helpful one, with their feelings and needs illustrated on a transition curve. Confidence is usually high at the outset, after having just got the job. However, at the beginning of the transition into a new situation feelings of competence fall. It is hard to negotiate a way into a new system with a unique culture and set of expectations, working practices and relationships. Induction is an influential way of reducing the possible negative effects of transition.

Further issues to consider relating to the importance of induction include:

(a)   the notion that first impressions persist;

(b)   the need for individuals to know the standards required of them;

(c)   the development of attitudes and loyalty. Within all organizations there will be a dominant set of shared attitudes and values as well as a minority. Learning will take place on two fronts—what is 'taught' or 'trained for' and what is 'learned in passing'. If the newcomer 'goes it alone' there will be no control over incidental learning and a lost opportunity to build up positive attitudes to work;

(d)   the effects of stress. New staff who experience uncertainty in many areas are more likely to experience stress and therefore feel dissatisfied and underperform.

If induction is defined as 'getting people to manage new demands', it is clearly an ongoing process. Induction and training are therefore inextricably linked. Important themes for managers to be aware of when addressing induction are:

(a)   it is more effective if planned as developmental rather than one-off;

(b)   there is a need for pacing to avoid overload;

(c)   the use of a 'sponsor' or 'mentor' from within the team can be an effective strategy;

(d)   checklists giving basic information for the new recruit and the timespan for learning key aspects are useful.

Appraisal

Appraisal seems to lead on quite naturally from induction. However, the whole area of appraisal is emotive and open to much debate. There appears to be no single, generally accepted use of the term, but there are a variety of approaches and definitions of the concept. The complexity involved has led to different approaches using different kinds of observation and different theoretical structures (Byrne Whyte, 1986, gives a comprehensive summary in relation to teacher appraisal). A more useful way of conceptualizing these approaches is in terms of the way they address the issues involved and formulate structures to explain certain aspects of behaviour. What aspects they choose to look at and what use they make of their conclusions are perhaps the most pertinent questions to ask.

A way of depicting some of the issues for a manager to address when developing an appraisal process is by identifying some of the driving forces and resisting forces (see Figure 6.2). One key issue is that appraisal is perceived as improving staff development but also as providing information for work-related decisions. There is a need to reconcile individual demands for development and organizational needs. A prior condition for an appraisal system, as has already been mentioned, is that the organization needs to have identified its priorities and timescales. This raises the issue of whether the organizational timescales are the same as those of the individual. Organizations tend to

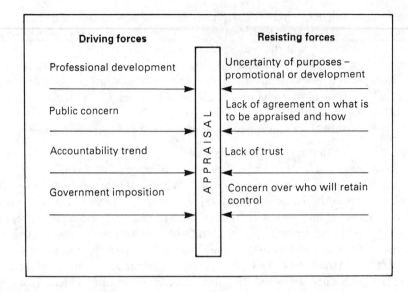

Figure 6.2   *Appraisal: a force-field analysis.*

be more concerned with the immediate here and now, whereas the individual may have a long-term perspective. An appraisal scheme has to reconcile these two demands. The notion of career anchor can be a useful analytical tool for the manager in understanding an individual's aspirations in this context.

Nuttall's (1981) research suggests that attention to the following characteristics promote good appraisal schemes:

(a)   *climate*: the scheme should be based within a tradition of trust and commitment to evaluation;

(b)   *formative and summative aspects*: there should be a clear separation of career/promotional aspects from the developmental/formative aspects;

(c)   *results and action*: the quality and nature of feedback is important, and joint problem solving is seen to be an essential aspect;

(d)   *appraisee involvement*: the appraisee must be involved in the scheme;

(e)   *autonomy*: the individual must retain autonomy over the process;

(f)   *criteria/processes*: there must be a shared understanding of the criteria used and the processes undertaken;

(g)   *team approach*: there should be more than one appraisor;

(h)   *adequate training*: there should be a discussion of values and assumptions within this.

Many of the above qualities relate directly to those factors previously described as affecting adult learning—motivation, relevance, involvement and feedback on performance. If services have developed their appraisal structures taking these key factors into account, negotiated learning opportunities which meet the needs of the individual and those of the organization are more likely to be realized.

Personal experience of being involved in a peer appraisal process that actively changed working practice reinforces the significance of this approach to human resource development (Bloom *et al.*, 1989). The appraisal process was formative but integrated into the service's summative context of annual professional development interview (see Figure 6.3). Time was set aside to debate the purposes of appraisal and how the needs of the individual and the service were to be met. Enabling structures were developed where individuals were able to come together to discuss concerns, debate the relative merits of certain approaches and plan a way forward.

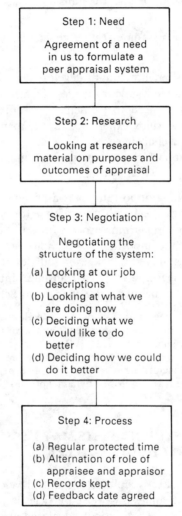

Figure 6.3 *Steps in a peer appraisal process.*

Coaching

The last staff development process to be discussed is that of 'coaching'. Central to the philosophy behind this technique is learning by doing, focusing directly on day-to-day work tasks, involving the learner in setting objectives and utilizing frequent informal contacts. Leigh (1987) describes coaching in the following way:

Every manager is a coach. Coaching is built into the job. Few organisations however formally acknowledge it, or deliberately try to develop the coaching role . . . It is a highly practical activity concerned solely with today's task . . . It is an informal, forward looking activity with no overtones of criticism. Its main focus is on helping people find solutions to current work problems, but in such a way that they learn whilst doing this. Thus the role of coach is not to hand out advice passively but to act as a partner and a catalyst. An effective coach is interested in people, recognizing their importance and potential. You need to know the desires, interests and capacities of your subordinates and above all to avoid doing their thinking for them. (p. 4)

Some of the main requirements for effective coaching listed by Leigh include the following:

(a)   recognizing that most of an individual's development occurs on the job;
(b)   recognizing that management style, priorities and attitudes influence employees;
(c)   accepting that employees need to participate in objective setting since this is motivating. It is also a learning experience for the manager, who may find his or her ideas questioned and challenged;
(d)   ensuring that information which assesses how well employees are doing is available to them and, preferably, devised by them.

The development of coaching opportunities is a powerful and effective method of staff development. It can also be highly motivating for individuals who find their autonomy increasing. It is, too, a learning process for the manager.

In concluding this section, the importance of human resource development for EPSs in the 1990s cannot be overestimated. Changes in individual educational psychologists brought about by effective learning is often translated into change at the point of delivery, and is thus a clear product of service change. As Schein (1978) states:

Neither organisational effectiveness nor individual satisfaction can be achieved unless there is a better matching of what the organisation needs and what the individuals who spend their working lives in those organisations need . . . Both the organisation and the individuals within it are dynamic, evolving systems whose needs change because of changing environments and changing internal factors deriving from age, life experience, and family circumstances. The matching of needs is therefore a dynamic process which must be periodically monitored and managed. (pp. 243–4)

WAYS EDUCATIONAL PSYCHOLOGISTS MAY FACILITATE STAFF DEVELOPMENT WITHIN SCHOOLS AND LEAs

The contribution of educational psychologists to staff development within schools and LEAs is well documented. An analysis of recent articles in *Educational Psychology in Practice* reinforces such a view. The particular training experienced, the specific role and relationships held within the LEA and the working practices developed with schools all help to locate the educational psychologist in such a role.

The survey by HMI on the range of activities carried out by educational psychologists in England and Wales during 1988 to 1989 (1990) described several ways in which educational psychologists were involved in facilitating staff development within their LEAs (paras 28, 31, 35, 55–9). Importantly, the range of work engaged in and observed related to both formal and informal approaches. Particular strengths identified referred to work where a careful analysis of participants' needs and requirements was undertaken.

Weaknesses were found where developments did not link with overall LEA strategic planning. The following outline encompasses the range of work.

Informal/incidental

> Inset is commonly regarded as that which is presented through attendance at courses based in centres or in the participants' own institutions. However, much of the inset provided by psychology services is informal and incidental. For example the discussion following an individual assessment allows opportunities for professional development, as does attendance at case conferences or reviews. Many written psychological reports provide a permanent record of the analysis of a pupil's difficulties and offer insights into assessment and treatment strategies . . . Much of the work observed during the inspection was of this nature, and although ephemeral, was considered to be fundamental to the development of expertise. (HMI, 1990, para. 59)

The acknowledgement by HMI of the fundamental contribution of educational psychologists to this form of adult learning is important. Probably the greatest amount of service time is invested in this development, and much of its success relates directly to the value given to those key features that characterize adult learning. The knowledge, expertise and perspective educational psychologists bring to these interactions is often at an implicit level and is difficult to articulate without considerable reflection and analysis. A key point, however, is the skill of generalizing from specific instances to wider principles, which give an understanding of the processes involved and help to change participants' perspective and behaviour subsequently.

Collaborative work

A further aspect of human resource development can be identified in many types of collaborative work undertaken by educational psychologists. Such work may have different purposes, but one of its aims is to help staff build on direct experiences, which they can then apply to similar situations in the future. Examples include a range of collaborative project work, interviews with parents, problem-solving sessions with other colleagues and running joint Inservice Education of Teachers (INSET) sessions. An important component of such work is the built-in analysis and reflection that is undertaken.

Consultation

A considerable amount of educational psychologists' time is devoted to consultation. Here the work ranges from informal opportunities to the more formal. The educational psychologist may have no direct involvement but may follow the individuals' personal agendas, helping them to find their own ways of solving problems. The role of the consultant is complex and needs to be skilfully handled, encompassing support and critical appraisal of a situation from an alternative perspective. The flavour of such work is well summarized by Roles (1986) with regard to the Derbyshire Secondary Development Project:

[Consultative visits] allowed for support of the school team in terms of understanding and advice from an individual who was ultimately involved in the project as a whole, but who was able to offer objective comments without being individually involved with the intricacies of the particular institution in a personal way . . . Skilfully this allowed for a blend of pressure on the schools . . . whilst also giving support when times were difficult, acknowledging that a breathing space may be necessary in order to work through some of the problems. The image is one of a relative, distant enough not to be over-personally involved, but close enough to offer advice in a knowing and supportive way. (pp. 1–2)

INSET

The range of involvement of EPSs in inservice training activities is wide and, as noted in the HMI report (1990), comments of those involved were

almost universally favourable, especially when it had responded specifically to stated needs and there had been a high degree of interaction. In most cases evaluation had been undertaken, ranging from course participants' initial reactions to a longer term estimation of the degree of change that had taken place. (p. 17, para. 53)

Characteristics of inservice activities that have had a direct impact on participants' development are:

(a)   It arises from a perceived need that is identified and located within an overall planning process for development for participants.

(b)   It addresses the difficulty of transferring theory into practice.

(c)   There are built-in opportunities for learning by doing.

(d)   It acknowledges that continuing support is required if participants are to implement what has been learned.

(e)   It recognizes the political dimension of change and that the structures and relationships of any organization may help or inhibit the transfer of learning into day-to-day practice.

In summary, this section has identified:

(a)   the role of human resource development as a core area of educational psychologists' practice;

(b)   that effective human resource development in a variety of contexts is based on the principles of adult learning, some of which have already been outlined. In particular, those involved need to ascribe a personal meaning to their experiences and have the opportunity to learn by doing. Resistance and anxiety about change are inevitable and the style adopted by the educational psychologist needs to enable people to learn from their mistakes as well as their successes;

(c)   individual learning needs to be considered in an organizational context if change in practice is to be maintained.

CONCLUSION

It has been argued in this chapter that the field of human resource development is one where educational psychologists have developed an expertise at both a theoretical and a practical level. Evaluation of such work has been positive. In the 1990s the importance

of services being able to communicate in a public arena the knowledge, skills and processes involved becomes imperative if a proactive stance is to be taken. The shifting
images of services and the values they attribute to aspects of work will consolidate
quickly. In such an environment, service members will also be affected by the unpredict-
ability and unstable processes of change. It will be important for services to apply the
expertise of human resource development to their own members so they are better
equipped to meet the challenges of new demands and requirements.

At the 1990 Association of Educational Psychologists' annual conference, a
workshop entitled 'Taking an educational psychology service into the 1990s' asked
participants what features and characteristics a successful service would embody. Key
features listed were:

- To have a clearly defined appraisal and professional development policy in order to
  identify service needs, individual needs and plan ways of meeting them.
- To make more explicit the skills psychologists have which could be essential in assisting
  the local education authority in its new role of enabler of change. Such skills identified
  were those of:
      Organisational development
      Learning theory
      Staff development models
      Appraisal processes
- To develop new areas of working by examining the current context, developing new skills
  and allocating time appropriately. (Gersch *et al.*, 1990, p. 129)

It is apparent that services and their members are forecasting possible opportunities
for themselves in the 1990s. The challenge is to act upon these scenarios in ways that are
practical and feasible within an ethos where individual needs are understood, valued and
integrated with those of the service.

REFERENCES

Argyris, C. and Schon, D. (1978) *Organizational Learning: A Theory in Action Perspective*.
  London: Addison-Wesley.
Bloom, J., McCarthy, M. and Townley, D. (1989) 'Peer appraisal: a summary of ideas and
  themes', in Asserting Psychology in the Market Place. *DECP*, **6** (4).
Boydell, T. (1976) *Experiential Learning*. Sheffield City Polytechnic. Manchester Monographs 5.
Byrne Whyte, J. (1986) *Teacher Assessment: A Review of the Performance Appraisal Literature
  with Special Reference to the Implications for Teacher Appraisal*. Manchester: Manchester
  Polytechnic.
Cline, T., Frederickson, N. and Wright, A. (1990) *Effective In-Service Training Resource Pack*.
  Resources for training LEA inset providers. London: Department of Psychology, University of
  London.
Department of Education and Science (1990) *Educational Psychology Services in England
  1988-1989*. A Report by HMI. London: HMSO.
Frederickson, N. (1988) 'Continuing professional education: towards a framework for
  development', in Jones, N. and Sayer, J. (eds) *Management and The Psychology of Schooling*.
  Lewes: The Falmer Press.
Gersch, I., McCarthy, M., Sigston A. and Townley D. (1990) 'Taking an educational psychology
  service into the 1990s', *Educational Psychology in Practice*, **6** (3), 23-30.
Handy, C. (1984) *Taken For Granted? Looking at Schools as Organisations*. Harlow: Longman
  Resources Unit.
Handy, C. (1985) *Understanding Organisations*. Harmondsworth: Penguin.

Knowles, M.S. (1973) *The Adult Learner: A Neglected Species*. Houston: Gulf Publishing Company.

Leigh, A. (1987) '20 ways to manage better IPM', as reproduced in Open Business School, *Managing People*. Milton Keynes: Open University Press.

McCarthy, M. (1987) 'Derbyshire Secondary Development Project', *School Organisation*, **7** (3).

Miller, A., Watts, P. and Frederickson, N. (1988) 'Planning professional development for educational psychologists: two case studies in implementation', *Educational Psychology in Practice*, **4** (2), 60–88.

Nuttall, D. (1981) *School Self-Evaluation: Accountability with a Human Face*. York: Longman.

Open Business School (1983) *Choosing and Developing Your Team*. Book 6 of 'The Effective Manager'. Milton Keynes: Open University Press.

Open Business School (1987) *Managing People. Book 2*. Milton Keynes: Open University Press.

Peters, T. and Waterman, R. (1982) *In Search of Excellence*. New York: Harper & Row.

Roles, D. (1986) 'Derbyshire Secondary Development Project: Long Eaton School evaluation report'. (unpublished).

Schein, E. (1978) *Career Dynamics: Matching Individual and Organisational Needs*. Wokingham: Addison-Wesley.

Smith, R. (1983) *Learning How to Learn: Applied Theory for Adults*. Milton Keynes: Open University Press.

Chapter 7

Connecting Organizational Psychology, Schools and Educational Psychologists

Mark Fox and Allan Sigston

THE EDUCATIONAL CONTEXT

In the last few years education in the UK has seen numerous, almost continuous external intervention designed to engender changes in schools. The Education Reform Act 1988 envisages a scenario where schools are quasi-autonomous bodies responding to the market pressures of open enrolment. Both institutions and local authorities have sought to meet these demands through applying 'business' models newly imbued with public sector ethics.

These approaches are well exemplified by the application of the idea of performance indicators which seek to objectify aspects of school effectiveness. Yet it seems that the easier these are to quantify the more ambiguous are the interpretations. The DES (1989) has published a list of features that schools might consider in reviewing their work; item 17 reads 'Incidence of special educational needs/learning difficulties including any provision made for pupils with statements'. If this incidence is 'high', does it indicate the failure of mixed-ability teaching, or the success of the screening procedures, or even the compliance of the educational psychologist that visits the school? Equally, if it is 'low' are the converses true?

For some performance questions the quantification of data may detract from its significance. For instance, item 16 on the DES *aide mémoire* asks, 'Cultural characteristics of the pupil population (e.g. percentage of pupils from homes where English is not the first language). Are there direct implications for the work of the school (e.g. the curriculum, support staff)?' Matters concerned with attitudes, beliefs and values are surely of greater importance in this respect than changes in percentage points.

In short, while discussion of performance indicators may have given a welcome impetus to the idea of schools appraising themselves, the most crucial educational issues do not seem susceptible to such quantitative assessment. If performance indicators imply a general selection of factors of conceivable relevance to school managers, then does it warrant the importation of such a potentially alienating term? It seems that the secret of the term's attractiveness lies in its connotations of commercial enterprise.

Etzioni (1961) has described how the types of psychological involvement of an organization's members relate to the type of power/authority that pertains. Schools would appear to be an example of what he termed normative organizations, composed of people who belong because they share the overall goals of the institution. Recent legislative changes have pressured schools toward being more utilitarian, through having to be more responsive to their economic relationships. Etzioni suggests that in utilitarian organizations, employees are more likely to show a calculative involvement where motivation is more closely linked to self-interest.

The tension between the normative and utilitarian forces, and their psychological concomitants, are vital new factors in the planning of change in schools that are unlikely to be addressed through the simplistic application of economic models borrowed from industry. These pose new dilemmas for all those concerned with initiating change within public sector education.

EDUCATIONAL PSYCHOLOGY PRACTICE AND ORGANIZATIONAL CHANGE

Educational psychologists' interest in the process of organizational change predates that of many of our colleagues in the education service and can be linked at least to Burden's (1978) call to 'systems' work. The attraction of organizational involvement for educational psychologists is the opportunity for what Caplan (1969) has termed primary prevention, the promotion of more psychologically healthy environments, in contrast to tertiary prevention, which attempts to mitigate the effects of established problems. Involvement in primary prevention projects implies a contribution beyond the margins of special educational needs and into the fabric of the school as a whole. Our colleagues in the education service might reasonably ask, 'What is the area of expertise that psychologists bring to such enterprises?'

While the intricacies of consultancy are addressed more fully in Chapter 5, it is worth reflecting on the functions of educational psychologists in this area of their work. Are they there as experts? If so, in what? After all, a boiled sweet manufacturer may want to buy expertise from an occupational psychologist, but not in concocting the recipe. Educational psychologists have direct classroom experience, but as their careers progress this seems less and less of an asset, and most schools are likely to have at least equally effective current teaching practitioners on tap.

There may be, though, certain areas where educational psychologists have expert knowledge either through experience of working with other schools or through awareness of relevant research. At the moment it is likely that such areas of expertise extend to special educational needs rather than organizational change.

Within the profession the debate about service delivery has been dichotomized crudely into preferences for clinical (individually focused) versus 'systems' (organizationally focused) approaches. The term 'systems' has come to be synonymous for educational psychologists with attempts at organizational change, but has sharply differing connotations. Although most psychologists would agree that a system constitutes fundamentally an enduring relation between input and output, for some the emphasis is almost entirely on mechanistic processes (for instance, Facherty and Turner, 1988) while for others the focus is on interpersonal process and subjective meaning (for instance, Dowling and Osborne, 1985).

These 'hard' and 'soft' systems represent only two of many schools of thought about the management of change, which is a field that has been richly endowed by psychology. Yet there is little evidence of this body of work being applied in the profession. In surveying 1989 articles in *Educational Psychology in Practice* (the house journal of the Association of Educational Psychologists), we found six out of a total of twenty-nine articles about projects intended to bring about higher-order change in identified organizations. Two of these do not make reference to any previous literature, and overall there are no citations of work on the management of change beyond the confines of education.

It seems fair to conclude that, despite a self-evident need, organizational psychology is having a limited impact in the field of education and that educational psychologists themselves have not significantly drawn upon this part of their parent discipline in their role. If educational psychologists are to offer a fuller contribution to the management of change in the 1990s and beyond, it is manifest that they will need to draw upon a wider knowledge base than appears to be the case currently. For it is clear that there will be opportunities for psychologists, educational or otherwise, who know schools to help with the process of change.

THEORIES OF ORGANIZATION

To have an understanding of an organizational context and insight into how participants construe their organizational lives is a key starting point for resolving both institutional and child-focused problems. While this chapter cannot hope to give a thorough resumé of the literature on theories of organization, it seems worth reviewing some of the major strands linking them to the profession of educational psychology. It is striking that while this theory base seems under-utilized by educational psychologists, many of its roots will be fairly familiar, drawing upon social psychology, sociology, cybernetics and, increasingly, biology.

Though commercial companies orientate themselves around clearly defined products/services and consumers, there is considerable ambiguity about how (or even if) these ideas apply to public sector education. For these reasons schools can be regarded as amongst the most complex of organizations and the need to have models to which their functioning can be related is inescapable.

Different explanatory models of organization have their own strengths and weaknesses in stressing objective or subjective features, process or outcomes. Perhaps most importantly, derivations and approximations of the models are part of the mythology of inhabitants and observers of institutions and services. Thus the models serve as constructs that help many educational psychologists, teachers, parents, and children to make sense of their experience of schools.

FORMAL-MECHANISTIC MODELS OF ORGANIZATION

Mechanistic models tend to be associated with the idea that institutions have clear purposes and boundaries that render their functioning relatively unaffected by the influence of the wider environment. The problem of design and change becomes one of how one arranges the division of tasks and responsibilities in order to optimize outcomes. This philosophy was most apparent in the growth of mass production earlier in this century. This endorsed the premises of scientific management proposed by F.W. Taylor (1911), which viewed workers as sophisticated machines that needed to be matched to and programmed for specific tasks. These principles spread beyond the factory floor into a general bureaucratization of employment that is a powerful force of social control (Weber, 1947). The notions of role definition, accountability and line and 'top down' management are all part of this approach.

It has been fashionable to criticize bureaucracies, and in their extreme they are a soft target, but they have certain strengths. Mechanistic organizations allow more complex activities to be routinized so that they can be carried out by less experienced or skilled staff, are less vulnerable to staff turnover and more immune to corruption. (These are all aspects that have endeared the model to the retailers of fast food!) These 'virtues' become hindrances when the tasks done by workers require initiative. As a consequence mechanistic organizations are less flexible in adapting to changing environments and less fulfilling for employees, because of their minimization of human creativity.

The concept of bureaucracy is deeply embedded in twentieth-century life, so it is not surprising that it is reflected to an extent in the way schools operate or at least describe themselves. Rigid divisions between pastoral care, faculties and special needs functions, prescriptive posts of responsibility, lists of pupil rules and regulations, the setting of organizational goals primarily by the senior management team, are all indicative of the hierarchy and role-boundedness found in bureaucracies. They carry with them the inherent problems described above, and will determine expectations of the role of the educational psychologist.

THE CONCEPT OF ORGANIZATIONAL CULTURE

Organizational theorists have broached the concept of culture in organizations under the guises of culture, climate and ethos. They have drawn heavily on sociology and anthropology in arriving at a conceptual paradigm applicable to organizations and institutions. The cultural approach underscores subjective elements in terms of the meanings and attributions used to make sense of life at the levels of nations, communities, organizations, groups and sub-groups. It is now considered almost axiomatic that once a group has experienced a shared history for a reasonable length of time a congruent, if unspoken, set of constructs of appropriate behaviour will develop.

Schein (1990) offers the following definition of organizational culture, as:

> (a) a pattern of basic assumptions, (b) invented, discovered or developed by a given group, (c) as it learns to cope with its problems of external adaptation and internal integration, (d) that has worked well enough to be valid and, therefore (e) is to be taught to new members as the (f) correct way to perceive, think and feel in relation to those problems. (p. 111)

Harrison and Stokes (1986) propose four generalized cultural orientations of organizations. In 'power cultures' control is invested in dominant individuals or coalitions. 'Role cultures' exhibit the characteristics of bureaucracy described earlier. 'Achievement cultures' are goal directed, so that human resources are aligned around tasks rather than structures. Finally, 'support cultures' stress mutual trust and informal alignment rather than organizing around goals and tasks. Hargreaves and Stokes have developed a questionnaire that clarifies both perceived and preferred orientations as a way of exposing issues for discussion among working groups.

At a finer-grained level, Schein (1990) suggests that a group's culture makes itself apparent at three levels of increasingly deep significance. First are artifacts, which include things like dress codes, modes of address and the folklore of the group (such as how people get promoted); second are values, reflected in norms, philosophy and ideology; third, and most difficult to decipher, are basic assumptions that guide action, thoughts and feelings.

The notion of culture seems immediately illuminating. Take, for example, grammar schools that have undergone the transition to become comprehensive schools. In responding to the needs of lower attainers a number of challenges to the dominant culture might be anticipated. New pupils and staff are likely to question artifacts such as uniforms for pupils and gowns for teachers. The values and norms of the original staff are likely to reflect academic excellence, expressed in events like speech days that may not be as cherished by subsequent pupils, parents or staff. Finally, basic assumptions about the purpose of teaching as cultivating the talents of the more able will be threatened by the greater prevalence of lower attainers. Experience suggests that these cultural tensions can persist for lengthy and painful periods.

The durability of cultures in the longer term stems from their ability to socialize new members. They provide stability and predictability for an institution's members and can facilitate or undermine change. Unfortunately the concept of culture seems a more satisfying framework for explaining why things do not change than informing how they might.

Rutter *et al.*'s (1979) research on secondary schools has emphasized the relevance of culture to schools. Generally more positive pupil outcomes were 'systematically and strongly associated with the characteristics of schools as social institutions' (p. 205). They collectively termed these characteristics of a school its ethos.

There are dangers in making too casual analyses of schools' cultures through projecting one's own basic assumptions on to them. Clearly educational psychology services have cultures too; including a culture about how to offer change in schools. The educational psychologist attempting to work at an organizational level, within, for example, a bureaucratic framework, without consideration of the issues culture raises can expect to waste a lot of effort.

UNITARIST VERSUS PLURALISTIC VIEWS OF ORGANIZATIONS: THE POLITICAL MODEL

A common assumption is often that all members of an organization share the same goals for it. Therefore if there is conflict it is presumed that it operates at a relatively superficial level, and that if the time and trouble is taken it will be possible to identify a bedrock of agreement about aims that serve as the premises for structure and action. On this supposition numerous educational psychology services in recent years have attempted to address issues of corporate identity through internal consultations over aims and objectives. This assumption of common goals and resolution of conflict through collaboration has been termed unitarist. In the wake of industrial strife in the 1960s and 1970s, Fox (1973) challenged the validity of the assumption, describing two other frames of reference: pluralist and radical.

The pluralist frame shows the organization as a coalition of individuals and groups who have divergent interests. Within the pluralist approach conflict is inherent and resolved through ongoing bargaining and negotiation. The radical perspective sees conflict within the organization as inevitable and part of the class conflict in society at large.

These views suggest that conflict can be seen as normal and even helpful: 'In a fragmented, dynamic social system, conflict is natural and not necessarily a symptom of breakdown in the academic community. In fact, conflict is a significant factor in promoting healthy organizational change' (Baldridge *et al.*, 1978, p. 35).

So ingrained are the assumptions of unitarism (or so great the avoidance of issues of power and control) that Hartley (1984) notes that, 'To develop a perspective away from unitarism is a significant development for most psychologists' (p. 159).

Yet for many educational psychologists the pluralist political scenario seems to fit many aspects of secondary schools certainly and even of the workings of local education authorities as a whole. Within schools the complexity of the task of teaching and the difficulty for senior managers of directly sampling classroom practice mean that changes are significantly affected by informal networks and alliances based on individuals' interests.

A head of a special needs department might demonstrate the significance of the political model if she or he were to suggest that the way to agree a new screening procedure was to talk it through informally over a drink with the head of English before formal discussions with the head. Here it is clear that there are coalitions that allow change to occur rather than a formal, 'goals of the school' perception. Theories of group cohesion and conflict (such as Sherif, 1966; Tajfel and Fraser, 1978) and of style of conflict management (such as Blake and Mouton, 1964; Rahim and Bonoma, 1979) are of direct relevance.

In the political model the decisions that get made depend on the power that different groups have. In considering issues of power within educational institutions and services it would be patently unjust not to note the massive imbalance in positional power between the genders (Weightman, 1989). The political model of organization reminds us of the ethical and practical naivety of ignoring the location of power, and the importance of distinguishing between it in its 'physical', 'positional', 'personal', 'legitimate', 'resource' or 'expert' forms (French and Raven, 1968).

THE SUBJECTIVE MODEL OF ORGANIZATION

In his book *Theories of Educational Management*, which is one of the most intellectually accessible works in the area, Bush (1986) provides an illuminating breakdown of differing organizational perspectives that have been applied to educational institutions. Bush describes what he calls formal and political models that correspond to the mechanistic and political frameworks described earlier. Additionally he refers to subjective and ambiguity models.

The subjective view of organizations rests in phenomenology. Essentially it is argued that organizations exist only in the 'eye of the beholder'. Through a pattern of interactions each individual builds up his or her own understanding of the nature and significance of events. Greenfield (1973) states that:

> Most theories of organisation grossly simplify the nature of reality with which they deal. The drive to see the organisation as a single kind of entity with a life of its own apart from the perceptions and beliefs of those involved in it blinds us to the complexity and variety of organisations people create around themselves. (p. 571)

For example, a staff meeting will have different meanings to the participants. For a new teacher it may seem long, tedious and irrelevant to the needs that are preoccupying her or him. A union representative might feel frustrated that important issues are rushed, perhaps assuming that this was a deliberate political strategy. A senior member of staff might enjoy the opportunity the meeting offered to embarrass the head publicly, while the head may see the staff meeting as a weekly, somewhat painful ritual.

The subjective model is in some respects the natural counterpoint to the cultural model described earlier, in that it highlights the way many assumptions are not shared. In a sense it is more of a denial of other explanatory paradigms than a competing theoretical framework. Its major implications are the importance of linking the goals of the individual to the focus of change and the difficulties of establishing shared meaning in working groups.

THE AMBIGUITY MODEL OF ORGANIZATION

The ambiguity model, as characterized by Bush, further stresses the complexity of institutions and the environments in which they are operating. He notes

> Ambiguity models assume that turbulence and unpredictability are dominant features of organizations. There is no clarity over the objectives of institutions and their processes are not properly understood. Participation in policy making is fluid as members opt in or out of decision making opportunities. (p. 108)

Endemic ambiguity means that change takes place through a coincidence of factors (often random) rather than by design. There are parallels with ecology: the reasons why a seed may flourish while many others perish can be seen to be related to the coming together of a number of necessary conditions, and the subsequent circumstances will then become part of a further pattern of mutual causality. The success and failure of organizational innovations can be seen in a similar light. It can lead to an apparent paradox: that everyone in an organization feels powerless.

Cohen *et al.* (1972) have produced a vivid image of organizations operating within this ambiguity as 'garbage cans'. It is postulated that solutions (such as timetable changes or appraisal schemes) to a large extent exist independently of problems. Problems and solutions mix together in the proverbial garbage can and get loosely attached to one another. When the organization is put into the position where a decision has to be made, choices are rarely made upon a considered resolution of the problem. More usually they are made via oversight (that is, speedily and without reference to other prevailing problems) or by flight (when the problem lingers on the back burner until a more palatable choice arises than the solution that was associated with the problem: Cohen and March, 1974). Not surprisingly, discussion of the garbage can model often raises a wry smile of recognition from teachers and educational psychologists.

THE RELATIONSHIP BETWEEN ORGANIZATIONS AND THEIR ENVIRONMENTS

The seminal work of Burns and Stalker (1961) provided one of the first articulated alternative organizational forms to the mechanistic variety. In a series of case studies of British companies, they proposed that the more successful companies working within less stable and predictable environments (in terms of technology and markets) tended to be those that could adapt more responsively, in an organismic fashion. The continual emergence of unfamiliar problems made the formal definition of responsibilities difficult to sustain. Communication and interaction became more 'lateral' than 'vertical' in order that the organizations' members could cohere around common problems, clarifying and mobilizing solutions. Organizations that failed to make such adaptive responses proved less likely to thrive, and as a result a process akin to Darwinian natural selection occurred.

The ideas triggered by Burns and Stalker have re-emerged repeatedly in differing guises. These have included Bennis's (for instance, Bennis and Nanus, 1985) notion of the 'adhocracy' (organizational structures that coalesce and dissolve in relation to particular purposes), Peters and Waterman's (1982) characteristics of excellent companies as being 'close to the customer' and 'biased for action', and Kanter's (1983) emphasis on organizations cultivating new ideas and not punishing their members for taking risks.

A practical problem with developing 'organic' organizations comes with size. Within a large secondary school, pragmatic constraints determine that some functions must be bureaucratized in order to ensure reliable functioning (for example, the timetable). The problem becomes one of minimizing the intrusions of such aspects while maximizing more flexible responses to change. One attempt has been the so-called matrix organization, which links its members into both bureaucratic and functional units. Secondary schools have long been pioneers of this arrangement in the way teachers form parts of both faculty and pastoral teams. The major problem with this framework has been in reconciling prescriptive membership of functional groups with the need for energy and commitment if the groups are to work well.

The premise of 'survival of the fittest' would suggest a proliferation of innovative institutions and 'flatter', more flexible hierarchies. It seems that as organizations grow there are inevitable pressures toward bureaucratization. A strategy of 'tightening up' is also a common response to survival-threatening crises, thereby often sowing the seeds of the organization's own destruction. In the wake of more recent evolutionary theory, Morgan (1986) has drawn upon the idea of autopoieosis, in particular the theories of Maturana and Varela (1980). In essence it is suggested that organizations seek to maintain their sense of identity through defining their relationship with the wider system of which they form a part. As a consequence, change is triggered by internal factors (often random) that lead to shifts in identity that in turn change transactions with other sub-systems. An example of this could be the case of having insufficient pupil numbers to maintain the viability of a number of local schools. The adaptational model suggests that the new environment would produce changes in all the 'competing' schools, to a greater or lesser degree. Autopoieosis suggests that only those schools whose personnel/ teachers redefine themselves in relation to parents, pupils and other schools, as a necessary precursor, will change their transactions with the wider community.

In working within schools, the issues raised by organic models for educational psychologists are to do with the goodness of fit between the functions of the school and its environment, and how the school defines itself through its perceived transactions with external elements. The Education Reform Act 1988 is a deliberate attempt to modify crucial aspects of the environment by making parents, in effect, the purchasers of school provision. Given the ensuing pressures the relevance of organic models seems obvious.

EDUCATIONAL PSYCHOLOGISTS' INVOLVEMENT IN ORGANIZATIONAL CHANGE

As we have seen, organizations are multi-faceted; all have formal, cultural, political, subjective and ambiguous aspects. All operate within some wider environment. All the models described have validity, but none alone could hope to give an all-embracing account. In his book *Images of Organization*, Morgan (1986) proposes that thinking of an organization as a machine or organism, cultural or political system (among others), provides a set of metaphors that can illuminate phenomena. By applying different metaphors to a given situation it is possible to find areas of good fit that inform action. Similarly Bush (1986) advocates taking multiple perspectives, but cites examples of their application in sequential phases of the management of change rather than the more open-ended 'diagnostic reading' proposed by Morgan.

In our view these different frames of reference offer an essential starting point for thinking about organizational change, for without them educational psychologists will be left viewing complex phenomena in limited ways. Not only, though, do educational psychologists need to be able to view the complexities of organizations in different ways; they also need to be able to link this to strategies for change. Otherwise, as Maslow was reported as saying, 'If the only tool you have is a hammer, you will treat everything as if it is a nail.'

In Chapter 5 the distinction has been made between expert and process consultancy. This is a particularly useful distinction for educational psychologists involved in organizational change. A second key distinction is whether the focus for organizational change is primarily on the objectives of the organization or a changed pattern of interpersonal relationships among the organization's members. These two dimensions give us four key areas that educational psychologists can be involved in when working on organizational change. This division of educational psychologists' involvement in organizational change is seen as a simplifying mechanism that is useful for illuminating how the profession has worked in this area (see Figure 7.1).

Strategies for educational psychologists' involvement

Educational psychologists' first move from individual children into organizational work is usually via Inservice Education of Teachers (INSET). Educational psychologists

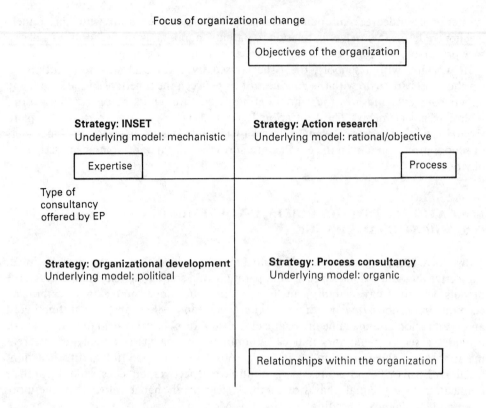

Figure 7.1   *Strategies for educational psychologists' involvement.*

have generalized from the expertise they have built up from their work with individual children to run courses for school teachers.

The development and delivery of INSET packages is a common method of service delivery (for instance, BATPACK: Merrett and Wheldall, 1990). This type of INSET is 'objectives driven' and the educational psychologist is seen as an expert in this area. The training is designed to teach skills and knowledge to teachers. The underlying assumption is that training teachers in a specific way will change their classroom practice and in the long run there will be a whole-school effect.

The often unspoken model underlying this strategy is that of a formal/mechanistic model. It is presumed that by training key members of staff, changes will occur. Mechanistic phrases such as a 'cascade' model of training are common.

The second strategy for educational psychologists has been to provide a process for change that the school can apply to specific areas of work; for example, training schools to use a 'problem-solving model' to sort out their own problems. Stratford (1990) describes how this was used to reduce 'discipline' problems in schools with the underlying aim of improving a school's ethos. System supplied information (Myers *et al.*, 1989) is similar in purpose in so far as it is designed to enable schools to specify their own needs and plan appropriate action to meet them.

Underlying these approaches is an action research model. This has a number of variations but rests on Lewin's (1959) assertion that implementing change is not only directly purposeful but enhances understanding of organizational functioning. Setting up a controlled intervention and analysing the theory against the intervention allows the organization to develop. Cowne (1989) used INSET to promote changes in policy and practice in schools. INSET was used as a basis for action research in the teachers' own schools. The INSET was content focused, as was the process of change (action research), but the actual change topic seems to have been left to the individual teacher.

For the most part, practitioners working within this part of the quadrant work upon the assumption that organizations can plan rationally and make objective decisions based on relevant evidence. The advocates of internal institutional review (such as McMahon *et al.*, 1984) either start from this premise or see it as a vehicle for helping schools to develop a problem-solving culture.

Action research is also considered a fundamental technique within the 'organizational development' strategy (Burke, 1987). Organizational development is one of the most rapidly expanding branches of applied psychology and builds on a perception of organizations as dynamic systems that are constantly in flux. The prime focus of the organizational development model is developing the human potential to respond to changes. It emphasizes the importance of interpersonal and intergroup tensions and so relates to the political and cultural views of organizations.

Organizational development theory also stems from the work of Lewin (1959), whose three-step model for change is still influential. Lewin believed that to bring about lasting change the present system needs to be unlocked or unfrozen through a re-educative process such as developing leadership skills. Next there must be movement in the system, made possible through the reorganization of tasks, functions or relationships. Finally these new changes need to be refrozen by supportive actions. The organizational development approach has been applied by educational psychologists when they are involved in courses on team building, team leadership, negotiation or communications skills.

The fourth and final strategy on the grid is process consultancy. The perspective here is of the educational psychologist approaching the task of organizational change with a completely open agenda on the content and method of change. In this way the educational psychologist is not acting as an expert on the contents of teaching or assessment or even on the best method of the organization of the school. The educational psychologist becomes the facilitator for the process of change rather than being seen as the expert on the contents or methods of the change. The direction, pace and meaning of change (to solidify, to loosen up) are set by the school.

The organizational model highlighted by process consultancy is the organic model. The process consultant's job is to ensure the organization breathes freely and is able to react healthily to environmental forces.

Phillips (1990) provides a useful description of how some educational psychologists are making the bridge between objectives on content-led and process-led organizational change. His objectives-led examination of a school's response to special educational needs was tied in with the educational psychologist's involvement in the process of the school organization. Phillips concludes: 'a key part of its task was to attend to the school's unique perception of itself. The illumination ("publication") and examination of this psychological distinctiveness is in our view a central contribution that educational psychologists are able to make to any organizational enquiry' (p. 73).

Process consultancy as a method of organizational change requires not only an understanding of how people in organizations work but also the skills necessary to help bring to the surface the issues that the individuals in the school face. The task is not to affect the direction that the school wishes to take but rather to help them take it more effectively by helping them see more clearly the process by which change happens in that school. The aim is simply one of improving the organization's ability to learn.

Among educational professionals, psychologists are particularly well placed and have a foundation of skills to work as process consultants. They are able to observe how people interact in an organization and, through reflection back, help its members understand it better.

THE CHARACTERISTICS OF LEARNING ORGANIZATIONS

In the last few years institutional development plans (IDPs) involving planning objectives and resource allocation have become *de rigueur* in the educational world, as was mentioned at the outset of this chapter. Like many other public service innovations, they have followed on from perceived good practice in the commercial and industrial sectors (such as appraisal)—though, perversely, the delay in the transition from industry to education is sometimes coincidental with a re-evaluation of the approach at its source. For while the idea of a 'business plan' on which IDPs are based has not gone out of fashion, it has been recognized that unpredictable environments require swift manoeuvring and that excessive advance commitment of resources can contribute to inflexibility. None the less, the idea of IDPs commands widespread support from education professionals who hold markedly different ideas about organizational functioning. *Aficionados* of the mechanistic approach may see IDPs as an opportunity to 'sharpen up' management in ways that draw on the 'management by objectives' approach (a mechanistic model of organization). Those who subscribe more to a participative approach to management may see the negotiation of content of an IDP as an opportunity to motivate and incorporate individuals' goals into those of the school (a subjective model of organization). It is therefore quite common to have agreement about the principle of having IDPs while uncovering fundamental and perhaps irreconcilable differences at the level of practice.

McGregor's (1960) distinction between two types of belief commonly held by managers well illustrates this point. McGregor's 'Theory X' suggested that many people believe that employees are by nature indolent, dislike responsibility, selfish and indifferent to the organization's needs. By implication they need to be persuaded, rewarded, punished and directed. On the other hand, 'Theory Y' supposes that employees do not inherently dislike work and all have the capacity for development and a willingness to work toward organizational goals. The role of managers holding this view is to arrange matters, as far as possible, so that workers can achieve personal goals through working toward organizational objectives. IDPs can be a vehicle for both Theory X and Theory Y.

IDPs are a means of ensuring the school is a 'learning organization', where the organization observes its environment, and self-regulates and adapts accordingly. Organizational theorists have drawn on ideas from cybernetics to illuminate the underlying processes. One critical distinction is between 'double-loop' and 'single-loop' learning. It is argued that relatively simple information processing systems are able to detect and correct deviations from a set goal or path (single-loop learning). What differentiates the intelligent system that survives in the long term is that it can also question those goals (double-loop learning). There are many instances in industry where adherence to goals proved to be the downfall of the organization itself. For instance, the British woollen industry suffered a severe and prolonged recession in the 1970s with the closure of almost half the factories in West Yorkshire. This was largely due to the increased competition from the development of synthetic fibres, in particular acetate and nylon, which emphasized easy care. The woollen industry had to focus on new goals, especially the easy care of garments, in order to compete again.

A great deal of work has been done on how double-loop learning can be achieved in organizations (notably Argyris, 1982; Schon, 1983). Fundamentally it involves the encouragement of questioning basic assumptions within the organization, especially about the culture and values discussed earlier. There is a further discussion of double-loop learning within educational psychology services in Chapter 8.

Morgan (1986) invokes the idea of a hologram to elucidate further characteristics of 'learning organizations'. This suggests the need for 'over-capacity' in sections of the organization, so that each sub-group or individual is able to undertake a wider range of functions than might normally be entailed. When this redundancy (as he terms it) is coupled with effective communication between these groups, the system attains a greater capacity to 'self-organize'. A major difficulty for schools is in the necessary commitment of time to organizationally distinct key tasks like lesson planning and presentation. These leave few time frames for 'self-organization'. The degree to which schools are able to optimize these opportunities is likely to be influential in determining their flexibility of response to outside pressures.

The conceptualization of schools as 'learning organizations' gives an interesting double meaning. The role of the process consultant involves ensuring that the surface structures, such as institutional development planning, connect with the deep structure required of successful 'learning organizations'.

INTERNAL V. ENVIRONMENTAL FACTORS

The specification of a school as a learning organization implies that change happens in a vacuum—it does not. As we have seen, the organic model highlights the need to look at organizational change within a wider pattern of relations with the environment.

Though there is no clear distinction between organizations and their environments, making the distinction draws attention to the key boundary transactions that ensure the survival of organizations. Dill (1958) highlights the distinction between the task environment and the contextual environment. The task environment consists of the people that the organization are in regular contact with outside of itself. For a school, the parents, governors and educational psychologist could all be considered to be part of the task environment. The contextual environment is the political, economic and demographic forces that extend beyond the task environment.

Task environment

As we have seen, educational psychologists have largely worked with internal factors (that is, people) when working for organizational change. It was a small step from educational psychologists' concerns with individual children to individual teachers, and from individual teachers to groups of teachers. The task environment factors have played a less important role in educational psychologists' deliberations.

The distinction between looking at the internal and external factors is mirrored in different orientations of work at a case level. Do educational psychologists work from an intrapsychic perspective with pupils—to help the pupil achieve self-development and change—or do they work in an interpsychic perspective (reciprocal determinism)—changing the environment in order to achieve change in the pupil? There is a danger that the educational psychologist may at times be coming in with the worst of both approaches, ignoring the environmental forces but at the same time intervening in a mechanistic way, working toward their own goals through dictating a corporate, goals-driven, content-led approach.

Georgiades and Phillimore's (1975) seminal paper warned of the difficulties for the potential 'hero innovator' by drawing attention to the futility of expecting organizations to change through training individuals in specific techniques without ensuring the host culture was cultivated. They emphasized the need to gain influence through expertise and ability, not through authority and power. It may be that expertise and ability are not enough if the psychologist, as the outsider, is trying to introduce a new technique into an organization. The educational psychologists may need to view the organization from within a political framework and acknowledge that they may need authority and/or power to effect change. Recognizing that there could be endemic conflict between groups of teachers, governors and parents may be necessary to ensure change. Instead of trying to facilitate harmony, the educational psychologist, if she or he is to work in the task environment, may need to ally herself or himself with other powers for change.

If educational psychologists are to continue to work in the school's task environment, they may need to consider how policy and politics are the basis for authority and power in attempting to change organizations. The other role is for educational psychologists to develop their expertise as facilitators for the process of change. To try to modify corporate goals as outsiders without authority to do so seems to be a recipe for no change.

The contextual environment

A 'top-down', content-oriented approach is the commonest LEA strategy for trying to influence schools. It draws heavily on the assumptions of formal/mechanistic organizational models. The LEA, in the form of officers, inspectors, advisors and educational psychologists, is there to inform the schools about the latest good practice and what they can do to implement it.

The part of the equation that is missing for educational psychologists is the organic factors (from the contextual environment) that effect change. Facherty and Turner (1988) provide one of the few descriptions of educational psychologists trying to achieve organizational change through policy change at an elected members' level. Their honest description bears witness to the difficulties. They acknowledge their lack of awareness of some of the critical forces at this environmental level, especially the financial underpinnings of policy.

Taking an 'organic' view of organizational interaction with the contextual environment, it is the throb of the resource blood that is so crucial. At the moment the contextual environment, the LEA, holds resources that it can use as levers for change in schools. These resources are assigned by the DES or the LEA for specific areas of change. There is a danger of overlooking the power of the contextual environment in terms of money and resources as the key factors in organizational change.

It may be helpful to see the validity of the perspective offered by the organic model for change and the importance of contextual environmental factors by considering changes in the organization of educational psychology services in the last ten years. What actually have been the forces for change in educational psychology services? How strong have been the internal forces such as professional development courses, team leadership or better communication? Or have environmental forces, such as the increase in staffing following the Education Act 1981 or the breakup of the Inner London Education Authority, been the forces for change? Will organizational changes in EPSs in the 1990s come about through changes of professional practice or the impact of LMS, delegated funding and the development of agency services? Though educational psychology services have changed because of factors at both ends of the spectrum, internal and environmental, the impact of environmental forces seems overwhelming.

Most radical changes occur because of external contextual factors rather than internal activities such as 'team building' or the annual service review that sets service objectives. Heller (1987), among others, has argued that psychologists' reluctance to focus on overall structure and environmental factors, such as policy and resources, is leading to serious difficulties in attempts to understand organizational change. Educational psychologists' reluctance to do so may stem from their lack of knowledge of economics and politics, but it may also in a more subtle way stem from our unwillingness or inability to conceive of human beings as not having control over their own destiny. An economic deterministic view of organizational change would not only shift people from centre stage, it would also shift educational psychologists from having a role in the change process. Nevertheless, if for example the future integration of children with special educational needs depends largely on factors external to the school, such as policy and resources rather than teachers' attitudes, knowledge and skills, it is important for us to recognize such phenomena and the implications for strategy, rather than becoming frustrated at our ability to help change organizations from the inside.

THE 1990s

It has been argued that, at least up to the implementation of the Education Reform Act 1988, educational psychologists may have seriously underestimated the impact of economic forces in attempting to achieve in schools goals with which they are sympathetic.

Educational psychologists have often regarded their role as slightly subversive, championing the cause of vulnerable clients within insensitive institutions that sometimes seem to value examination success and compliance above all else. Within this scenario, educational psychologists' work at an organizational level was conceived of as developing expertise or helping reactivate schools by siphoning resources and effort towards children with difficulties. It was usually argued that improved quality of education for the most needy pupils would result in beneficial changes for all. Indeed there is quite a lot of evidence for the proposition that institutions that are well organized, have high expectations and emphasize achievement, rather than stressing failure and misdemeanours, show more positive pupil outcomes as a whole (for instance, Rutter *et al.*, 1979; Mortimore *et al.*, 1988). No doubt many educational psychologists could cite anecdotally how they were instrumental in such changes, usually where a significant group of school staff have been of similar mind. However, it has also been argued that in their other common role as the arbiters of resources for individual pupils, the profession (along with others) has undermined the need for schools to make more inclusive arrangements for all pupils (for instance, Reynolds, 1987; Dessent, 1987).

There is a naivety in the conception of the educational psychologist as a corporate subversive that has been clearly exposed in the UK by the implications of local management of schools emanating from the Education Reform Act 1988. In casework there are readily apparent arguments as to why the school cannot be regarded properly as the client and should not, therefore, hold the purse-strings. In matters of organizational consultancy the school is the client, particularly where it is not pursuing change that directly impinges on specific responsibilities or strategic objectives of the local education authority.

More clearly than ever, educational psychologists require mandates based on the informed consent of 'school members' (though there may be arguments about quite whom this group constitutes) in order to offer organizational consultancy to schools. It can even be argued that determining a fee does much to clarify matters. In short, educational psychologists work on organizational problems at the invitation of the client institution, which also owns the subsequent process and outcomes.

In our opinion the major contribution of psychology to such enterprises is the way it can inform and facilitate the process of change. Educational psychologists obtain frequent and at times unique insights into organizational functioning, through regular collaboration with school staff on the needs of pupils perceived as being the most problematical. These features indicate a potential contribution to organizational problem solving that is unmatched by any other professional group working in the educational field.

In the 1990s schools are becoming self-regulating. While there may be some simplification and rationalization of the way this is done, few people would anticipate a wholesale return to the pre-1988 Act position. Local management of schools will affect the balance of power in terms of the forces for change. If in future the school holds the resources, the LEAs will have few forces that will allow them to influence change in schools. The key focus in the contextual environment will be demographic. The building of a new estate will more directly affect the success or failure of a school than its policies or structure.

In Lewin's terms, schools have had a blast of hot air; they are now unfrozen. The involvement of educational psychologists needs now to be towards school-centred, process-orientated change; the role of educational psychologists is towards helping schools undertake change, facilitating the process.

CONCLUSIONS

This chapter has outlined the importance of having different frames of reference to understand organizations. By being aware of these different frames of reference, educational psychologists can view organizations as complex and dynamic phenomena. Of necessity, the overview of models of organization presented does little justice to them. It is hoped that it may help educational psychologists to become more generally aware of the large body of organizational and management literature that can offer valuable perspectives on the functioning of the institutions in which educational psychologists work.

Perhaps the most fundamental lessons for educational psychologists are that if they are to be involved in organizational change in different ways they need to change themselves. All too often educational psychologists see the need for change in other people: 'If people want to change their environment, they need to change themselves and their actions—not someone else . . . Problems that never get solved, never get solved because managers keep tinkering with everything but what they do' (Weick, 1979, p. 152).

The key is for educational psychologists to work in school in different ways. In order to do this two environments need to be scanned. Firstly the school as an organization, in order to create initiatives that will resonate with the needs of the school. It is suggested that schools in the 1990s will largely need help with the process of change, not the content. Secondly, educational psychologists need to be scanning their own LEA environment and, by establishing key relationships, actually begin to shape that external environment so that educational psychologists are seen to carry the LEA's authority in organizational change.

This scanning does not take place by gathering facts. The models outlined above have indicated both the complexity of organizations and the interpretive nature of their operation. The scanning process, therefore, is one of trying to make sense of a chaotic, changing world through the enactment of models that give some shape or form to the organization and the environment. A phenomenological approach that recognizes the levers of power in the environment makes some small sense to us.

Finally, educational psychologists need to be considering the health of their services' response to change. There is no better place to start understanding organizational change than by changing one's own organization. Schein (1988) has derived the following criteria for a healthy organization, which we have adapted for educational psychology services. How does your service match up?

(a) *adaptability*: the ability to solve problems and to react with flexibility to changing environmental demands

(b) *a sense of identity*: knowledge and insight on the part of the educational psychology service of what it is, what its goals are and what it is to do. Pertinent questions include: to what extent are goals understood and shared by all members of the educational psychology service? To what extent is self-perception on the part of the educational psychology service in line with perception of the educational psychology service by others?

(c) *capacity to test reality*: the ability to search out, accurately perceive and correctly interpret the properties of the environment, particularly those which have relevance for the functioning of the educational psychology service

(d) *integration*: a state of 'integration' among the sub-parts of the total educational psychology service, so that parts or individuals are not working at cross-purposes (adapted from Schein, 1988, p. 232).

REFERENCES

Argyris, C. (1982) *Reasoning, Learning and Action*. San Francisco: Jossey-Bass.

Baldridge, J., Curtis, D., Ecker, G. and Riley, G. (1978) *Policy Making and Effective Leadership*. San Francisco: Jossey-Bass.

Bennis, W.G. and Nanus, B. (1985) *Leaders: The Strategies for Taking Charge*. New York: Harper & Row.

Blake, R. and Mouton, R.S. (1964) *The Managerial Grid*. Houston: Gulf Publishing.

Burden, R. (1978). 'Schools systems analysis: a project centered approach'. In Gillham, R. (ed.) *Reconstructing Educational Psychology*. Beckenham: Croom Helm.

Burke, W. (1987) *Organisational Development: A Normative View*. Wokingham: Addison-Wesley.

Burns, T. and Stalker, G.M. (1961) *The Management of Innovation*. London: Tavistock.

Bush, T. (1986) *Theories of Educational Management*. London: Harper & Row.

Caplan, G. (1969) *An Approach to Community Mental Health*. London: Tavistock.

Cohen, M.D. and March, J.G. (1974) *Leadership and Ambiguity: The American College President*. New York: McGraw-Hill.

Cohen, M.D., March, J.G. and Olsen, J.P. (1972) 'A garbage can model of organizational choice', *Administrative Science Quarterly*, **17**, 1-25.

Cowne, L. (1989) 'Managing change through INSET', *Educational and Child Psychology*, **6** (3), 13-23.

DES (Department of Education and Science) (1989) 'Development of performance indicators key to effective management says Education Minister'. Press Release 382/89. DES, Elizabeth House, York Road, London SE1 7PH.

Dessent, T. (1987) *Making the Ordinary School Special*. London: The Falmer Press.

Dill, W. (1958) 'Environment as an influence on managerial autonomy', *Administrative Science Quarterly*, **2**, 409-43.

Dowling, E. and Osborne, E. (eds) (1985) *The Family and the School*. London: Routledge & Kegan Paul.

Etzioni, A. (1961) *Complex Organizations*. New York: Holt, Rinehart & Winston.

Facherty, A. and Turner, C.D. (1988) 'Changing at the top? An attempt by EPs to influence special education policy within an education authority', *Educational Psychology in Practice*, **4**(2), 99-104.

Fox, A. (1973) 'Industrial relations: a social critique of pluralist ideology', in Child, J. (ed.) *Man and Organization*. London: Allen & Unwin.

French, J.R.P. and Raven, B. (1968) 'The bases of social power', in Cartwright, D. and Zander, A. (eds) *Group Dynamics*. New York: Harper & Row.

Georgiades, N. and Phillimore, L. (1975) 'The myth of the hero-innovator and alternative strategies for organisational change', In Kiernan, C. and Woodford, F. (eds) *Behaviour Modification with the Severely Retarded*. Amsterdam: North-Holland Elsevier/Excerpta Medica.

Greenfield, T. (1973) 'Organisations as social inventions: rethinking assumptions about change', *Journal of Applied Behavioural Science*, **9** (5), 551-74.

Harrison, R. and Stokes, H. (1986) *Diagnosing Organization Culture*. California: Harrison Associates.

Hartley, J. (1984) 'Industrial relations psychology', in Gruneberg, M. and Wall, T. (eds) *Social Psychology and Organizational Behaviour*. London: John Wiley.

Heller, F. (1987) *Another Look at Organisational Change*. Paper delivered at the Third West European Congress on the Psychology of Work and Organisations.

Kanter, R.M. (1983) *The Change Masters*. London: Unwin.

Lewin, K. (1959) *Field Theory in Social Science: Selected Theoretical Papers*. London: Tavistock Publications.

McGregor, D. (1960) *The Human Side of Enterprise*. New York: McGraw-Hill.

McMahon, A., Bolam, R., Abbott, R. and Holly, P. (1984) *Guidelines for Review: Internal Development in Schools*. London: Schools Council Publications.

Maturana, H. and Varela, F. (1980) *Autopoiesis and Cognition: The Realization of the Living*. London: Riedl.

Merrett, F. and Wheldall, K. (1990) 'Does BATPACK training of teachers lead to higher pupil productivity?', *Educational and Child Psychology*, 7 (1), 31–43.

Morgan, G. (1986) *Images of Organization*. London: Sage Publications.

Mortimore, P., Sammons, P., Stoll, L., Lewis, D. and Ecob, R. (1988) *School Matters*. Wells: Open Books.

Myers, M., Cherry, C., Timmins, P., Brzezinska, H., Miller, P. and Willey, R. (1989) 'System supplied information (SSI): how to assess needs and plan effectively within schools/colleges', *Educational Psychology in Practice*, 5 (2), 91–6.

Peters, T. J. and Waterman, R. H. (1982) *In Search of Excellence*. New York: Harper & Row.

Phillips, P. (1990) 'Consultative teamwork in secondary schools: a training exercise', *Educational and Child Psychology*, 7 (1), 67–77.

Rahim, A. and Bonoma, T. V. (1979) 'Managing organisational conflict: a model for diagnosis and intervention', *Psychological Reports*, 44 (3), 1323–44.

Reynolds, D. (1987) 'The effective school: do educational psychologists help or hinder?', *Educational Psychology in Practice*, 3 (3), 22–8.

Rutter, M., Maughan, B., Mortimore, P. and Ouston, J. (1979) *Fifteen Thousand Hours*. London: Open Books.

Schein, E. H. (1988) *Organizational Psychology* (third edition). Englewood Cliffs, NJ: Prentice-Hall.

Schein, E. H. (1990) 'Organizational culture', *American Psychologist*, 45 (2), 109–19.

Schon, D. A. (1983) *The Reflective Practitioner*. New York: Basic Books.

Sherif, M. (1966) *Group Conflict and Cooperation*. London: Routledge & Kegan Paul.

Stratford, R. (1990) 'Creating a positive school ethos', *Educational Psychology in Practice*, 5 (4), 183–91.

Tajfel, H. and Fraser, C. (1978) *Introducing Social Psychology*. Harmondsworth: Penguin.

Taylor, F. W. (1911) *Principles of Scientific Management*. New York: Harper & Row.

Toffler, A. (1982) *Future Shock*. London: Pan.

Weber, M. (1947) *The Theory of Social and Economic Organization*. London: Oxford University Press.

Weick, K. E. (1979) *The Social Psychology of Organizing*. Reading, MA: Addison-Wesley.

Weightman, J. (1989) 'Women in management', *Educational Management and Administration*, 17 (3), 119–22.

Chapter 8

The Paradoxes of Organizing and Managing Educational Psychology Services

Mark Fox

INTRODUCTION

This chapter is concerned with how educational psychology services (EPSs) are organized. It takes as its starting point the premise that there are difficulties with the organization of EPSs as there are fundamental paradoxes about the way services are perceived. By bringing these paradoxes into focus it is hoped that educational psychologists will develop a clearer perspective of the difficulties their services face in the 1990s.

Argyris (1983) defines a paradox as that which 'occurs when individuals are in a situation in which whatever response they make in order to be constructive is also counterproductive' (p. 10). This chapter can be seen as an example of such a paradox. A simple, clear chapter on how EPSs are organized and managed at the present would not have been constructive. Instead, in order to be constructive, the chapter is written as a series of paradoxes that in itself can also be seen as counterproductive, since it raises issues that some educational psychologists would rather ignore.

Since psychology is about understanding people, then psychologists should have the basis for understanding how their own person-based services operate. However, psychologists differ greatly in their understanding of people and therefore any description of EPSs must start with a recognition of these differences. This chapter's starting point is the assumption that individuals create their own reality and therefore see the world differently. People create their own world, which has meaning and makes sense to them. In other words people create frames of reference or constructs about the world. These frames are necessary in so far as they give some power to predict what is going to happen. The assumption is that educational psychologists construct EPSs which may have different meanings to different educational psychologists, and certainly have different meanings to other people in the local education authority (LEA) as well as in the world at large.

The principal difficulty for educational psychologists is to communicate their view of their services not only to each other but also to significant others in the LEA. This is particularly important as the EPS is a person-to-person service. Educational psychologists do not make a product, nor do they deliver any service apart from a greater understanding of how people learn and develop. The whole EPS therefore depends on effective communication with other people.

In order to communicate, educational psychologists must share their frames of reference with other people. If, however, educational psychologists have different frames of reference and therefore different meanings for EPSs, then there is a likelihood that there will be misperceptions and miscommunications. This can be considered a paradoxical problem. People's meanings must be communicated, but if educational psychologists have different meanings, the more they communicate the clearer these differences become. If we try to communicate with someone who does not share our perception we tend to attribute the problem to them: 'They don't understand us.' This means that it is likely that we will try to get them to see it from our point of view by restating our position more forcefully. If they do not respond we may stop communicating with them and consider them stupid because they do not see our point of view. We also, of course, never see their point of view and therefore we are equally incomprehensible to them.

Paradoxes can only be broken by accepting the validity of all perspectives. The chief education officer's perspective on the EPS is just as valid as that of the principal educational psychologist. The newly qualified educational psychologist's perspective is just as valid as those of the seniors close to retirement. The task is to understand the other perspectives and to communicate that understanding. This communication is the only way to resolve paradoxes—it is not done by ignoring or castigating other people's perspectives of EPSs.

What are the paradoxes that underlie the management and organization of EPSs? Five key areas which contain paradoxes can be identified:

(a)   the identity paradox;
(b)   the career paradox;
(c)   the client paradox;
(d)   the professional paradox;
(e)   the management paradox.

The rest of this chapter explores these five areas. It explores different views of each area—to show that the issues make more sense, not less, by shifting positions.

THE IDENTITY PARADOX: PSYCHOLOGISTS OR EDUCATORS?

One of the central paradoxes for educational psychologists is whether they are educationalists with a particular expertise in psychology or whether they are psychologists who work in education.

The paradox of being identified as 'educationalist' or 'psychologist' goes right back to entry into the profession. To work as an educational psychologist in England and Wales, one is required to have an initial degree in psychology (or its equivalent)—clearly a psychology component. This must be followed by at least two years' teaching experience—clearly an educational component. Finally one requires professional training as an educational psychologist. This is the final anomaly, as it mixes psychology and educational theory to try to inform a practitioner's perspective—and it can take place in either an education or a psychology department within a university or polytechnic. The point that is being made here is not the appropriateness of training but rather how training leaves educational psychologists with different meanings for the title 'educational psychologist'.

When educational psychologists began to be employed by LEAs they were usually deployed in child guidance clinics. These clinics had grown up during the 1930s and 1940s, and usually comprised a child psychiatrist, psychiatric social workers and an educational psychologist who would work with children and their families (Ford *et al.*, 1982). Educational psychologists began to question the psychiatric domination of these clinics, and in the 1960s and early 1970s began to work increasingly in schools—as a method of moving out of the clinic. The Summerfield Report (DES, 1968) recommended increasing the numbers of educational psychologists. As the numbers grew, they formed a critical mass in some LEAs and began to agitate for their own service outside the child guidance clinics. Thus the first school psychological services started and educational psychologists began to be identified with school work.

Increasingly educational psychologists have moved out of child guidance clinics and are now more likely to be seen as part of the school support services, and certainly as part of the education department within the local authority (DES, 1990). This then becomes a paradox: can EPSs be a central and integral part of LEAs and yet at the same time retain their distinctive psychological element? As the EPS works closely with the LEA, do the norms, values and language of education begin to predominate in such a way that the psychological component is lost?

From another perspective one can also ask if there is even the need to have EPSs. How essential is it for educational psychologists to retain their own separate service within the LEA? Does the basic concept of an EPS ensure the employment of educational psychologists, but actually stop psychology being used within an LEA? This may be, because the application of psychology within the LEA may be seen as the province of the educational psychologist rather than as a body of knowledge that all personnel should draw upon. In addition, as educational psychologists are only seen to work in particular areas within the LEA, large areas of psychological knowledge never have ready access to the educational world. Have separate EPSs a function that protects educational psychologists, or is this their Achilles heel, which in the end will lead to their demise? The paradox is, of course, that by talking about it as a possibility one can give hostages to fortune.

Is the real way forward the decoupling of educational psychologists from EPSs, thus ensuring that psychology is taken on board through the LEA? The issue here is not about delegating the budget for EPSs to schools—that is a separate matter. The question is more fundamental—should educational psychologists work as a distinct professional group, or would psychology have a greater impact on the educational system if psychologists were working as education welfare officers, inspectors, LEA officers and teachers?

Having an EPS has different meanings for the chief education officer and elected members. Certainly it is likely to have a different meaning from having psychologists who are employed as individuals in their own right. Having a service gives structure, and therefore educational psychologists can be seen as a group of people with a single purpose, rather than acknowledging that within an EPS there are different individuals who can offer different services. Schools have always recognized this latter fact and are increasingly aware that they receive different services from different educational psychologists. So having an EPS allows the LEA to make assumptions about how educational psychologists operate. It diminishes the purpose of the individual educational psychologist and allows a collective accountability to take over.

Psychology has power in many people's eyes. It is, though, often a negative power in so far as it is associated with problems. Psychologists are seen by the general public as being concerned with helping people who have difficulties, often through some sort of counselling or therapy. It is still often associated with Freud and the subconscious—the belief is that psychologists can understand people's hidden selves. Psychologists are used by UK institutions to try to predict people's behaviour; this is as true of forensic psychology as it is for psychologists working in marketing. Most psychologists will have experienced the hush that falls at a dinner party on the disclosure of one's profession. For many people psychology is something to be feared—it may seem to touch aspects of the self which one does not really want to examine or know about. Psychologists are also aware, though sometimes dimly, that this is happening, and move to work in safer areas of the educational environment. So, for example, some educational psychologists have moved into curriculum-focused work and played down their ability to deal with problems of complex interpersonal relationships.

So another paradox is whether educational psychologists have to disavow their roots in psychology in order not to threaten themselves as well as others within the LEA. Clearly, however, by doing so they also reduce their own ability to offer services that are meaningful to other people's perception of the role of the psychologist. In Britain at the moment, educational psychologists are working in large and complex organizations in times of increasing change, surrounded by children and adults who are stressed, depressed, anxious, lonely, insecure and vulnerable. And what do educational psychologists focus on? The assessment of special educational needs! What is educational psychologists' fear of offering psychological services to the education world—and what is the educational world's fear when they are offered?

Educational psychologists need to address the paradox of being seen as either psychologists or educators, and the implications of being seen in these roles for the services they deliver.

THE CAREER PARADOX: MOVING IN OR OUT OF MANAGEMENT?

There are usually three types of post within educational psychology services: main-grade, senior and principal. Educational psychologists entering the profession are appointed to main-grade posts. Promotion is possible after approximately three to five years—though there is considerable variation. Principals are nearly always appointed from seniors with substantial experience. This career structure is common throughout England and Wales and it contains certain paradoxes.

The first step on the career ladder, a senior position, can be viewed from contradictory viewpoints. On the one hand it is seen as a career step that gives the promoted educational psychologist higher status. By definition, therefore, it can also be seen as simultaneously downgrading main-grade educational psychologists. The more steps there are on the ladder, the greater the differentiation between educational psychologists. Senior educational psychologists can therefore be viewed with hostility by main-grade educational psychologists, who find senior posts a threat to their position.

This might be resolved if there were a clear understanding of the role of senior educational psychologists. In many LEAs this is confused. Some seniors clearly have management responsibilities for leading a small team of educational psychologists, and in some shire counties this can in fact mean leading as large a team as a principal does in some metropolitan boroughs. The educational psychologist will still be a senior, however—not a principal. In other EPSs seniors have specialist functions; for example, pre-school or social services work. These posts may be linked to other departments, and even paid for by them. Here it appears that educational psychologists have been promoted for working with difficult client groups. But even this is not clear, as some of these specialist seniors do not take on the direct work with the difficult client groups but instead take on a management or coordinating role.

The first paradox is whether educational psychologists are promoted for management or practitioner skills. This paradox exists in many professions. Social workers are often quickly promoted to a position where they can use their management and organizational skills and away from the day-to-day contact with their clients. It will be increasingly true of teachers, where promotion to headship will depend less on teaching ability than on ability to manage a school. Many people would argue that this is sensible—that you need efficient managers to run efficient services. The paradox is, of course, that because they are not necessarily the most efficient practitioners, their view on the delivery of services may not be the same as the skilled practitioner. The skilled main-grade psychologist delivering quality services may have a completely different perspective on what and how quality services need to be delivered from that of the manager. If promotion depends on management skills it may also mean that it is not in educational psychologists' interests to develop their practitioner skills, as it does not lead to movement within the career structure.

There needs, therefore, to be greater clarity about the role of seniors. Are they senior executives with management responsibilities? Or are they leading professionals dealing with the most complex and difficult problems? By clarifying their LEA's and their own expectations the value of senior posts can be judged more accurately.

It may well be in the 1990s that one of the key tensions in educational psychology services will be between senior and principal educational psychologists. With the increased devolution of management responsibilities under local management of schools, many LEAs are slicing down their central functions; officers and offices are being moved to area or community bases. Within shire counties the power of the area senior may be increased, with direct responsibility for an area service. The shire principal may take on a role as 'head of profession', but with no management responsibilities. On the other hand there is a tendency for organizations to move to flatter structures with a decrease in the number of management tiers. From this perspective it may well be the middle managers—the seniors—who find their management responsibilities taken away from them. Senior and principal educational psychologists need to be aware that there may be inevitable tensions in the present management career structure, given the inherent conflict in the move to flatter structures and devolution in LEAs.

So it is important for educational psychologists to think about the paradoxes they face in career development. There are ways forward. One way is to expand on the perception of how educational psychologists might develop from the simple career-management-orientated three-tier system: main-grade, senior, principal. It is important to acknowledge that there are other ways of developing as well as in the direction of management responsibilities. Schein (1978) has outlined two other ways: development of expertise/specialism and movement towards the centre. Development must be allowed within the specialist practitioner field, where educational psychologists can receive rightful recognition for their contribution without having to take on management responsibilities. Properly accredited professional development, either through the British Psychological Society or through universities and polytechnics, should be increasingly important in the 1990s. The initial practitioner status should be seen as a qualification that can be built on by acquiring expertise in particular fields. This is not an argument for more academic qualification but rather for proper recognition for expertise in the field (Frederickson, 1988).

The other method of development, movement towards the centre, is more nebulous. Movement towards the centre is the recognition of the importance of people's experience in organizations. It is movement to a position where educational psychologists feel they have a voice and influence. To be marginalized and shut out by an LEA's hierarchical system is not productive for either the LEA or the educational psychologist. This third type of development is useful for all educational psychologists. It may be particularly important for principals to recognize that this is how their careers can develop. At the moment too many principals can feel they have reached a plateau—trapped by their position—with a belief that they have nowhere to go. Greater recognition that this is the time they need to move towards the centre of power and really ensure that psychology has an effect in the LEA could be liberating.

Another way forward for educational psychologists is to clarify exactly what the meaning of career development is for them. Whose needs are they serving when considering career development: those of the educational psychology service, the LEA or themselves? Recognizing the motivations behind applying for promotion is particularly important if educational psychologists are to match their individual needs to opportunities within an LEA.

Career development in the public sector contains a number of paradoxes. By recognizing these it is possible to go some way towards reconciling these differences and accepting that promotion has different meanings for different people.

THE CLIENT PARADOX: PUPIL, SCHOOL, OR LOCAL EDUCATION AUTHORITY?

The educational psychologist's role in the child guidance clinics in the 1940s and 1950s was to provide information, normally psychometric, on the child's educational attainments and abilities. Referrals were made to the psychiatrist in charge of the child guidance clinic. Despite the difficulties and disagreements on many other issues, it was quite clear that the client was the child. The educational psychologist's role was to provide information on the child that would be helpful—either directly for the child, or for those who were responsible for his or her education.

In the 1960s, educational psychologists had begun to work outside the clinic, in schools. Many educational psychologists viewed schools as a more normal working atmosphere, not dominated by the medical model. Educational psychologists began to set up their own referral system and pupils were referred directly to them. However, in the 1970s it was still not uncommon to have two sets of files in an office filing system—the school psychological service's and the child guidance clinic's.

The educational psychologist's first tentative steps alone into the world outside the clinic were not trouble-free. Headteachers with sudden access to this new service ensured that the educational psychologist visited their school by referring pupil after pupil. So started the infamous educational psychologist's waiting list. From the educational psychologists' point of view this was a treadmill which they could never get off—from the headteacher's point of view it was a holding system whereby she or he could refer the responsibility for a problem onwards and then, rightly, complain if it was not dealt with.

An additional problem for the waiting list was the confusion about who was the client. The powerful psychiatric medical model had a very clear understanding of who the client was. Educational psychologists suddenly found they were under pressure to consider the teacher as client within a school context. The shift is clearly evident when considering issues where the schools' and pupils' needs do not coincide; for example, with pupils suspended from school. Is the head the educational psychologist's client, or is it the pupil? Is the educational psychologist meant to view the situation from the head's perspective, or see what is best for the pupil? Trying to reconcile these different perspectives has been one of the key paradoxes of educational psychologists' work.

This shift from viewing the pupil as the client was due not only to the development of school psychological services separate from child guidance, but also to the development of behavioural psychology as the dominant psychology of the profession. Fuelled by the enthusiasm of a number of tutors on the professional training courses, behavioural psychology, with its emphasis on external determinants of behaviour and its reluctance to see internal child factors as modifiable variables, moved many educational psychologists to consider that teachers were responsible for a pupil's difficulties and that, therefore, they were the educational psychologist's clients. This is not the place to unravel the conceptual confusion between the 'causes' of behaviour and the responsibility for change—an area that is well explored in the literature on attribution theory (Farr, 1987). It is sufficient to point out that, for many educational psychologists, behavioural psychology became the professional justification for considering teachers as their clients in terms of the focus for change. It is interesting to note the very different behavioural path clinical psychologists have taken.

This move to work with teachers as well as pupils was helped by the development of an indirect consultation framework. Relying on Tharp and Wetzel's (1969) triadic consultation model, educational psychologists distinguished between the 'consultant', the 'mediator' and the 'target'. The consultant (the person with the knowledge or skills or vision or methodology; for instance, the educational psychologist) offers services to the mediator (the person with the influence; for instance, the teacher or parent) to help him or her affect the learning of the target (the person with the problem; for instance, the pupil). (See Chapter 3 for a description of the educational psychologist as consultant.)

Consultation services were offered on a time-contracted basis to schools; for example, one visit a month or a term. The concept of time contracting emerged as a way of cutting the waiting list and managing referrals (Born and Sawyer, 1979). Instead of heads referring pupils (usually on a specially devised form), they now consulted on their difficult pupils when the educational psychologist visited their schools. One of the services the time-contracted consultation service offered was a way of dealing with the pupil pre-referral. It was not uncommon to find a situation in which the educational psychologist insisted that the teacher had to consult about the pupil before a referral could be made.

Following on from this consultation/time-contracted model of service delivery, educational psychologists started different ways of recording their work. Instead of the individual pupil report by the educational psychologist, school reports were produced. This also helped the educational psychologists' myth that the school was their client. However, most school reports simply turned out to be a record of pupils' names (or initials if it was pre-referral) and details of the individual's problems. None the less, the illusion of offering a different sort of service continued.

It is debatable whose problems, if anybody's, these new styles of service delivery actually helped resolve. The problems did not go away (except by spontaneous remission). All that happened was that teachers did not refer. It did not affect the number of children with difficulties or the way of resolving the problems (Knapman *et al.*, 1987). One of the original hopes of the time-contracted consultation model was that it would enable educational psychologists to work on changes in school systems (see Chapter 5). This seems largely to have been a fruitless wish, and educational psychologists mainly merely worked the time-contracted consultation model with individual cases.

The client dilemma remained. It seems that some educational psychologists still saw the client as the pupil, and consequently alienated teachers by not doing what they thought the educational psychologist should be doing—recommending extra resources or removing the child to a special school. Or the educational psychologist sided with the teacher, and disenfranchised the least powerful person in the situation, the pupil, in some way or other. One of the key paradoxes is the belief that a consultation model can help both the teacher and the pupil. It is important to acknowledge that this sometimes is not possible given that there are conflicting needs to be met, the pupil's and the teacher's. The educational psychologist may be able to aid both parties by helping shift the perception of one about the problem, but the starting point for this may be the realization that there are conflicts of interests that cannot be resolved.

The pupil is, by definition, causing worry to the teacher. Usually that worry centres on the belief that the pupil needs more help or expertise than the teacher has available in the class. The educational psychologist is seen to have the power to resolve the problem by removing the pupil or by obtaining extra help. The educational psychologist's failure to do so inevitably means the teacher is dissatisfied with the educational psychologist, who finds it difficult to communicate his or her actual powerlessness to the teacher, as it would mean giving up what is perceived as power. There is a feeling of being helpless if one gives away the one power that is readily recognized by the teacher. The teacher, in turn, finds it difficult to communicate her or his helplessness—to do so would increase feelings of vulnerability. A readily identified paradox, therefore, develops whereby neither side talks about their real concerns.

The Education Act 1981, implemented from 1983 onwards, caused another set of problems that exacerbated the question of who the client is when considering service delivery. The move to integrate pupils with special needs in ordinary schools, while not reducing the number of pupils in special schools, did at the same time lead to the growth of resources available to mainstream schools. These resources were normally in the form of teaching support time or welfare hours. As we have seen, teachers now felt that educational psychologists could respond to their requests for more resources. Educational psychologists' responses to these requests and their continued ambiguity about who their clients were gradually brought a new player into the game.

The new player was the LEA, which had been a sleeping partner until now. The

Education Reform Act 1988 has already begun to change all that, and the 1990s will really emphasize that change. Educational psychologists have always been employed by LEAs—their salaries are paid for by the borough or county council. With LMS beginning to take effect this may no longer be the case.

Two scenarios begin to unfold before us. The first is that educational psychologists continue to be employed by the LEA: the educational psychologist is the consultant, the LEA the consultee and the school (or teacher) the client. Or the school will employ the educational psychologist as the consultant, the teacher as consultee and the pupil as client. It may well be that in the future there will be two educational psychologists involved with a pupil—one employed by the LEA, the other by the school. This scenario is not too far away. Already we have the situation where private educational psychologists are employed by parents to prove that their child has special educational needs—normally specific learning difficulties—in order to obtain access to greater resources. The position can soon be foreseen where it is the school that is employing an educational psychologist, maybe through an agency, to back its claim for extra resources, or for the disapplication of pupils from the National Curriculum. The LEA educational psychologist's position would be to validate the school's claims. The LEA would view the educational psychologist as able to give valid professional advice which would justify its resource-backed responses.

In this scenario educational psychologists' reports would become more adversarial, with tighter, more objective assessment procedures. The pressure to produce valid and reliable psychometric assessment would be intense. This can be clearly seen in the United States, where the pressure for access to resources has moved most of the states to produce clear, unambiguous psychometric criteria for access to resources (Boyan, 1985).

THE PROFESSIONAL PARADOX: CREDIBILITY THROUGH DISASSOCIATION?

EPSs are considered to be professional services, and this has major implications for the way they are organized. It has been suggested by Goode (1960) that the two central characteristics of professions are a lengthy period of training in a body of abstract knowledge and a strong service orientation. This definition has been challenged by Johnson (1972), among others, as it is not critical enough of what professionals actually do. He has suggested that: 'While the service ethic may be an important part of the ideology of many professional groups, it is not clear that practitioners are necessarily so motivated'(p. 25). It may be that professional behaviour is not so much a descriptive term but one that claims value and prestige by emphasizing a service orientation. It is important not to ignore the differences between the label of 'professional service' and the real characteristics of professional groups.

There are a number of characteristics of professional groups that suggest they exhibit complicated motives. Numerous studies of professional groups—doctors, social workers and teachers—suggest that professionals resist administrative control. All groups display 'similar patterns of latent and actual conflict between the occupational group and organisational requirements which cannot be simply explained away in terms of the recalcitrance of awkward individuals' (Hughes *et al.*, 1985, p. 271). This arises from two interlocking themes: the professionals' claim to autonomy within the organization, and the problems arising from an external orientation towards their professional group.

Educational psychologists are employed by LEAs with the clear expectation that they can give valid professional recommendation on children's needs. Each educational psychologist is expected to be able to make judgements on his or her own, and this autonomy is part of the argument not only for the long training, but also for the high salary grading within an LEA structure. The ability to make independent judgments is considered crucial. It can be contrasted with other local authority departments. Social workers, for example, have much clearer supervision and lines of accountability which stretch up through social work departments. The expectation that independent professional judgments will be made can be seen to be at odds with any highly structured, management-orientated system. This may be exacerbated by the previously argued point that educational psychologists may often not be promoted for their practitioner skills, thereby increasing tension in a line management structure. Many educational psychologists are therefore reluctant to accept the legitimacy of a hierarchy of authority.

Underneath this is the fundamental desire that most people have to retain some control over their lives. This is a very strong motivator for many professionals. Any increase in bureaucratization will threaten professional autonomy and will therefore be resisted by educational psychologists. The key issue is to recognize that autonomy and accountability are not opposites, but the different sides of the same professional coin.

The paradox here is that the strength of the educational psychologist as far as the LEA is concerned is to be perceived by the general public, schools and parents as being an independent professional. Through the perception of independence, the educational psychologist is able to act genuinely in the LEA's interest. The LEA could gain greater control over educational psychologists by imposing standardized procedures, but by doing so it would also throw away the benefit of educational psychologists being seen as independent by the public. Is professional variability too great a price to pay for perceived independence? Different LEAs and educational psychologists have different views on the answer.

There is another problem for professionals—the need to look outwards rather than inwards. An educational psychologist gains credit and self-esteem from being in contact with developments in the profession. Professional skills are measured not against other skills in the LEA but against educational psychologists' skills from other services. The educational psychologist needs to keep up to date with the professional developments in the field. LEA officers concerned with the tasks of organizational maintenance may question the loyalty of educational psychologists who seem to have as a reference group their professional association rather than the LEA. This perceived disloyalty to the LEA, because of the educational psychologist's strong sense of commitment to the profession, can cause a paradox. The educational psychologist cannot develop professionally without making reference to educational psychologists outside the LEA but, by definition, this can appear destructive to the officers in the LEA as it militates against the LEA's socialization process.

So it seems that to function effectively educational psychologists need to be seen to work independently but in order to be given independence they must be clearly accountable and unambiguous in their practice. Educational psychologists can only maintain their independence if they are able to demonstrate that their procedures are unambiguous, fair and purposeful, when they are rigorously scrutinized.

THE MANAGEMENT PARADOX: THE ULTIMATE
ACCOMMODATION TECHNIQUE

One of the key questions that will be answered in the 1990s is that of who will manage EPSs. Will it be a principal educational psychologist or will it be another officer within the LEA? The issue is about whether managers of educational psychology services are chief executives or leading professionals, and whether these two roles can be combined. Hughes (1976) identified for headteachers a number of characteristics of these dual roles, which can also be applied to principal educational psychologists.

Within the 'leading professional' role, principals are expected to have strong affinities with the general body of educational psychologists; that is, they are required to look out-wards. They are expected by staff to take an innovatory stand on the actual practice of educational psychology—to introduce new ideas and techniques. They are also expected to provide expertise and advice for educational psychologists who want professional guidance on difficult problems. Within the 'chief executive' role, principals are expected to organize the delivery of services and to delegate tasks and responsibilities effectively to service members.

It is no accident that in the last few years some LEAs have begun to uncouple these two functions. As some of the larger county authorities begin to break their centrally based structure into area teams, principal educational psychologists' responsibilities are changing from those demanded by the dual executive/leading professional role to simply those of the leading professional. It will be interesting to note how effective (in the light of the subsequent developments) such management is. Certainly there is sup-port in education for the splitting of functions. Handy (1984) has argued that in schools there should be two leaders, senior professionals and administrators: 'To combine the two roles in one person is an invitation to stress' (p. 23).

Three separate management functions can be distinguished in educational psychology services: task achievement, team maintenance and development, and external represen-tation of the service. By examining these functions for management within the EPS as a professional organization, we can uncover some of the paradoxes that presently occur, and are thus better able to judge whether these may disappear in the future.

Task achievement

Educational psychologists, following the lead of most LEAs, tend to believe in a ratio-nal model of planning, where a 'vision' for the service is turned into broad aims which are then formulated into objectives. In the last few years this has been further refined into performance indicators and critical success factors. This is the rhetoric. The para-dox is that the reality is often very far removed, not only for educational psychologists but also for most LEAs when they talk about rational planning. Given the present culture within Britain it is, though, anathema to suggest that rational planning is not valid. High credibility is given to services that have clear aims and objectives.

The reality is, however, that service objectives are often kept inconsistent and unclear—thus allowing all aims to be non-operational in so far as they neither require nor exclude any particular behaviour. In this way the different demands from different groups in the LEA can all be satisfied. The danger in times of turbulence and change is that pressure mounts to clarify the operational parameters of EPSs. This includes clarity over services that are being delivered, time-contracting procedures, referral systems and interlinks with other agencies. The problem with this is that the EPS can become locked into a mode of responding that was useful at a certain time and from a certain perception. As times, and perceptions (new educational psychologists, new LEA officers) change, the former clear objectives become increasingly off key in the context of a need for flexibility and rapid change. The question is how far both the EPS and the LEA will accept the ambiguity that allows service delivery to reflect the complexity and shifting nature of the educational world: 'Professionals themselves argue that it is impossible to meet the heightened societal expectations for their performance in an environment that combines increasing turbulence with increasing regulation of professional activity' (Schon, 1987, p. 7).

Educational psychologists need to plan, but they would do well to question the view which suggests that rational planning models are the most effective. As with most things in life, there are alternatives. The educational psychologists who understand the ambiguity and political aspects of planning may have models which help ensure that tasks are actually achieved.

Another aspect of task achievement for managers is ensuring that educational psychologists are skilled enough to undertake the tasks that the service has planned to deliver. This is a very loose notion that causes all sorts of difficulties, but it is clearly ingrained and needs to be examined. What paradoxes face the manager trying to monitor the effectiveness of a service through such management tools as performance indicators or critical success factors?

First there is the point, which this chapter has emphasized, that there are different models of psychology—effective practice within one model will be considered mumbo-jumbo in another. This can be clearly seen in such a common problem as non-school-attendance. An educational psychologist working within a behavioural framework who decides on 'flooding' the pupil as a method of resolving the problem will be completely incompatible with an educational psychologist who sees the problem from a family therapy framework, and believes that the pupil should not be forced to school. How does the manager monitor the effectiveness of the service? Not by such a simple performance indicator as return to school—the family therapist (and the family) might not even see this as a goal of the intervention.

These conflicts do not only arise in the field of behaviour and emotional difficulties. They are equally prevalent in the learning field, where debates continue to rage—real reading v. direct instruction is just one example. Critical success factors depend intimately on the political issues, such as who is the client. This can be clearly seen in the Health Service, where critical success factors such as reducing the waiting list and keeping within set budgets are in diametric opposition to each other.

The concept of performance indicators and critical success factors may work well in industry where the product is readily identifiable. In a person-to-person service they seem less meaningful unless one denies the individuality of each person's perception.

This is in no way, however, an attempt to deny the responsibility of educational psychologists or their need to be accountable. It is, though, an attempt to face up to some of the paradoxes managers encounter when monitoring task achievement—whether they are psychologists or not.

Team maintenance and development

The argument for appointing educational psychologists as managers is often advanced on the grounds that they will have the confidence of educational psychologists and therefore be better able to influence them as a team of professionals. One of the difficulties of viewing the EPS as a team is that there is a continuum of concepts about what a team is. At the tight end there is the concept of a football team—a number of players all on the pitch together, with complementary skills, working to each other's strengths, all trying to kick a ball into the same net. At the loose end of the continuum of teams is the golf 'team': golfers may play the same course but not necessarily together, and often they do not even consult and communicate—apart from a few distorted reminiscences in the clubhouse afterwards.

Educational psychologists have very different perceptions on how the EPS should operate as a team. The task then becomes not simply to develop a team, but first to analyse genuinely if an EPS team is necessary. Clearly it is necessary for the principal to develop a team if part of his or her *raison d'être* is to lead a team. The inability to create one in this circumstance will be seen as a sign of failure. But this, in itself, is no justification for considering it essential that educational psychologists need to act as a team.

Teams can be seen to serve two functions: a task function and a psychological support function. To have a task function there must be areas of work which the team tackles together. This could be project work, action research, organizational change or individual pupil work. The present model for service delivery, where individual educational psychologists work their own school area, militates directly against any sort of team work developing.

Do educational psychologists have psychological needs for a team? The complexity and ambiguity of the job would seem to create the need for human contact. Without the opportunity to test their view of reality, educational psychologists are likely to find themselves in increasingly paradoxical situations—unable to understand what other educational psychologists are doing and unwilling to discuss their differences.

Managers need to have a clearer conception of the function of the educational psychology team which they wish to develop before they consider how the service could be organized to ensure that it does develop.

External representation

The 1990s is going to be a period of rapid change. No longer can people think of themselves within fixed positions in a hierarchy. Power groups are forming, both in the larger political world and within smaller pressure groups within the LEA. Clearly one of the important roles for any manager is as representative or ambassador. The manager is asked to represent the service to pressure groups like the local dyslexic association and headteachers' committees, and it is here that the role of leading professional becomes crucially important. The manager becomes the personification of the service—becomes the reality by which the service is judged. The manager has a duty to make visible the concept of the educational psychologists and to network with influential people in the environment. He or she will in future need to spend considerable time working on the external environment to make the EPS visible in this rapidly changing world.

As we have seen, professionals have always prided themselves on the ability to self-monitor and self-regulate their work—their autonomy is defined by this. The more management there is the less professional the service is. So managers have a paradox. If they are to be successful managers within a bureaucratic perception, they are likely to need to reduce autonomy, increase uniformity and set performance indicators for service delivery. Paradoxically the more they take on this role, the more they diminish the status of their EPS and therefore themselves.

Even if they manage to resist the culture that calls for 'scientific' management, they may face a second paradox. The less management they are seen to do, the less justification there is for their post. The good manager within a professional organization facilitates, creates opportunities and helps the EPS develop its own vision of the future. The better the manager does this, the more likely the LEA and even the EPS are to discount her or his contribution. It is a dilemma many other people face. If you have a healthy society, do you really need doctors? If you do not have wars, do you really need so many diplomats? The more efficiently the job is done, the more likely the manager will be to be seen as redundant, even if not actually out of a job.

Having psychologists managing services can, however, be viewed in another perspective. It can be seen as the ultimate accommodating technique in so far as it legitimizes hierarchy, legitimizes having a single reference point for outside representation, and helps ensure that the needs of the LEA are translated into terms acceptable to the professional sensibilities of the educational psychologists. The LEA, by having an educational psychologist managing the service, effectively neutralizes the powerful challenging influence the service may have on the LEA. Challenging here is seen as a positive influence—the ability of individuals within the LEA to question the basis for operations—and therefore survive.

This ability to survive by challenging existing practices has been described as two separate ways of developing (Argyris *et al.*, 1985). A distinction can be made between single-loop and double-loop learning. Single-loop learning is when a problem is solved or fixed; it has been described as adjusting the thermostat to a standard that has already been set. In the educational psychology world it would mean the manager ensuring that the 1981 Education Act assessments are completed in a set time. Double-loop learning, on the other hand, means examining the more fundamental questions of why the thermostat has been standardized in this way. In educational psychology terms, it is the manager questioning the need for speed when completing the 1981 Act assessments. Double-loop learning is about questioning the values and assumptions that drive our behaviour.

Argyris argues that for organizational development and long-term survival to occur in a changing environment, single-loop learning is inappropriate—there must be double-loop learning. He suggests that the conditions necessary for this are:

(a) valid information;
(b) free and informed choice;
(c) internal commitment to the choice;
(d) constant monitoring of implementation.

The question is, therefore, whether psychologists as service managers are the best people to ensure that double-loop learning will occur. What sort of manager will ensure that the necessary questioning, challenging stance will actually be taken in EPSs in the 1990s?

The ultimate paradox may be to enjoin psychologists to let go of striving to run psychological services and instead to move into LEA positions which allow them to use their psychological skills to ensure that double-loop learning occurs. In the end, the whole question is not about the survival and function of EPSs in isolation—it is about the survival and function of LEAs if EPSs as a free public service are to continue.

CONCLUSIONS

This chapter has taken as its starting point the premise that EPS organization and management are problematic. There are therefore paradoxes contained within the ways that EPSs are organized and managed to deliver services. These paradoxes are defined as those issues where every attempt to communicate to be constructive is also counterproductive. It is counterproductive unless educational psychologists share the view that people have different views, and that underlying those different views are theories or constructs that are held about the way the world operates.

These constructs not only shape the way educational psychologists see the world: they are also the basis for theories of action (Argyris, 1989). Theories of action are like key programmes that are carried around in people's heads, which they use to try to bring about intended changes in others. Argyris calls the theories in action that people actually use their 'theories in use'. He distinguishes these from their 'espoused theories'—what people say they use.

Understanding this distinction between espoused theories and theories in use is critical. Espoused theories can be defined as what people say guides their behaviour. Theories in use are what actually guide it. People's theories in use can be inferred from their action. Educational psychologists who say that equal opportunities is a key concern of theirs (espoused theory) but who have case loads that are 90 per cent boys and 10 per cent girls can be inferred to have a theory in use that ignores equal opportunity issues.

In summary, there are inherent paradoxes with the organization and management of EPSs. Educational psychologists construct EPSs that may have different meanings to different educational psychologists, and certainly have different meanings to people in the larger world. In addition, there is also a discrepancy between educational psychologists' espoused theories and theories in use when it comes to explaining their view of services.

The way to break the paradoxes is through what Argyris *et al.* (1985) call action science. Essentially this requires educational psychologists to reflect upon the inconsistencies in their behaviour and especially between their espoused theories (what they say they do) and their theories in use (what they really do). By recognizing the gaps between espoused theory and theory in use, educational psychologists will begin to become more aware of different perspectives on their practice.

Educational psychologists need to inquire into others' views—those of teachers, parents and LEA officers, as well as of their educational psychologist colleagues—and to bring into the open previously undiscussable inferences about how others see EPSs. Only by doing this can educational psychologists break some of the organizational and management paradoxes that they presently face.

In the same way educational psychologists need to challenge others in the LEA to make theories in use match up to espoused theories. By recognizing people's strategies to try to gain unilateral control over others, educational psychologists can help create the conditions necessary for double-loop learning to occur.

The difficult part is that this means breaking out of the vicious circle which is characterized by a desire to control the situation. It may mean letting go of some preciously held beliefs about the organization and management of EPSs, thus allowing educational psychologists to learn and develop in the 1990s.

REFERENCES

Argyris, C. (1983) *Making Social Science Research More Usable: Maps to Action*. Presentation to Center for Effective Organizations, University of Southern California.

Argyris, C. (1989) *Reasoning, Learning and Action—Individual and Organizational*. San Francisco: Jossey-Bass.

Argyris, C., Putnam, R. and Smith, D. (1985) *Action Science*. San Francisco: Jossey-Bass.

Born, R. and Sawyer, C. (1979) 'Time contracting: a method for controlling referral from schools', *Association of Educational Psychologists Journal*, 5 (1), 17–20.

Boyan, C. (1985) 'California's new eligibility criteria: legal and program implications', *Exceptional Children*, 5 (2), 131–41.

DES (Department of Education and Science) (1968) *The Summerfield Report*. London: HMSO.

DES (Department of Education and Science) (1988) *Education Reform Act*. London: HMSO.

DES (Department of Education and Science) (HMI) (1990) *Education Observed—Special Needs*. London: HMSO.

Farr, R. (1987) 'Misunderstandings in human relations: a social psychologist perspective', *Education Management and Administration*, 15, 129–39.

Ford, J., Mongon, D. and Whelan, M. (1982) *Special Education and Social Control: Invisible Disasters*. London: Routledge and Kegan Paul.

Frederickson, N. (1988) 'Continuing professional education: towards a framework for development', in Jones, N. and Sayer, J. (eds) *Management and the Psychology of Schooling*. Lewes: The Falmer Press.

Goode, W. J. (1960) 'Encroachment, charlatanism and the emerging professions: psychology, sociology and medicine', *American Sociological Review*, 25, 194–209.

Handy, C. (1984) *Taken for Granted? Understanding Schools as Organisations*. London: Longman.

Hughes, M. G. (1976) 'The professional-as-administrator: the case of the secondary school head', in Peters, R. S. (ed.) *The Role of the Head*. London: Routledge & Kegan Paul.

Hughes, M. G., Ribbins, P. and Thomas, H. (1985) *Managing Education: The System and the Institution*. London: Cassell.

Johnson, T. J. (1972) *Professions and Power*. London: Macmillan.

Knapman, N., Huxtable, M. and Tempest, A. (1987) 'Redecorating educational psychology?: an alternative approach to service delivery', *Educational Psychology in Practice*, 3 (3), 29–33.

Schein, E. (1978) *Career Dynamics: Matching Individual and Organizational Needs*. London: Addison-Wesley.

Schon, D. (1987) *Educating the Reflective Practitioner*. London: Jossey-Bass.

Tharp, R. and Wetzel, R. (1969) *Behaviour Modification in the Natural Environment*. New York: Academic Press.

Section III

Focus on Community

Chapter 9

Educational Psychologists Working in a Biased Society

Trevor Bryans

INTRODUCTION

Social science has an implicit responsibility to explain and make sense of the world even though the pathways to explanation are both discontinuous and elusive. It is also problematic for social science practitioners because frequently they must engage in what Hall (1980) called 'deconstructing the obvious'. The obvious in the context of this chapter includes most aspects of belief in relation to race, gender, disability or the rights of all individuals to have access to equality of opportunity in health, wealth or education.

Each of these areas requires a massive and detailed analysis. In this chapter the intention is to focus primarily on issues of bias or disadvantage which directly impinge on the work of educational psychologists, but with a primary focus on race and cultural issues. This is because race and culture in relation to educational issues are of over-riding importance to educational psychologists in multicultural Britain. Of course, class issues are perennial in their juxtaposition with education and these too will be addressed, if implicitly, throughout this chapter.

Many educational psychologists choose to limit their field of operations to what they believe are 'manageable' dimensions of the presenting problems, so that when confronted, for example, by a partially hearing Asian child of six, living in bed-and-breakfast accommodation with a young mother, the educational psychologist and the teacher may only focus on helping the child learn to read or enjoy books in school. Yet this particular example contains almost every dimension of disadvantage associated with bias in our society—race, sexual inequality, disability, poverty, culture clashes within the family and a loss of control over life choices.

Within most human societies there are identifiable issues of bias, inequality or direct discrimination by some groups or individuals against others. In most cases the bias is ultimately rooted in the political and societal infrastructure, in such a way that peripheral tinkering with presenting symptoms of discrimination may only serve at best to change a few surface features or, at worst, invert the problems so that the bias simply shifts to operate against some other minority group.

Moral awareness does not appear to be endemic to most political systems (Rawls, 1972). Rather, shared human concerns, empathy and active citizenship require generations of political and social lobbying before there is an awareness of the problem which in time results in agreed action. Thus individuals or groups claiming the right to be viewed by the majority as 'special' in some way or another must ultimately be able to prove their case politically.

In the West over the past thirty years or so there has been massive public support for increasingly open debate about minority rights issues. Black or gay rights, feminist perspectives, the rights of the disabled or individuals with severe learning difficulties have all been given prominence. Both in the United States and in Britain there is legislation to ensure equality of opportunity for all regardless of race, creed, religion or sexual orientation. Indeed, there is now a considerable and thriving industry in equal opportunities across the industrialized West, with many professionals employed in organizations to ensure that there is equal access for all citizens to services and/or material wellbeing.

Most Western democracies now accept that 'minority rights' issues are important enough to be given recognition in nearly all aspects of social policy or planning; for example, in education or housing. But in a way, the philosophical underpinning for such equal opportunities practice may have been left some way behind.

Equality and quality in public services such as education present any analyst with a multilayered problem. In the first instance, as Cooper (1975) has pointed out, equality in education is spurious and can only relate to relativities of performance. Thus, if school A is seen as better than school B, equality of opportunity for the pupils who attend each school can only be achieved by raising standards at school B or by lowering standards at school A, so that parity and equality is offered to all pupils in both schools. Secondly, quality (or excellence) and principles of equality for all do appear to be relative concepts (Mackinnon, 1987). Each is desirable, but each is relative and dependent on polar opposites in order to be self-defining, as well as contingent on many other factors in differing situations. It is precisely because neither excellence nor equality is an absolute that logical explanation may only increase the logical tension between them. In concrete terms, should the outcome of equal opportunities policies in education mean that all pupils go to university? Does it mean that all pupils of all ethnic backgrounds, boys as well as girls, should achieve the same standards across every area of the curriculum? How much diversity of performance can be accepted before lack of opportunity is used as the explanation for the observed diversity?

The Education Reform Act 1988 was proposed partly to give power of choice to the consumers of education—parents and children. It was also enacted to reduce the powers of local education authorities (LEAs) by increasing centrally the powers of the Secretary of State for Education and those of governors of schools and headteachers. On the surface the Act does not offend the Western view that educational policy should enhance equality of opportunity (Rawls, 1972). But not only is there an intrinsic difficulty with the concept of equality, outlined above, but the tremendous structural inequalities within society have immense impact on the outcomes of the educational system. For most parents the notion of education as a facilitator of upward mobility for their children simply does not occur (Halsey *et al.*, 1980). Instead, the vast majority of children are restrained within the system, while the children of the middle classes generally find their status confirmed by their educational experiences (Robinson, 1989). The framing of the

Education Reform Act (ERA) tends to reinforce the view that it pays surface attention to equality of opportunity by using a market-force model to improve schools and therefore improve the quality of education—but probably only for those who are most likely to succeed in it anyway.

Earlier reference was made to the fact that, in this chapter, there would be less emphasis on bias issues in sex equality, as far as these affect the work of educational psychologists. That is not to appear indifferent to the need for analysis of assumptions made about male/female roles in society. Some of the conceptual dilemmas in defining equality in this domain are apparent, although the dominant view is that equal means the same (Bryne, 1985) and that, for example, in education, the curriculum for boys and girls should be identical. However, simply making these provisions again feeds into the 'surface' equality noted earlier. The outcome is different in educational terms in that sex differentiation affects option choices made by girls and boys, as well as examination successes or failures (Weiner, 1985).

Within special education, biases are apparent, but they tend to be inversions of what might normally be thought of as discrimination. Boys are massively over-represented in most forms of special education (Fish, 1985). Some of the unofficial categories of special education, namely pupils with emotional or behavioural difficulties, exhibit this bias very clearly indeed and are discussed later in the chapter.

Focusing attention on the actual or potential bias operating in society fuels debate around the perennial question of many support services, including educational psychology services: who is the client? Before exploring some of the relevant themes of bias in the work of educational psychologists, it is proposed to examine briefly some of the issues to do with conceptualizing the notion of 'client' or, to use contemporary 'free-market' terminology, the 'customer'. Many of the historically significant shifts of awareness in public provision for racial equality or for groups seen as disadvantaged have usually been preceded by a change of attitude about the status of the client.

Educational psychologists may initially adhere to the view that ultimately their client is the child. But it soon becomes clear that adherence to this notion is strategically naive and politically self-defeating. The child does not pay for educational psychologists' service. The child's parents may pay through their local tax for some local services, but the institutions and systems paid for through such taxation have a professional logic of their own. Furthermore, such services are not usually amenable to rapid or idiosyncratic changes or demands. Service delivery is also subject to legislation, which reinforces the view that many services are delivered to client groups irrespective of whether or not the client either wants or needs them—by people who are acting on behalf of a primary client because they are paid to do so.

Many professionals, including educational psychologists, are involved with clients who have relatively little power in the system. From the 1960s onwards, there has been an increase in the numbers of professionals recruited to help people. Many of these professionals view themselves as acting on behalf of the client. In reality they are also creating a more complex network of service delivery systems which must be negotiated by all other professionals before the client can be helped. Thus, in a real sense, there is no such single entity as a 'client', in this case a child. The child's teacher, parent, social worker, learning support worker and welfare assistant may also be the educational psychologist's client, as well as each other's, in many individual situations. Each professional may have assumed responsibility for the child and each of the professionals may need advice from another on aspects of care, teaching or management of the child. The client notion is, of course, complicated by the fact that there is also a power and professional status hierarchy between and among the professionals, each of whom will have expectations about the kinds of service to be delivered to the child by each of the other professionals, and also about the particular outcome of an individual case. These outcomes and the professional decision making leading to them can in some cases almost exclude the primary client, further reinforcing the existing bias in the system.

It may also be that at the very centre of the debate the truth is that the client may not be the same as the customer, for it is the customer who pays and decides in some cases which services the client receives. This distinction exposes one of the flaws of the market-forces model being applied to all areas of public service and particularly to education, for the notion of parents as customers is clearly at odds with the professional conception of 'a client', who likewise receives services but may not pay for them.

RACE AND EDUCATION

It is now over twenty-five years since public consciousness about race and equality issues became enshrined in government policy (HMSO, 1965). Over that time there have been phases in race relations from assimilation through integration to notions of cultural pluralism (Mullard, 1985).

Specifically, within education there has been a continuing debate about the causes of the observable under-achievement of some groups of black children, particularly Afro-Caribbean pupils. There are two opposing explanatory viewpoints. For some, including some psychologists (Jensen, 1969), the explanation, whether acceptable or not, is straightforward. They believe that some racial groups are simply not as intelligent as others. Other observers (Wright, 1987) locate the blame firmly in racist institutions such as schools or in white racist teachers.

Whichever of these two points of view is held, until the mid-1980s 'the fallacy of the single factor' (Parekh, 1983)—that is, racism or lack of intelligence—appeared to achieve and maintain explanatory status. Thus on the one hand, if a child or adult were black then they were likely to be less intelligent than a white person. Alternatively, the greater the degree of racism experienced by particular groups the less likely they were to achieve in white-run schools, businesses or higher educational establishments. The more strident advocates of the racism-based thesis often achieved success in bringing racism to the top of (usually) a local agenda. Often this involved confronting white groups with their own racism in awareness training courses and, in some spectacular cases well reported in the press, individuals (usually professionals) were identified as having made racist remarks and were brought to book.

But Parekh has noted that the single factor theory of either simple racism experienced by black people, or their lack of intelligence, very quickly breaks down as an explanation for under-achievement in the light of the evidence (Mortimore *et al.*, 1988). Looking at the racism causation thesis specifically, it is extremely difficult to assess what is actually going on in any situation in terms of racist content or racism experienced, whether at the individual, institutional or structural level. Ethnicity is itself a far from absolutely precise concept. Furthermore, gender, age, geographical location, social class and family circumstances, family motivation and composition all interact with each other and with a whole series of school variables in a complex and dynamic way, putting possible outcomes far outside the domain of a single, simple explanation.

More importantly, acknowledgment of race issues has opened up a more substantial and perhaps more constructive debate about culture and what Syed (1989) calls 'dislocations and discontinuities in the negotiation of black children's identity'. Opening up the debate on issues of culture may be the only way to elucidate and clarify some of the presenting phenomena. It is clear that many black children's experiences of white society are not coterminous with their own family culture, and there is no database to clarify exactly what many black or Asian children actually feel about their parents, their family philosophy and religion, counterpointed with Western white materialism. What we do know (Gibson and Barrow, 1986) is that black children have to make many choices between and among the material trappings of Western society and the values, which are often discontinuous, evident in their own families. While designer track suits and trainers seem impervious to the ethnicity of their teenage wearers, it is just possible that many youngsters are at odds with many aspects of the hidden curriculum of Western society. It may also be that in many cases something has to give in the child's developing self at the point where home culture and religion are clearly at odds with general, secular, social behaviour and norms. Personal individual choices implied by Western societal notions of equal opportunities, such as those at school, may have no place and make no real sense in the family value system, where an entirely different order of priorities is maintained. Such individual expression in some cultures implies taking on board secular or irreligious values, tantamount at the extreme to blasphemy and disloyalty to the group (Troyna, 1979). Gibson and Barrow (1986) have likewise detailed aspects of West Indian or Caribbean home culture which may play a part in producing discontinuity between home and school, particularly in child-rearing inconsistency, punishment and externalization rather than internalization of control.

Whatever these factors may be within individual home cultures, all the available evidence points to the differential pattern of educational achievement by different cultural groups in British schools (Mortimore, 1988; Swann Report (HMSO, 1988)) and the pattern of achievement or under-achievement is not solely distinguishable along black/white lines. Some British-Asian groups are much more successful at school than any of the white groups, while Afro-Caribbean pupils as a group continue to under-achieve at every level after entry to school through to public examinations (Troyna and Carrington, 1990). Here again, neither the simplistic effects of racism nor lack of intelligence even begin to explain the presenting phenomena.

RACE AND THE PRACTICE OF EDUCATIONAL PSYCHOLOGY

How appropriate is the psychology delivered to children in multi-ethnic areas of Britain? As has been stated elsewhere (Bryans, 1988) the question is probably meaningless to a large number of educational psychologists nationally, whose contact with black or Asian children is minimal. But in inner city areas where between 70 per cent and 90 per cent of an entire LEA or individual school's intake may be non-white and perhaps non-English-speaking, addressing that question is crucial. If educational psychologists do not do so, there is a risk that they may continue in some places to be viewed with suspicion by black parents and 'compared to the police as agents of black oppression' (Booker *et al.*, 1989).

The making of the idea that 'black equals problem' has been documented elsewhere (Bryans, 1988), and educational psychologists must share some of the responsibility for that situation, in which disproportionate numbers of black pupils were placed in various forms of special education (Fish, 1985). The issue on this particular question of educational psychologists acting as the 'gate-keepers' to special education has been addressed in the past by educational psychologists themselves. Perhaps it is worth stating yet again that the entitlement curriculum for all pupils is, on one level at least, fundamentally an equal opportunities issue.

Having acknowledged, however, that many educational psychologists do not necessarily have much professional contact with black children and their families, an initially attractive notion might be for all of them to have some sort of racism awareness training (RAT), to open up the debate at least. Unfortunately, this area of RAT is fraught with problems. Many awareness courses have tended to focus on issues of individual or personal racism, in aiming to identify aspects of one's own behaviour or attitude as a white person which could be construed as racist. But many attenders at such courses are liberal, white, middle-class professionals, and it is frequently difficult to envisage precisely what is achieved by attendance at such workshops. A significant number of the attenders are also at different stages of self-awareness or self-appraisal of their attitudes to race. For them a blanket starting assumption that each attender is racist by virtue of attendance at the course amounts to what Jeffcoate (1985) calls 'anti-racism as illiberalism'. Indeed there is a body of evidence (Jeffcoate, 1985) to suggest that race awareness training may be counterproductive. The main reason for this is that RAT may not deal at all with the more complex, subtle and specific aspects of individual professional practice, including those of an educational psychologist, that contribute to institutional racism, which is in itself more damaging to the life chances of black children.

It is at this precise level of understanding and practice about race and culture that educational psychologists, like many other professionals, may be in danger of misunderstanding exactly what is at issue. Individual and institutional racism can be confused and compounded by RAT because not being a racist at the individual level has little to do with the effects of institutional, structural or indeed professional racism. Hence the commonplace experience of many educational psychologists, individually white, liberal and non-racist, as documented by Booker *et al.* (1989), is of guilty, defensive bewilderment in the face of black outrage at what educational psychologists actually do in their daily practice. The individual, liberal, non-racist educational psychologist may in practice have used a variety of inappropriate strategies feeding into the institutionalized racism and the inappropriate professional handling of the child. This could include such factors as inadequately detailed casework, inadequate knowledge about the home culture or inappropriate assessment, which may result in a premature termination of proper intervention with a black child and could result in the pupil being placed in some form of specialized, off-site or unit provision, restricting access to normal schooling. It is possible that a focus on personal racism may have distracted professionals from looking in depth at practice issues which contribute to institutional racism.

But what are the issues for educational psychologists, given that there is great uncertainty about what is actually occurring in society generally in terms of race and cultural pluralism? Cline and Lunt (1990) have drawn attention to a number of areas of concern for educational psychologists, including:

(a)   educational developments in multicultural society;
(b)   second language learning;
(c)   bilingualism;
(d)   social/cultural/ethical aspects of assessments;
(e)   total factors in therapeutic intervention;
(f)   multicultural and anti-racist education;
(g)   equal opportunities issues;
(h)   working in multicultural communities.

Over the years there has been a steady stream of writers cautioning educational psychologists to exercise greater care before making transcultural assumptions based on white, Eurocentric psychology (Coard, 1971; Cummins, 1984).

EDUCATION IN A MULTICULTURAL SOCIETY

Banks (1988) outlines three main ways in which multicultural education as a process can occur. Curriculum content is the first way in which cultural or gender factors may be incorporated into curriculum. Secondly, achievement approaches may also be observed, in which strategies are employed to improve the achievement of lower-class or black students. The last way is by intergroup education approaches in which all students are facilitated to develop more positive attitudes towards people from different cultures and backgrounds. Most multicultural education in both Britain and the United States is subsumed by these approaches.

As noted earlier, there are many difficulties with any holistic curriculum content initiative. In inner-city Britain many cultures and languages are represented in a single school or institution, and any attempt at acknowledging the cultural diversity could simply turn out to be a superficial romp through different ethnic cultures, resulting in a reinforcement of stereotypes. During Diwali celebrations in one London primary school recently, a Caribbean boy approached his teacher and said 'Miss, I shouldn't be here, I'm a Christian!' In that particular primary school there are around eighty spoken languages and dialects, as well as almost seventy recently arrived Somali and Eritrean children. In such a context, achieving a transformational approach, in which different cultural perceptives on history, music, dance or the arts are incorporated to enable diversity of viewpointing, does seem a very difficult task indeed.

ISSUES IN ASSESSMENT

Consideration of the question of assessment is fraught with intrinsic difficulties in any situation where equality of opportunity is also mentioned (Gipps, 1990), largely because at least one of the functions of any form of assessment is to rank order individual performance. Furthermore, assessment is one of the underpinning tenets of value attribution in almost every area of human endeavour and is a feature of almost every human society. As noted earlier, the contention is that excellence and equality may remain as ideals towards which all may aspire, but the achievement of both simultaneously may well prove to be almost impossible.

There is therefore a central paradox in balancing societal requirements, and perhaps even the necessity of assessment of all pupils at some key stages in their educational lives, with the fact that all educational experiences and the assessments contingent upon it are culture bound (Joyce, 1988). In the past, the role of the educational psychologists as assessors of special educational provision (Booth and Statham, 1982) did give rise to problems, in that psychologists appeared at times to be friendly police guarding the special school gates and escorting pupils away from the mainstream school into special educational provision.

The debate about the relevance of standardized tests to non-white pupils has been under way for a long time and is aptly summed up by Cummins (1984). Most educational psychologists are now wary about using these tests with black children because they are likely to show that pupils from other cultures have low cognitive or academic achievement or potential. Most psychologists, too, would regard IQ tests in particular as a maintaining factor in the Anglocentric educational status quo (Cummins, 1984). Yet when faced with a child in an assessment situation they will probably resort to some form of standardized assessment of the child, perhaps ignoring the complexity of skills and knowledge acquisition of the child's home culture.

Joyce (1988) has summarized some of the main issues to be acknowledged in considering any form of assessment by an LEA educational psychology service with black children. These are:

(a)   All assessment is culture based.
(b)   Tests are culture bound by virtue of content, standardization, population and situations in which they are administered.
(c)   Norm-referenced tests are biased in favour of the majority group.
(d)   Knowledge of the cultural background of the child combined with observation of the child is essential before assessing the pupil's needs.
(e)   Criterion-referenced tests should be specific to the child's own progress—not against or compared to other pupils.

What are the alternatives, given that both in the United States and in Britain much legislation (PL 94–142 and the 1981 Education Act) posits a core concept of learning difficulty? In both cases this is located in or around the child in question and only by assessment can the child's difficulty be identified and dealt with.

In the first instance, educational psychologists must accept a number of basic principles. Firstly, psychometric standardized assessment with most non-indigenous, non-white groups is irrelevant and misleading and should be discontinued. Further use of such tests simply confirms that educational psychologists are maintaining the psychometric world view alluded to by Cummins; that is, that 'intelligence' as measured by an intelligence test underpins every aspect of human achievement. But there might need to be a more radical reappraisal of the testing/assessing function of the educational psychologist. If many tests are thought to be inappropriate for black children, another question readily emerges: that of the appropriateness of these assessment instruments with any children at all.

Over the years there has been a continuing search for a culture-fair test (Gupta, 1984), usually focusing on a global notion of a child's ability to learn. However, most of these tests do not seem to produce results which are in any sense meaningful, since they are often assessing skill areas which have little to do with real-life situations (Desforges *et al.*, 1985).

Secondly, the making of 'black equals problem' paradoxically occurred at precisely the same time in English education as liberal, progressive notions were being adopted by schools. Hence the relative educational failure of some groups may not be conceptualized in crude psychometric terms, but rather in the views that any form of diversity away from the dominant expectations of the white middle class is unacceptable. This could include bilingualism, non-standard English use or non-standard cultural affiliations. Appending learning difficulties or deficit special educational concepts to black children is therefore doubly disadvantaging and divisive, since these concepts, no matter how subtle in their application, reinforce abnormality. Educational psychologists must therefore abandon learning difficulties deficit views of all pupils, particularly if they are not white.

Thirdly, assessment which is not based on the context and content of real-life learning cannot be sustained. Many educational psychologists have of course moved towards criterion-referenced or 'hand-made' checklists or 'test-teach-test' materials in specific areas of language, number or reading, and this is to be welcomed. Continuous skill assessments in individualized settings are generally emerging as one of the most equitable means of assessing a pupil's progress. But such criterion-referenced assessments are not without difficulties as well—mainly in the areas of the prejudices of the tester and the appropriateness of the teaching style.

One example of such emerging practice is the document (University College, 1989) on the assessment of bilingual pupils. In this are many suggestions for assessing systematically the needs of bilingual pupils. The key issue with pupils who are from a non-English-speaking home background is that of determining whether the child has 'special educational needs' within the framework of the 1981 Education Act, or whether the child's needs are cultural and linguistic, requiring different educational provisions to be made under Section 11 funding.

Using an approach such as Domico and Oller's pragmatic approach to language proficiency with bilingual pupils is clearly a vast improvement over the outdated practice of using some verbal sub-tests of the WISC-R. However, it must be noted again that assessment with all pupils is complicated enough. With black or Asian pupils the range of variables operating multiplies considerably, to the point where it is no longer clear precisely what is being assessed. At the time of writing it is too early to record what the implications of the ERA will be in terms of equality of opportunity. The implementation of the National Curriculum and associated standard tests of attainment will inevitably encounter the kinds of difficulty outlined above, in that not all students can initially have equal access to or opportunity in that curriculum, by virtue of their cultural background, language and affiliations (Tomlinson, 1989). How can SATs testing be fair to a large group of Asian students and pupils, in particular when we know that non-English-speaking pupils usually acquire surface language skills within about two years, but literacy and written language skills may take at least another five years to develop adequately (Cummins, 1984)? Assessments across a range of curriculum areas at 7, 11, 14 and 16 years of age will almost certainly delineate the lower achievement of some groups of pupils and, in the free market of schools competing for pupils, could lead to 'white flight' from inner-city schools in particular.

FORMAL ASSESSMENT

Wider issues of assessment, as in Section 5 Formal Assessment (under the 1981 Education Act), pose a number of problems.

Educational Opportunities for All?, an account of special education in inner London (Fish, 1985), is one of the few sources of information in which the ethnic composition of pupils of special schools and special needs populations was ever detailed. One significant factor (p. 47) was the general disquiet about the outcome of assessment as well as the great confusion and anxiety which can occur with parents whose English is poor. It was noted that 57 per cent of Afro-Caribbean parents were totally dissatisfied with the way they had been informed about their child's special educational needs and with all the services working with their children. Many parents simply did not understand what the assessment was about or what it was for (Rehal, 1988). Once again, cultural assumptions by professionals may play a considerable part in creating the confusion.

The point was made earlier in this chapter that educational psychologists and other workers who service clients have to negotiate their way through a complex network of professionals. Parents too have to negotiate their way through the professional network, so that what seems to them to be a relatively simple presenting problem at the outset—'Darren isn't learning to read'—has become, after the intervention of half a dozen professionals, a near incomprehensible, jargon-ridden range of bureaucratic procedures. Meanwhile, Darren still is not reading. There is quite a wide variation nationwide in the quality of information given to parents whose children are undergoing a formal assessment (Bradley, 1988). Furthermore, there is an equally wide variation in the extent to which parental contributions are seen as important by different LEAs. In some authorities the parental contribution was as low as 5 per cent.

The only solution to lack of parental comprehension of, and participation in, assessment is to:

(a)   ensure that parents are properly briefed and informed about what is going to happen from the outset;
(b)   ensure that *every* parent makes a contribution to the assessment.

Frameworks and guidelines exist that facilitate this process (Wolfendale, 1988), and indeed, several of these have been translated into Asian languages.

Parents also need to know that formal assessment may not only give the protection of a statement but may also take away parental rights over choice of school. But the most important feature—that of observing the child and parents together and listening to what the parents say about their children—is overwhelmingly important, particularly in the case of black or non-English-speaking parents.

Questions raised by this are to do with variations in the numbers of statements held by individual local authorities and what criteria are used to initiate Section 5 assessments (Select Committee, 1987). It seems reasonable to suggest that where statementing procedures are involved most commonly the decision to effect a formal assessment/statement is taken by an administrator (Goacher *et al.*, 1988), but that it is usually a fairly subjective decision based on advice taken from other professionals, including the educational psychologist. At the point where the decision is made to assess formally, clearly it must be jointly formulated, involving parents, teachers, the pupil himself or herself where appropriate and the officers of the authority. Lack of consultation is still a feature of some LEA practice (Goacher *et al*., 1988), and educational psychologists who are caught up in this lack of consultation at LEA level are very likely to be singled out by parents, among all of the professionals involved, as the ones most guilty of duplicitous dealing. Frequently, then, it is likely that the procedure has become mechanical, minimizing parental contributions and wishes, unless there is a prior agreement about possible outcomes of the assessment. Such an *a priori* agreement is, of course, most likely in those cases where extra resourcing for the pupil is forthcoming to support a mainstream placement.

Dovetailing with this issue is that of the LEA's providing appropriate sources of advice and support to parents in the form of the named person or befriender (Circular 22/89), for even with good written information available, as was noted above, a large percentage of parents are still unhappy with the assessment outcome, particularly in the case of pupils with emotional, behavioural difficulties or moderate learning difficulties. Because of the direct involvement of the educational psychologist in assessment, it is unlikely that the role of the designated person or befriender could be an educational psychologist—rather, an advising officer who is available to parents, but in such a way that her or his views are independent of the assessment process.

There are many examples of LEA practice (Goacher *et al*., 1988) which have excluded parents from the decision-making processes involving their children. For example, informal placements for 'assessment' were noted as a common practice in the majority of placements in authorities' MLD schools. Some authorities hold back placement of five-year-old pupils until the parents have agreed to an assessment. In such a situation the educational psychologist allocated to the case has little prospect of winning parental confidence by accepting a role in assessment which is itself being used coercively by the LEA. Educational psychologists who do not have an active role in shaping policy decisions at the LEA level inevitably find that such decisions as those outlined above totally undermine their credibility as 'objective' assessors of the child's special educational needs.

To ensure professional integrity of educational psychologists' involvement in formal assessment procedures would require the following. Educational psychologists should:

(a)　participate fully in LEA policy making on special needs issues;
(b)　ensure they are not coerced into carrying out unreasonable, discriminatory professional practices, reinforcing institutionally or structurally racist outcomes of assessment;
(c)　ensure total parental cooperation at all stages of informal and formal assessment;
(d)　give unbiased evidence of assessments.

In the case of 'difficult' pupils the decision-making process by professionals is often, if not nearly always, within this displacement framework, involving more negative administrative actions to remove the student in question from the school (Mongon, 1988). If an educational psychologist becomes embroiled in such a case, it often proves difficult to maintain a neutral position. Indeed, the issue is again raised: who is the client?

The hugely disproportionate numbers of Caribbean pupils in various non-mainstream provisions suggests that teachers, educational psychologists and others have been negligent in pursuing sufficiently detailed policy and practice in the assessment of Caribbean pupils' learning and behaviour.

EDUCATIONAL PSYCHOLOGISTS AND THE ASSESSMENT OF BEHAVIOUR DIFFICULTIES

One of the more contentious areas of special educational provision is that for pupils with emotional behavioural difficulties. Experience suggests that many educational psychology services differ considerably in the degree to which psychologists become involved, and at what stage, with pupils who are posing a problem for the school. Some educational psychologists may be involved with a pupil who is on the point of suspension or exclusion. Other educational psychologists are not happy to be associated directly with a system which finds it necessary to exclude pupils from full participation.

If racial considerations and statistics are included, then there is evident cause for concern. The Fish Report (1985) indicated that Caribbean pupils in London were fifty times more likely than Asian pupils to be placed in units for disruptive pupils or in educational guidance centres. Several interpretations of this fact are feasible, including the possibility that Caribbean pupils are perceived by teachers to be potentially more difficult, aggressive or disruptive (Gillborn, 1990). Gillborn notes from his research that in multi-ethnic schools pupils of Afro-Caribbean origin come into conflict with teachers more often than pupils from other ethnic groups. Afro-Caribbean pupils are also more likely to be excluded or suspended from school. They are also likely to be in receipt of more detentions. The issue at the crux of the matter is that much more research is needed to highlight the complex interplay between and among the crucial home–school as well as teacher–pupil variables, before it is possible to add much of substance to the debate. One interpretation which must be considered is that there are specific factors within Caribbean culture which predispose Caribbean pupils to behave in a way which clashes with the predominantly white or middle-class norm of school (Wright, 1987) in ways which other black groups do not. Furthermore, the behavioural patterns probably do serve as a focus for negative attention by teachers (Gillborn). But what are the behaviours? How do black pupils view the rules of the school system? Do teachers systematically pick on black pupils? Gillborn thinks not, but many pupils do think so (Wright, 1987).

In such a confused and embattled arena the naive educational psychologist is likely to be in some difficulty very quickly. Without a database it is impossible to guess how often psychologists are carefully manipulated by schools to ease the perceived difficult pupil out of school by the process of gradual displacement, a process legitimated by the educational psychologist becoming involved.

The Elton Report (HMSO, 1989) takes a wide-ranging look at the many factors which need consideration if schools are to be orderly, with good academic achievements. There are a number of specific recommendations included in the report which link to race and gender issues: 'We recommend that teachers should take account of the gender differences involved in pupils' behaviour—by not reinforcing attention seeking and aggressive behaviour' (p. 159), or 'Teachers should recognise the potential for injustice and the danger of stereotyping certain kinds of pupils as troublemakers' (p. 159). The report also recommends clear strategies for dealing with racial harassment by teachers and pupils alike (p. 160). For educational psychologists it is clear that referral of pupils, even at an informal level of discussion, could be a racist projection by the teacher, and some educational psychology services have codes of practice to which their service delivery adheres.

SUMMARY

In this chapter an attempt has been made to elaborate on issues of equality and cultural awareness and the work of educational psychologists.

The profession has moved on from simplistic, global, psychometric views of the educational world and of children, but it is probably true to say that indicators of good practice to replace outdated professional responses are still unclear in some areas of work. Unintentional and subtle racist practice in educational psychology services is still commonplace (Desforges *et al.*, 1985), and it is hoped that some surface-underpinning professional practices which could be construed as racist have been discussed in this chapter.

One must return again to the notion of deconstructing the obvious, as outlined by Hall (1980), quoted at the beginning of this chapter. Bedrock assumptions on intelligence, race or gender, from whichever point of view, do tend to achieve explanatory status—largely because they fit in with existing precepts. Replacing these with informed and sensitive practice is a priority not only for educational psychologists but for others in the education service. Being sympathetic to black or cultural issues is simply not enough to help black children's chances in life, if one maintains a professionally outmoded and subtly racist practice based on prior Eurocentric assumptions on the nature of intelligence, achievement or behavioural norms. It is only through greater professionalism in maintaining a high level of knowledge and skills that educational psychologists can avoid repeating the mistakes of the past, no matter how these occurred.

The issue is finally about delivering a relevant service to *all* children and their families. As Davis (1984) has noted, 'black people do not want favours or privileges from education authorities. What they want is to be accorded their statutory rights under the law. If officers, advisers, inspectors, headteachers and teachers in multiracial areas paid serious attention to their statutory obligations . . . there would be no need for separate policies' (p. 511).

REFERENCES

Banks, J. (1988) *Multiethnic Education*. London: Allyn & Bacon.

Booker, R., Hart, M., Moreland, D. and Powell, J. (1989) 'Struggling towards better practice', *Educational Psychology in Practice*, **5** (3).

Booth, T. and Statham, J. (1982) *The Nature of Special Education*. London: Croom Helm.

Bradley, H. (1988) 'A survey of the documents published by the LEAs of England and Wales to help parents through the assessment and statementing procedures of the 1981 Education Act'. Unpublished MSc Educational Psychology dissertation, North-East London Polytechnic Psychology Department.

Bryans, T. (1988) 'Educational psychologists working in multicultural communities', *DECP*, **5** (2), 8–18.

Bryne, E.M. (1985) 'Equality or equity—a European over-view', in Arnot, M. (ed.) *Race and Gender*. Oxford: Pergamon Press.

Cline, T. and Lunt, I. (1990) 'Meeting equal opportunities criteria: a review of progress in educational psychology training', in *Training for Professional Practice, DECP*, **7** (3), 59–66.

Coard, B. (1971) *How the West Indian Child Is Made Educationally Sub-normal in the British School System*. London: New Beacon Books.

Cooper, D. (1975) 'Quality and equality in education', in Brown, S.C. (ed.) *Philosophers Discuss Education*. London: Macmillan.

Cummins, J. (1984) *Bilingualism and Special Education Issues in Assessment and Pedagogy*. Clevedon: Multi-lingual Matters.

Davis, G. (1984) 'How pervasive is white superiority?', *Education*, **22** (6), 511.

Desforges, M. F., Goodwin, C. and Kerr, A. (1985) 'Do you work in a subtly racist psychological service?', *Educational Psychology in Practice*, **1**, 1.

Fish, J. (Chair) (1985) *Educational Opportunities for All?* London: Inner London Education Authority.

Gibson, A. and Barrow, J. (1986) *The Unequal Struggle*. London: Centre for Caribbean Studies.

Gillborn, D. (1990) 'When cultural display is seen as a challenge', *Times Educational Supplement* (30 November).

Gipps, C. (1990) *Assessment—A Teacher's Guide to the Issues*. London: Hodder & Stoughton.

Goacher, B., Evans, J., Welton, J. and Wedell, K. (1988) *Policy and Provision for Special Educational Needs*. London: Cassell.

Gupta, R. (1984) 'The longitudinal predictive validity of the learning efficiency test battery: psychologists and ethnic minority groups', *Educational and Child Psychology*, vol. 1. Leicester: British Psychological Society, p. 1.

Hall, S. (1980) 'Teaching race', *Multicultural Education*, **9** (1), 3–13.

Halsey, A. M., Heath, A. F. and Ridge, J. M. (1980) *Origins and Destination: Family Class and Education in Modern Britain*. Oxford: Clarendon Press.

HMSO (1965) *Race Relations Act*. London: HMSO.

HMSO (1988) *Education for All*. London: HMSO. (Swann Report)

HMSO (1989) *Discipline in Schools*. London: HMSO. (Elton Report)

Jeffcoate, R. (1985) 'Anti-racism as an educational ideology' in Arnot, M. (ed.) *Race and Gender*. Oxford: Pergamon Press.

Jensen, S. (1969) 'How do we boost IQ and scholastic achievement?', *Harvard Educational Review*, **39**, 1–123.

Joyce, J. (1988) 'The development of an anti-racist policy in Leeds', in Wolfendale, S., Lunt, I. and Carroll, T. (eds) *Educational Psychologists Working in Multi-cultural Communities*, *DECP*, **5** (2).

Mackinnon, D. (1987) 'Is equality necessarily incompatible with quality?', *Journal of Philosophy of Education*, **23** (2).

Mongon, D. (1988) 'The role of teachers in issues', in Smith, J. and Bryans, T. (eds) *Statementing Children with Educational and Behavioural Problems*. Windsor: NFER-Nelson.

Mortimore, P., Sammons, P., Stoll, L., Lewis, D. and Ecob, R. (1988) *School Matters: The Junior Years*. Wells: Open Books.

Mullard, C. (1985) 'Multi-racial education in Britain: from assimilation to cultural pluralism', in Arnot, M. (ed.) *Race and Gender*. Oxford: Pergamon Press.

Parekh, B. (1983) 'Educational opportunities in multi-ethnic Britain', in Glager, N. and Young, K. (eds) *Ethnic and Public Policy*. London: Heinemann, pp. 108–23.

Rawls, J. (1972) *A Theory of Justice*. London: Oxford University Press.

Rehal, A. (1988) 'Involving Asian parents in the statementing procedure—the way forward', *Educational Psychology in Practice*, **4** (4), 189–97.

Robinson, P. (1989) 'Whose Act is it anyway?', in Evans, R. (ed.) *Special Educational Needs—Policy and Practice*. Oxford: Blackwell Education.

Select Committee (1987) *Report on the 1981 Education Act*. London: HMSO.

Syed, R. (1989) 'Ethnic persona in the self perceptions of the Asian child', personal communication.

Tomlinson, S. (1989) 'The origins of the ethno-centric curriculum', in Verma, G. (ed.) *Education for All?* London: Falmer Press.

Troyna, B. (1979) 'Differential commitment to ethnic identity by black youths in Britain', *New Community*, **7** (3), 406–14.

Troyna, B. and Carrington, B. (1990) *Education, Racism and Reform*. London: Routledge.

University College Department of Psychology (1989) *Assessment of Bi-lingual Pupils*. University College London.

Weiner, G. (1985) 'The Schools Council and gender', in Arnot, M. (ed.) *Race and Gender*. Oxford: Pergamon Press.

Wolfendale, S. (1988) *The Parental Contribution to Assessment*. Developing Horizons No. 10. Stratford-upon-Avon: National Council for Special Education.

Wright, C. (1987) 'The English culture is being swamped: racism in secondary schools', in Booth, T. and Coulby, D. (eds) *Producing and Reducing Disaffection*. Milton Keynes: Open University Press.

Chapter 10

Psychologists, Child Law and the Courts: Contexts and Professional Advice

William Conn

INTRODUCTION

This chapter explores the complex area of psychologists in relation to child law. The area is sometimes referred to as forensic child psychology, the word 'forensic' merely meaning 'of or pertaining to the courts'. While it is possible to debate the issue of whether forensic child psychology represents a separate specialism within applied psychology, such a debate would be rather sterile in the context of this volume. The primary purpose of this chapter is to look at the role of the psychologist in regard to child law. The issues, anxieties and dilemmas of this role remain the same whether one specializes in the area or has only the occasional case.

Much of what I am proposing to say applies to the role of psychologists whatever their sub-discipline. By psychologist I mean (in UK terms) someone who has obtained an honours degree in psychology and has further undertaken an advanced course approved by the British Psychological Society and usually leading to the award of a higher degree. In the case of educational psychologists there is an additional requirement for a teaching qualification and at least two years' teaching experience.

Whatever their particular orientation it seems to me that applied psychologists all access the same core discipline. They have a knowledge of major psychological theories and a training that permits them to apply a range of validated techniques and approaches to the identification and solution of difficulties, including the generation of unique solutions to novel problems. They will have an awareness of and usually experience in research. In the case of psychologists working with children and families, the major psychological domains sampled will include developmental psychology, family functioning and dynamics, abnormal psychology, including constraints of development, and, importantly, a need for a developed contextual awareness of major social institutions and influences, such as cultural and ethnic background, economic influences, etc. An examination of the notion of awareness of these social institutions is in my view crucial to psychologists locating themselves and their roles within a set of systems. It is helpful to conceptualize this essentially ecological notion into the component parts of a microsystem, a mesosystem, an exosystem and a macrosystem. (Also see Chapter 4.)

The microsystem in this context is the actual, immediate social and psychological environment of the child. It is the perceived reality for an individual. Family and school represent two important microsystems.

The mesosystem is the interconnectedness of the various microsystems in which the child is located. Few would argue about the importance of the major interfaces between home and school or school and peer group. An evaluation of the degree to which there are links, the number of different linkages and their positive or negative loadings is plainly of importance.

The exosystem is a yet wider notion. There is no requirement for the individual to 'know' systems of this type, but they are none the less important influences. An LEA and its policies are an example of an exosystem. So too are the courts.

Finally in this analysis there is the largest system—the macrosystem. The previous systems are set within a matrix of broadly based and pervasive influences including cultural, economic and political aspects. These influences define the collective social heritage of beliefs, symbol systems, ideas, values, etc. and are powerful normalizing influences. The macrosystem need not be thought of as deliberately created to a blueprint or plan but includes unforeseen interconnections and consequences. Under normal circumstances it undergoes change in a slow and evolutionary manner.

It is at the macrosystem level that the notion of the child evolved. Childhood is essentially a social construct. Childhood legally begins at birth (not conception) and comes to an arbitrary legal end at the age of 18 years. At different points in British history 10 years and 12 years have been the age of majority. In medieval times a distinction was drawn between the sons of knights and the sons of inferior classes: the former came of age at 21 years and the latter at 14 or 15 years (Freeman, 1983). Childhood has different meanings depending on cultural context (Mead and Wolfenstein, 1955). Aries (1962) argues with scholarly eloquence that childhood was 'invented' in Europe in the seventeenth century.

In this chapter, it is proposed to begin by looking at the wider legal responsibilities of psychologists. I will then indicate the types of case in which psychologists are involved and list the major legislation pertaining to this. Because of its recency and pervasiveness I shall give special attention to the Children Act 1989 with its new conceptual notions. Following this the role of the psychologist as expert witness will be discussed, with special emphasis on practical courtcraft issues. Finally I will say something about the role of guardian *ad litem* and furnish some advice on the preparation of reports.

THE LEGAL RESPONSIBILITIES OF PSYCHOLOGISTS

Broadly speaking the essential legal responsibility of psychologists relates to the notion of a 'duty of care'. Basically this requires psychologists (like all professionals) to 'take reasonable care in all the circumstances' in dealing with their clients. The requirement is to act with due care considering all the circumstances and to act within the realm of one's own competence. Anything that violates these principles would render the psychologist liable to a charge of professional negligence. In my view it is good practice for psychologists to have personal indemnity insurance that includes cover for legal fees. Though psychologists are covered in most cases by employers' insurance, I feel that it is prudent to ensure that one has one's own coverage even if working in the state sector and essential if in private practice.

Psychologists working with children have a special problem in relation to consent. Certainly one needs to have the consent of the child's parent(s) to undertake direct work with the child, and one hopes, implicitly at least, to have the consent of the child (see later section on the Children Act 1989).

There is also the issue of confidentiality. Psychologists' notes, reports, test pro-formas etc. are technically the property of the employer. They must be handed over if required, however 'private' the information contained therein. Of greater concern is the fact that psychologists have no privilege in court regarding information given to them, even when it was given to them with an agreement of confidence. If the court demands information in your possession, even if it is in your head, you must give it or be in contempt of court.

This understandably and rightly causes many psychologists a high degree of consternation. It is particularly an issue when the psychologist was seeing the child and/or family as a 'routine' part of his or her daily work rather than specifically to prepare a report for the court. There is no easy answer here. If there are very special circumstances—for example, if revealing what a child said would expose him or her to danger—then one could make representations to the court. It is wise to do so as soon as you know you are to be called to court rather than waiting till the day of the hearing. The fact remains, however, that you can still be required to say what you know (see McCloskey *et al.*, 1986, for a detailed discussion of the ethical issues).

Many local authorities have policies in regard to their staff appearing in court. Most require a witness summons or subpoena to be issued. The issuing of such a subpoena can be helpful in that it makes it very clear to the child and family that there is no choice for the psychologist but to attend. It can also be helpful to let the child and/or family know you are being called to court. There is nothing improper in this, and it may reduce the degree of shock and anger on the day.

THE MAJOR LEGISLATION

The major legislation with a direct bearing on children and which might involve psychologists is as follows: the Education Act 1944, the Education Act 1981, the Education Reform Act 1988 and the Children Act 1989. The last is new legislation, with a date for implementation of October 1991. It is a very important piece of legislation aimed at consolidating a disparate array of child law. It also introduces some important new concepts, ideas and changes of nomenclature.

It is not proposed here to attempt to summarize all this legislation, merely to flag these Acts as the most important. Most educational psychologists will be familiar with the primary education acts and aware of their implications. It is not usually the Education Acts which cause the most psychologically complex issues to emerge and which create the greatest difficulty in marrying psychological and legal concepts.

It may be helpful here to list the types of case in which psychologists in Britain are most likely to be involved. It is difficult to do this in a very thorough manner since to my knowledge there has only been one survey of this sort in Britain, that of Gudjonsson (1985). She undertook this survey at the request of the Division of Criminological and Legal Psychology of the British Psychological Society. She reports that of the 185 psychologists who completed the questionnaire 181 had appeared in person as an expert witness during the previous five years, either in court or tribunal. Of these, 51 per cent had appeared in civil cases such as matrimonial, childcare and custody proceedings, head injury and compensation cases, and 50 per cent in criminal cases, with 18 per cent having appeared in both civil and criminal cases. The majority (67 per cent) had appeared in court only once or twice.

My own experience is probably not typical in that I specialize in cases of child abuse and neglect. Inevitably this involves several court appearances each month. However, within this context I do meet a number of other psychologists and have kept loose records of the sorts of case involved. As in Gudjonsson's survey, the majority of cases involving children are civil cases, mostly childcare cases. There is a tendency for psychologists in private practice to be more frequently involved in divorce cases where the issues are of custody or access or in compensation cases. A higher proportion of state-employed psychologists are involved in the juvenile justice system, usually reporting on individual children and their families in criminal proceedings.

Of cases with a more obviously educational flavour, by far the commonest reason for psychological involvement relates to non-attendance at school. I shall devote a separate section to this issue following the discussion of the Children Act. Clearly, too, psychologists are involved in appeals against decisions in the whole arena of special educational needs. It is, however, relatively rare for such appeals to reach the courts, though nationally several more dramatic cases do occur each year.

THE CHILDREN ACT 1989

I provide separate comment on this Act for reasons hinted at above. It represents the most fundamental change in child law for a hundred years. It radically changes many established notions and creates a new philosophical and conceptual apparatus. Its intention is to provide a comprehensive and integrated statutory framework for children. (Also see Chapter 11.)

Section 1 of Part I begins with an uncontentious assertion of the dominant principle of the Act, namely that:

> When a court determines any question in respect to—
> (a) the upbringing of a child; or
> (b) the administration of a child's property or the application of any income arising from it,
> *the child's welfare shall be the court's paramount consideration.* (my italics)

Section 2 states, again laudably, that

> In any proceedings in which any question with respect to the upbringing of a child arises, the court shall have regard to the general principle that any delay in determining the question is likely to prejudice the welfare of the child.

Also of very great relevance to psychologists in working with children in a legal context is the introduction of a checklist of considerations to be borne in mind by the court. Psychologists should bear this fully in mind either when preparing a written report or when giving oral evidence. The checklist is set out in Section 1(3) and consists of eight items:

(a) the ascertainable wishes and feelings of the child concerned (considered in the light of his age and understanding);
(b) his physical, emotional and educational needs;
(c) the likely effect on him of any change in his circumstances;
(d) his age, sex, background and any characteristics of his which the court considers relevant;
(e) any harm which he has suffered or is at risk of suffering;
(f) how capable each of his parents, and any other person in relation to whom the court considers the question to be relevant, is of meeting his needs;
(g) the range of powers available to the court under this Act in the proceedings in question.

The role for psychological advice in deciding on these issues is fairly clear. Psychologists have (or should have) a special facility in terms of ascertaining the child's wishes and feelings. They are also the professional group best suited to establishing his or her emotional and educational needs and the likely effect on him or her of any changes. Also uncontentious is their potential role in looking at harm or risk of harm (see below for the definition of harm, which includes harm to physical, intellectual, emotional, social or behavioural development). The psychologist's knowledge of family dynamics and of how child need can be met, too, will be of undoubted use in helping courts reach a determination, especially in more complex and contentious cases.

As part of the general intention of the Children Act to consolidate existing legislation, a number of new orders are introduced. These are known collectively as Section 8 orders. Two of these orders, namely residence orders and contact orders, replace the concepts of custody and access orders respectively. They are, however, not exact equivalents. Of greater interest is the introduction of two entirely new orders, namely a prohibited steps order and a specific issue order.

A prohibited steps order places a specific embargo on a defined course of action which would otherwise be within the parents' right to determine. A specific issue order can deal with any point or question which has arisen in connection with any aspect of parental responsibility for a child. This could include such matters as whether or not there should be an assessment of the child under the 1981 Education Act or whether the child should be sent to a boarding school.

It is interesting to note that the wording of Section 10 of the Children Act would entitle children to apply for a Section 8 order in regard to themselves. The court's leave is needed for the child to apply and the court may 'only grant leave if it is satisfied that he has sufficient understanding' to make the application. No definition of sufficient understanding is offered. One can well see the advice of psychologists being sought in some such situations, and indeed there is the prospect of some psychologists advising a child to apply for such an order to prevent something to which the child has strong objections being arranged for him or her, or to permit something to occur which is being unreasonably denied.

In regard to new orders it is perhaps, in the interests of completeness, worth pointing out here that a family assistance order is introduced. This order basically replaces the former matrimonial supervision order. A family assistance order can only be made with the consent of all those involved.

Part III of the Children Act makes frequent reference to 'children in need'. This is a phrase in common colloquial use and is accessible in meaning. However, the act actually provides a definition, which again has important implications for psychologists. Section 17(10) states:

For the purposes of this Part a child shall be taken to be in need if—
(a) he is unlikely to achieve or maintain, or to have the opportunity of achieving or maintaining, a reasonable standard of health or development without the provision for him of services by a local authority under this Part;
(b) his health or development is likely to be significantly impaired, or further impaired, without the provision for him of such services; or
(c) he is disabled,
and 'family', in relation to such a child, includes any person who has parental responsibility for the child and any other person with whom he has been living.

Section (11) states that

For the purposes of this Part, a child is disabled if he is blind, deaf or dumb or suffers from mental disorder of any kind or is substantially and permanently handicapped by illness, injury or congenital deformity or such other disability as may be prescribed; and in this Part—
'development' means physical, intellectual, emotional, social or behavioural development; and
'health' means physical or mental health.

We turn now to compulsory powers in regard to the removal or protection of children and the likely role of psychologists in such proceedings. This is dealt with in Section 31 of the Act. This makes it clear that a court may only make a care order or supervision order if it is satisfied:

(a) that the child concerned is suffering, or is likely to suffer significant harm; and
(b) that the harm, or likelihood of harm, is attributable to—
   (i) the care given to the child, or likely to be given to him if the order were not made, not being what it would be reasonable to expect a parent to give to him; or
   (ii) the child's being beyond parental control.

This single category of significant harm replaces the six categories under which a child could come into care under the Children and Young Persons Act 1969.

The Children Act goes on to define 'harm' as meaning 'ill treatment or the impairment of health or development', and 'development' as meaning 'physical, intellectual, emotional, social or behavioural development'. 'Health' is defined as meaning 'physical or mental health' and 'ill treatment' is defined to include 'sexual abuse and forms of ill-treatment which are not physical'. Interestingly, the Act goes on to consider the issue of how to determine significance:

Where the question of whether harm suffered by a child is significant turns on the child's health or development, his health or development shall be compared with that which could reasonably be expected of a similar child.

One should note here that many of the words and concepts used are psychological in flavour. It seems probable that courts will increasingly look to psychologists for opinions on such matters.

It is also very important to note that this legislation, unlike the previous legislation, allows the court to look to the future by considering the 'likelihood of harm'. Under the 1969 Children and Young Persons Act the child's 'proper development' had to be currently 'neglected or impaired'. It seems to me that one of the more principled ways of looking at the likelihood of harm is to address the research literature, especially longitudinal work. When we come to deal with the psychologist as expert witness I shall say more about his or her right in that regard to quote research.

It is worth pointing out another change in regard to care proceedings. Under this Act children can no longer come into the care of the local authority on the grounds of non-attendance at school alone, and there are no more care orders in criminal proceedings.

Before turning to procedural issues, courtcraft and the role of the psychologist as expert witness, I shall say something about the emergency protection of children.

Most practitioners with children are aware of place of safety orders, whereby a juvenile magistrate, sitting alone and hearing only the social-work side of the case, could make an order for the immediate removal of a child for his or her protection. Under the Children Act the place of safety order is replaced by an order called an emergency protection order. The court has to be satisfied that the child is likely to suffer 'significant harm' (or that access to him or her is being denied and she or he may be suffering such harm). The order is limited to eight days, with a possible extension of a further seven days. Certain persons, including the parents, may apply for the discharge of the order after seventy-two hours. An emergency protection order can also be used to keep a child where he or she is by preventing removal; for instance in a foster home. As with the former place of safety order, anyone can apply (psychologist, teacher, neighbour) but in practice it will be the social services department or the NSPCC. The police may also take a child 'into police protection' for up to seventy-two hours if they have grounds to believe that he or she would be likely to suffer significant harm.

One other new type of order which it is worth mentioning here as it may have implications for psychologists, especially those working closely with social services departments, is the child assessment order. Following the report on the death of Kimberley Carlile (Blom-Cooper *et al.*, 1987), the need for such an order was even more manifest. The sole purpose of a child assessment order is to be able to complete an assessment of the child. According to Section 43(5) of the Children Act, a child assessment order must specify the date by which the assessment is to begin and shall have effect for a maximum of seven days. No parental consent will be needed for the assessment. However, it is very interesting to note that Section 43(8) indicates that 'if the child is of sufficient understanding to make an informed decision he may refuse to submit to a medical or psychiatric examination or other assessment.' Once again there is no definition of 'sufficient understanding', and this is clearly left to the professional judgment of those involved.

Under a child assessment order a child may only be kept away from home if this is necessary for the purposes of the assessment, and only for such a period as is specified in the order. Though primarily aimed at obtaining medical opinions, there seems to be little doubt that it will be used also to obtain psychological opinions about a child's welfare. One has to note here, however, that many forms of psychological assessment require a rather longer time-frame than that allowed for under a child assessment order. None the less, it will at times be the only means of having access to a child in order to investigate his or her circumstances and to determine aspects of his or her development.

In order to make a child assessment order the court must be satisfied that there is reasonable cause to suspect that the child 'is suffering or likely to suffer significant harm', or that such an assessment is necessary to ascertain whether the child's health or development is suffering significant harm or is likely so to suffer, and that it is 'unlikely that such an assessment will be made or be satisfactory in the absence of an order under this section'.

THE PSYCHOLOGIST IN COURT

Whatever the grounds for the psychologist being involved in proceedings and whoever it is who is calling the psychologist to give evidence, there are certain common elements in what happens. I list below the major procedural issues.

Firstly there is the oath or affirmation (affirmation is used for those who do not profess any religious belief). Secondly you will be asked for your name and professional address and your qualifications and experience. You may also be asked to say what your involvement has been, who referred the child or family to you and with what brief.

The evidence you give at the instigation of the person who called you to give evidence is referred to as your 'evidence in chief'. After giving your evidence in chief you are then subject to cross-examination by the legal representatives of the other parties.

Witnesses are sometimes confused as to how to refer to the magistrates or judges. Technically magistrates are referred to as 'Your Worship' or 'Your Worships'. However, it is perfectly permissible to refer to the chair of magistrates as 'Sir' or 'Madam'. Crown court and county court judges are addressed as 'Your Honour', while high court judges (in wardship proceedings, for instance) are referred to as 'My Lord' or 'My Lady' or 'Your Lordship' or 'Your Ladyship'.

Given the magnitude of the decisions being made it is appropriate to dress soberly and respectably. If you do not you may well affect your credibility as a witness and thus adversely affect the outcome.

Within the court setting the psychologist is regarded as an expert witness. Sometimes a distinction is drawn between a professional and an expert witness; more usually the words are used interchangeably. Where the distinction is adhered to, it seems to be as follows. The professional witness is one who stood in some form of professional relationship to the subject of the proceedings before the case started. Thus if a psychologist were working with a child in a school or clinic on the basis of a previous referral and during this time court action was instigated then he or she could be called to give an opinion. This is the situation where the previously addressed issue of confidentiality arises. Psychologists, like medical practitioners, are obliged to answer questions under oath even if the information was given to them on the understanding that it would be treated confidentially. An expert, on the other hand, might not have seen the child or family but has specialist knowledge of an area of work; for example, child abuse, sensory impairment, mental handicap etc. Frequently psychologists occupy both roles.

Being an expert witness is not solely a matter of prestige and status. Very real 'rights' come with it. Firstly an expert may, with the consent of all the parties, be present for other people's evidence and may comment upon it. Thus I have often sat through social work accounts of a home situation or access visits and been asked to comment as to the likely effect of the described behaviour on the child's emotional development.

Secondly, and very importantly, an expert is not restricted to matters of fact but may express a professional opinion. Most other witnesses are prevented from straying into the arena of opinion. Thus the expert witness might say that in his or her opinion the child's developmental delay, behavioural problem, etc. is likely to have been caused by the abusive situation in which he or she was living at home. One notes here that Section 31 of the Children Act requires only that the harm or likelihood of harm 'is attributable to' the care given to the child.

The expert witness may refer to his or her case notes providing that these were contemporaneously made or made very shortly after the interview. Notes referred to with the court's permission can be viewed by the legal representatives of the parties. It is, however, very rare for the notes or records of an expert to be viewed, as they are assumed to require technical understanding. Sometimes one of the other parties employs their own expert to sit in court and advise them.

Another important aspect of being regarded as 'expert' is that the witness can refer to published research findings. In my view this should only be done when the research genuinely elucidates a pertinent point, rather than as a vague appeal to an unspecified other authority to enhance the status of what is being said. It is good practice to re-read the research before going to court if you intend to quote it. This is for two main reasons: firstly we do not always correctly remember findings, and secondly those specialist solicitors and barristers cross-examining you may also know the work in question if it is genuinely relevant. It is possible to be asked if you know of any research pertinent to a particular point.

Older children who are thought to be of an age to instruct their own solicitor often sit in court during proceedings. If you feel as an expert that hearing your views on prognosis for them or on an aspect of their parents' life would be damaging for them, you can ask the court that they be excluded. If this is likely to be an issue you should inform the solicitor calling you before the proceedings so that she or he can canvass colleagues' opinions about the matter. This can save valuable court time. It is important to bear in mind, however, that the child's fantasy about what is said might have an effect as bad as or worse than hearing the actual evidence. The decision is the court's.

Finally the expert can be asked to base an opinion purely on a synthesis of other evidence available without having seen the child or family. This will clearly be based on the expert's overall knowledge of such cases and can, when handled with due circumspection, be helpful to courts.

Over a number of years of providing expert testimony both in state and independent practice, prevailingly in cases of child abuse and neglect, I have identified a number of strategies that can help.

It is important to be familiar with your own evidence before taking the stand. Your own opinion should never come as a surprise to you. Thus if the matter before the court is care proceedings you should have sought to be clear for yourself whether you feel that the child has suffered significant harm that is attributable to the quality of care he or she has received. However, if it is not possible to form such an opinion on available evidence, that is what you must say.

It is very easy to get drawn in as though on one side or the other. Your status and usefulness as an expert depend on being able to form a balanced, independent opinion. Thus you should give credit where credit is due and praise good aspects of a situation where this is fair, even though your overall view might be negative.

It is helpful to anticipate likely questions in order to sort your thoughts out. It is not in my view helpful to prepare set answers. Not only can these sound stilted and artificial but, since the question is hardly ever going to come up in exactly the form you have anticipated or can mean something different in terms of preceding evidence, a prepackaged answer can be misleading.

It is also appropriate to have your file, notes or records with you. If you wish to refer to them you should ask permission from the magistrates or judge, explaining that the notes were contemporaneously made. Remember that, though it is unlikely, legal representatives of the other parties can ask to see your notes.

One strategy that many psychologists find facilitating is to write a list of questions for whoever is calling you as a witness. This is perfectly ethical. You know what your knowledge base is and what your views on the case are. In your evidence in chief you need this to come across as clearly as possible.

Inexperienced witnesses often have initial difficulty in knowing to whom they should address their replies. Regardless of who asks the question, the replies are addressed to the magistrates or judge. This requires a little practice at first since all our social training and experience guides us to look at the person who asked the question. I find it helpful to position myself so that I am basically facing the bench or judge and only look round, without changing my overall body position, to signal that I have completed my answer. Besides being congruent with established court etiquette, such a position makes it harder for the solicitor or barrister questioning you to interrupt.

It is obviously important to speak clearly. We all tend to speed up when we are anxious. If you do go too fast you will be asked to slow down. In the juvenile court a handwritten record of the evidence is made by the clerk to the court. Keeping an eye on the clerk's pen is a useful strategy. In higher courts evidence is usually taped.

It is worth mentioning here that court clerks are not secretaries or administrators. They are lawyers (solicitors or barristers) who advise the lay bench on legal matters.

Though perhaps one should not need to say this, it is important in giving evidence to be as direct as you can and avoid evasion. Jargon too should be kept to a minimum; if technical words need to be used, provide a definition.

When you are asked a question, listen carefully. Try to answer the question asked. Wait for the question to be completed before you begin. Take thinking time. If you feel a question is unfair, loaded or misleading, you are entitled to say so—to the bench or judge. Similarly, if you are being pressed for a yes/no answer on a question that does not lend itself to such a dichotomy, say so to the bench or judge. If in the course of your evidence you make a mistake or are being misinterpreted, again say so to the bench or judge.

You are in court to help clarify matters. An easy mistake to make might be to mix up some information about children of the same gender and similar in age from a large sibship. Keep an eye out for the 'deliberate' distortion of your previous evidence, such as a question being preambled by phrases which purport to summarize several things you have said. If you feel such a distortion is creeping in, you can, and I feel should, say so. Very long questions can be confusing: what exactly is being asked? You can ask for questions to be repeated. If the question is inaccessibly opaque, again say so. It is as likely to have confused everyone else in court.

There is no doubt that being in court can be anxiety inducing. If you feel that your mouth is going dry, you are entitled to ask for a glass of water or even a minute's break. If you are desperate to go to the toilet you may ask for a 'natural break', or words to that effect.

By their nature courts are adversarial. If people were in agreement on matters we would hardly need them at all. However, a special issue for the expert witness is when there is another equally well-qualified expert who comes to quite a different conclusion. If in conflict of opinion, do not berate or belittle your colleague, however much you might privately think he or she is inviting this. There is nothing so unedifying as a verbal brawl in a courtroom. In my view expert witnesses are ambassadors for their profession.

The best strategy is to give your views clearly—repeat them if necessary. Accept calmly that you are in disagreement. Give your reasons for having reached the conclusions you did. If pressed on the other expert's views you can say that he or she will be the best person to explain his or her position.

Finally, when you have finished your examination in chief and all the cross-examination, you may remain in court if you wish. However, if you have had enough of the court for that day or have other appointments you should ask the bench or the judge if you can be 'released'. Technically, until you are released in this way you should not go. Often the solicitor who calls you as a witness will ask this for you. If you prefer this, ask them to do so when you first go to court.

Depending on the complexity of the case and the centrality of the experts' opinion, their evidence can last from a few minutes to two or three days. In care proceedings where it is proposed to remove a child or children from their parents' care, psychological evidence of the 'harm' the child has received, its 'significance' and the likely cause are very potent. These are not decisions to be taken lightly. It is correct that such views be subjected to systematic examination.

As an expert witness you will in most cases be treated with great dignity and courtesy. Most courts will not allow witnesses of any variety to be bullied. Good preparation and a proper, balanced view of the matter in hand are your best protection.

LEGAL ASPECTS OF SCHOOL NON-ATTENDANCE

School attendance in Great Britain first became free and compulsory with the Forster Education Act of 1870, though it was not until the Education Act of 1918 that half-time education was finally abolished and all elementary education made entirely free till the age of 14 years.

Section 36 of the Education Act 1944 lays the duty to ensure that every child of compulsory school age attends a school 'suitable to his age, ability and aptitude and to any special educational needs he may have' upon the parent. Thus non-school attendance is an offence committed by the parent, not the child.

This section further talks of 'efficient full time' education, but does not define 'efficient'. Nor is 'full time' defined, though the Education (Schools and Further Education) Regulations 1981 prescribe at least three hours of secular instruction per day for classes of under 8 years old and four hours for those over 8 years in schools operating on a five-day week.

Section 36 also states that the child must receive his or her education by 'regular' attendance at a school 'or otherwise'. Regular attendance is generally taken to mean attendance at times determined by the LEA and in a technical sense does not include times of arrival after the register has been closed. The 'or otherwise' option, always problematical, may prove even more so now that we have an entitlement National Curriculum under the Education Reform Act 1988. The organization Education Otherwise advises parents on their rights under this section.

There is a set procedure to be followed when the LEA wishes to take action against the parent in response to non-school attendance. Firstly under Section 37 of the Education Act 1944 the authority must serve upon the parent a notice requiring the parent to satisfy the authority within a specified period, which will not be less than fourteen days, that the child is being properly educated. This notice must also state the school likely to be named in the school attendance order.

If the parent fails to satisfy the authority it must then serve a school attendance order. If the parent names a school he or she would like the child to attend within the specified period, the LEA must decide whether the school is suitable to the child's age, ability and aptitude and to any special educational needs she or he may have. If the school is not deemed suitable because the child has special educational needs which cannot be met there, a separate procedure is followed. In this procedure (spelled out in Sections 15 and 16 of the Education Act 1981) the authority may, after giving due notice, apply to the Secretary of State for a 'direction' determining which school is to be named in the order. The decision of the Secretary of State is final.

The penalties for failure to comply are laid down under Section 40 of the 1944 Act. They are the same for children with and without special educational needs, and involve a fine. Under previous legislation (Children and Young Persons Act 1969 Section 1(2)e), the LEA could apply to the juvenile court for a care or supervision order. These specific grounds which allowed for a care order to be sought have been repealed by the Children Act 1989.

Section 36 of the Children Act empowers LEAs to apply for a new order, known as an education supervision order. This will only be granted if the court is satisfied that the child (who has to be of compulsory school age) is not being properly educated. An education supervision order cannot be made against a child already in local authority care.

Whether an LEA prosecutes the parents under Section 40 of the Education Act 1944 or applies for an education supervision order under Section 36 of the Children Act will depend upon whichever is deemed most likely to be effective. The Children Act imposes a duty on the LEA to decide whether it would be appropriate instead or in addition to apply for an education supervision order. However, if it proceeds under Section 40 it is open to the courts to direct that the LEA apply for an education supervision order.

If, in consultation with social services, the LEA determines that other action is under way and that the child's welfare is being protected in these ways, it need not comply with the order but must inform the court of its reasons. When proposing to apply for an education supervision order, the LEA is required to consult social services.

An education supervision order lasts for up to a year initially, but may be extended by up to three years at a time. It requires the supervising officer to advise, assist, befriend and give direction to the child and her or his parents in such a way that her or his proper education is secured. The supervisor is required to ascertain the wishes and feelings of the child and parents before giving directions. If a parent fails to comply with a direction he or she is liable to prosecution and can be fined up to £400. This is the same fine as can be imposed when a parent is prosecuted under Section 40 of the Education Act 1944.

If, despite the best endeavours of the supervisor, the child or parent fails to comply, the supervisor can apply for the order to be discharged. At that point the court hearing the facts of the matter can direct that the social services department investigate the circumstances of the child.

How does all this affect psychologists? Firstly we need to have an understanding of the processes described here, since we may be working with a child or family and need to advise other agencies or authorities as to an appropriate course of action. Likely issues to be considered are whether the child might have special educational needs within the meaning of the Education Act 1981 or whether the child might be school phobic. There are many complex issues surrounding school attendance at a family and school level. These issues I have explored in more detail elsewhere (Conn, 1983).

If a psychologist is involved in legal action in regard to these matters the guidelines provided in the earlier part of this chapter apply equally to these 'educational' issues. The psychologist's view is that of an expert witness and will be taken seriously by the courts.

THE ROLE OF THE GUARDIAN *AD LITEM*

Guardians *ad litem* are independent workers whose primary task is to ensure the informed representation of child subjects of civil proceedings where the central issue is the child's welfare. They are appointed by the court from specially set up panels of guardians and are answerable to the court. By professional background the vast majority of guardians are social workers who have not only good experience in working with children and families but also detailed knowledge of childcare law and legal processes.

The thrust for the appointment of guardians in care cases followed the committee of enquiry into the death of Maria Colwell in 1974. Maria died after an uncontested parental application for the discharge of a care order. In the manner of such things it was not until 1984 that local authorities in England and Wales were formally required to establish country-wide panels of guardians.

Many guardians work for the state system, usually in social services departments, and are part-time guardians. An increasing number, however, are full-time guardians practising on a self-employed basis. They must not be employed by the local authority which is taking the proceedings or is in any way a party to the proceedings.

Guardians are charged with the duty to provide 'a close independent investigation of the facts'. Under Section 42 of the Children Act 1989, guardians have a right to inspect and take copies of any records of or held by the social services department compiled in connection with the proceedings in which they are appointed. This includes any report furnished to social services by a psychologist in regard to the proceedings. Besides reading the social services record, guardians meet the child and family and interview other professionals involved. This includes psychologists where one is involved. Guardians may request the involvement of a psychologist as an independent expert witness.

Though, like all professional groups including psychologists, guardians reflect a range of professional competence, they are a powerful voice in the various forms of proceedings in which they are appointed. They are there for the child—representing his or her best interests. I strongly recommend that psychologists cooperate closely with guardians and share whatever information they have which they feel to be relevant.

WARDSHIP

I propose here to comment only very briefly on the wardship jurisdiction since, under the Children Act, there will be considerably less use of this by local authorities. Essentially, in wardship the high court becomes in effect the child's parent and has to be consulted on any important decision that a parent would have to make, such as starting a full assessment under the Education Act 1981 or being interviewed by a psychologist at all. Use of wardship both in terms of frequency and of complexity of cases involved has, in my experience, shown wide variation across local authorities.

One of the strengths of wardship is its immediacy. A child is warded by the application to make him or her a ward. Thereafter the situation is as it were frozen until a judge has time to hear the matter. A judge in wardship could make a care order if he or she felt it appropriate. This led many local authorities to ward children when they failed to prove a case in the juvenile case, in order to get a 'second go'. Often these were cases of great complexity. However, the Children Act imposes on all courts the same requirement of 'significant harm' under Section 31. Thus the high court can only make a care order if the threshold conditions laid out in this section are satisfied.

It should be noted that the Children Act limits only local authorities in the use of the wardship jurisdiction. It does not so restrict individuals' right. Some 60 per cent of wardships are not instigated by a local authority. However, it seems likely that with the availability of such new orders (under Section 8 of the Children Act) as prohibited steps orders and specific issues orders, these will be the recourse of first choice by many families.

PSYCHOLOGICAL REPORTS

The writing of reports is a much-debated issue among psychologists. Many psychologists prepare reports which they are aware will be submitted to courts without due regard to the facts that (a) the parent and child will see them, and (b) without the consent of all the parties to the proceedings—parents, child, possibly grandparents and the local authority—the report cannot be presented to the court until the case has been heard and proved. Oral evidence is thus called for. This then renders psychologists available to cross-examination on what they have said. In an age in which psychologists are increasingly taking the issue of accountability seriously, the court setting is an interesting arena in which these issues are explored.

From my experience of preparing reports for court and of giving oral evidence, I have compiled the following suggestions on good practice in writing reports. Most psychologists familiar with writing professional advice to LEAs in regard to special educational needs will not find anything too contentious here.

To begin with, the date, source and reasons for referral should be specified. You should say in what capacity you act; for instance, for a local education department, for a social services department, for a child guidance clinic or as an independent expert. If the last, you should say who instructed you; that is, who commissioned the work. You should also indicate at this stage whether you were asked to investigate any specific areas or issues, such as sexual abuse or emotional trauma.

Next it is important to indicate any relevant position or positions held, such as senior psychologist with responsibility for sensory impairment or under 5s, generic psychologist working mainly within a school system, etc. You should list your qualifications and experience. Though, among the most specifically qualified workers in the system, many psychologists are coy about specifying their academic and professional qualifications, such modesty is more misleading than touching. It can give the impression that you have no qualifications or that you have very many. By causing people unfamiliar with your discipline to guess what level of training you have had, you potentially disadvantage your client.

Having established what you were asked to do and by whom, and your qualifications for undertaking the task, it is helpful to provide the names, dates of birth and addresses of the family members you assessed and the legal status of the children—wards of court, on interim care orders, etc. It can be helpful also to indicate any placements that are relevant, such as names of schools, playgroups, etc.

Given that we seldom go cold to an interview or assessment of a child or family, it is important to list the sources of information available to you, such as discussion with foster mother, report from school, case conference minutes etc., as well as your own direct contacts with the child and family.

In writing your report it is important where possible to remember to distinguish matter of fact from matters of opinion. As indicated previously, you are entitled to furnish an opinion. Indeed it is a very important part of the evidence you provide. Thus the child's school attendance record is a matter of fact, but it may be your opinion that he or she is school phobic or is somehow entrapped in a complex family dynamic.

While it would plainly be foolish to try to summarize every report you have read or encounter you have had, it is helpful to abstract psychologically relevant aspects of the background information, especially those features to which you attach special weight, possibly such as the number of unplanned separations from the mother in the first few years of life. In regard to your own direct contact with the child or young person it is good practice to indicate where and when the child was seen, for how long, the level and quality of rapport and any special constraints, such as a noisy room or the child fearfully glancing at the door when answering questions. Similarly with other people interviewed: dates, time and durations of interviews are helpful, as is a comment on level of perceived cooperation.

If you are doing a long report with many sections or referring to many children it can be very helpful to include a summary at the end of each section. Sub-headings, such as developmental status, school reports, observations of access, etc., can be used constructively. Some people number the paragraphs, which can greatly ease referencing particular points in contested hearings. As when giving oral evidence, one should where possible avoid very complex sentence structures and the use of jargon. Any technical words which you need to use should be fully explained.

It can be immensely helpful to a court (and indeed to others) if you specify the child's social, emotional and educational or other needs from your perspective. It is a good point to include the child's views on what is happening, too. You should also indicate any issues of gender, ethnicity, culture, language, class, etc. that seem to you to have a bearing.

Having identified the child's needs it becomes relevant to indicate the sorts of support, facility or resource that are required to meet these needs. In care proceedings under Section 31 of the Children Act, you may comment as to the likelihood of the parents meeting the identified needs or the degree of help they would need in order to become able so to do. When commenting on parental competence it is also relevant to give the parents' views on what is happening, including their comments on your opinions. Again, within care proceedings you need to indicate whether from your perspective the child has suffered 'significant harm' or is likely to suffer such harm, and whether in your view this harm is 'attributable' to the quality of parenting he or she has received, or whether you feel the child or young person to be beyond parental control.

I find it helpful to include a 'conclusions' sub-heading. Within this, if it is possible to make a clear recommendation to the court, then you should do so. If you feel a care or supervision order is required (or any other order) you should say so. In keeping with the fact that it is the court which makes the judgment, it is important to address its ultimate responsibility by using a phrase such as 'It is thus my respectful advice to the court'. However, if it is not possible to come to a conclusion on the information you have, then you must honestly say so. As a psychologist you are an independent and autonomous professional. You carry the grave responsibility of the power of your professional label. The courts and the child or children have a right to expect you to resist pressure. If you need time to make more detailed assessments or observations, then you should indicate this.

Right at the end it is useful to suggest the likely effect on the child and family if your recommendations are accepted. Indeed, there is no reason why you could not say what the effects of making an order would be and the effects of not making an order.

The above sounds an onerous and rather idealized description of producing what could become a rather hefty tome. In practice this need not be so. I have said nothing about length of reports since this depends on the size and complexity of the family and the degree of investigation undertaken. Reports should, however, only be as long as they need to be. Courts receive a deluge of papers and it is hard to read and take in all the information. I have seen psychological reports one or two pages long which present with great clarity what needs to be said, and equally forty-page reports which obscure the intended meaning by the inclusion of excessive detail. Again, I have seen reports of two or three pages on a large and complex family which in their brevity trivialize the issues.

Finally, it is important to remember that the report is the part of your contribution which survives the court case. It is important to signal that it is strictly confidential. Though the insertion of the phrase at the start of the report has no legal status, I often say 'This report is restricted to those professionally concerned with the child(ren). It should not be further copied or distributed without reference to the writer.'

Good proof-reading of your report is in the mutual interest both of you as the psychologist and of the client. Well-typed or word-processed reports which are free of messy corrections will have a more 'professional' feel and be likely to be taken more seriously. Despite the reservations of Parker (1987) as to the impact of psychological reports or their selective use by magistrates, my experience is that they are increasingly called for and taken very seriously.

CONCLUSIONS

The whole area of psychologists, children and the law is rich, complex and developing. It is difficult to do justice even to part of this in a single chapter. There are many levels of analysis to consider, from the ontogenetic accounts of how an individual became the sort of person he or she is through comments on the increasing layers of organizational complexity (with our growing awareness of institutional dynamics and effects) to the most abstract levels of socio-economic and political deliberation.

Lloyd-Bostock (1988) well represents this range of levels. She notes research on eye-witness reliability, interrogation and confessions, the courtroom itself, jury selection and children and the law. On the last of these she points to evidence that psychologists are being increasingly involved in cases and legal issues concerning children. In the same year, however, Richards (1988) pointed to concern about the small degree of use that is made of psychological work in judicial decision making.

While not all psychologists work within a forensic context, all work within legal constraints. Educational psychologists, with their dual citizenship in the domains of education and psychology, are in a unique position to provide a comprehensive view on child and family matters. My own experience has led me to the view that all psychologists need a thorough familiarity with this area at initial training level and that there should be routinely available opportunities for updating at a post-experience level. There is likely to be a significant sub-group of psychologists who specialize in this work, and increasingly the courts will seek psychological input in a wider variety of cases and range of issues. The coming of the Children Act will in all probability accelerate this effect.

Given this, it is rather surprising to note how little British work is published on the practice issues, though many training courses are now introducing the major themes. One should mention the helpful article by David Cooke, 'On being an "expert" in court' (Cooke, 1990). This has many useful ideas and a good list of references. One proviso, however: Cooke, in talking about dealing with esoteric questions, picks up an idea from Blau (1984) on using a 'cue book' of notes or references. Blau was writing from an American perspective. I have never known a cue book to be used and doubt whether it would be permitted in British courts.

There are many issues with which I have been unable to deal in a chapter of this length. I have, for example, concentrated on civil proceedings rather than criminal proceedings, where the standard of proof is different. In civil proceedings, such as care proceedings, one has to show that something is the case on the 'balance of probabilities', whereas in criminal cases the requirement is 'beyond reasonable doubt'—a much tougher standard. Furthermore, I have not dealt with themes such as the detailed management of child sexual abuse (for a helpful account of the issues see Cullen *et al.*, 1990): or child eye-witness testimony (see Ceci *et al.*, 1987).

Though few areas of our professional work are likely to engender as much anxiety as the thought of appearing in court, with the correct information and appropriate preparation psychologists can make a useful and professionally rewarding contribution. Many of the children whose welfare is decided by the courts are among the most vulnerable in our system. Making the best of our professional skills available to them to secure their futures is the task in hand.

REFERENCES

Aries, P. (1962) *Centuries of Childhood*. Harmondsworth: Penguin.

Blau, T.H. (1984) 'Your day in court', in Blau, T.H. (ed.) *The Psychologist as Expert Witness*. New York: Wiley.

Blom-Cooper, L., Harding, J. and McC. Milton, Elizabeth (1987) *A Child in Mind*. London Borough of Greenwich.

Ceci, S.J., Toglia, M.P. and Ross, D.F. (eds) (1987) *Children's Eyewitness Memory*. New York: Springer-Verlag.

Conn, W. (1983) 'Truancy: the ball in whose court?', in Geach, H. and Szwed, E. (eds), *Providing Civil Justice for Children*. London: Edward Arnold.

Cooke, D. (1990) 'Being an "expert" in court', *The Psychologist: Bulletin of the British Psychological Society*, **3**, 216–21.

Cullen, C., Frude, N., Peake, A., Sambrooks, J. and Stratton, P. (1990) 'Psychologists and child sexual abuse: the report of a working party', *The Psychologist: Bulletin of the British Psychological Society*, **8**, 344–8.

Freeman, M. D. A. (1983) 'The concept of children's rights', in Geach, H. and Szwed, E. (eds), *Providing Civil Justice for Children*. London: Edward Arnold.

Gudjonsson, G. H. (1985) 'Psychological evidence in court: results from the British Psychological Society survey', *Bulletin of the British Psychological Society*, **38**, 327–30.

Lloyd-Bostock, S. (1988) 'The benefits of legal psychology: possibilities, practice and dilemmas', *British Journal of Psychology*, **79**, 417–40.

McCloskey, M. E., Egeth, H. and McKenna, J. (eds) (1986) 'The ethics of expert testimony', *Law and Human Behaviour*, **10** (1 and 2) (special issue).

Mead, N. and Wolfenstein, M. (1955) *Childhood in Contemporary Cultures*. Chicago: University of Chicago Press.

Parker, H. (1987) 'The use of expert reports in juvenile and magistrates' courts', in Gudjonsson, G. and Drinkwater, J. (eds), *Psychological Evidence in Court-Issues in Criminological and Legal Psychology*, No. 11. Leicester: British Psychological Society.

Richards, M. (1988) 'Developmental psychology and family law: a discussion paper', *British Journal of Developmental Psychology*, **6**, 169–81.

Chapter 11

Boundary Issues: Multidisciplinary Working in New Contexts—Implications for Educational Psychology Practice

Philippa Russell

INTRODUCTION

The current debate about definitions of professional roles and the nature of collaborative and interprofessional working is not new. The Court Report (for Child Health Services: Court, 1976) and the Warnock Report on special educational needs (Warnock, 1978) together emphasized the need to work with children in a holistic and truly collaborative way. However, over a decade further on, we have seen radical changes in legislation which have tended to reinforce the rhetoric, rather than the reality, of teamwork and the blurring of identities between different professional groups. The biggest unifier of all professionals has probably been the generally shared concept (albeit varied in interpretation) of 'parents as partners'. Indeed Britain, a country which has neither a formal constitution nor a bill of rights, has introduced a whole range of new duties on statutory agencies and professionals to satisfy their customers and to reinforce 'parent power'. Again, although the 1987 Select Committee (House of Commons Education, Science and Arts Committee, 1987) noted that there 'is widespread support for the comprehensive nature of assessment processes under the 1981 Act', the *comprehensive* nature of all human services in an increasingly complex and litigious society has been more and more difficult to achieve. Indeed, 'parent power' itself often leaves parents bewildered and powerless as they struggle to understand complex procedures and wonder which will be the 'best buy' in a market-orientated culture.

The outlook for educational psychology is not, however, all bleak in this brave new world. All other professions, including education, medicine and social services, are similarly undergoing fundamental changes. The 1981 Act, for all its bureaucracy and lack of resources, has forced new groups of professionals to work together. It has also, by removing the old convenient 'categories', created a new sense of individual needs and the 'packages of care' which form the basis of the new community care arrangements. It is interesting to reflect how many major pieces of recent legislation affecting children have contained duties for a number of professional groups and services—and require collaborative working as an integral part of implementation. The Education Act 1981 was probably the first. But the NHS and Community Care Act will also necessitate joint assessment and management by all three statutory agencies, with inbuilt mechanisms for independent inspection and quality control. The Children Act 1989, the most important piece of childcare legislation of this century, is an act for the *whole* local authority (housing, recreation, leisure and education as well as social services). It also lays duties on child health services, and the statutory assessment orders require a range of professional expert witnesses from *all* professions to attend court hearings on demand. The Register of Disabled Children will, according to the guidance, best be developed as a joint endeavour between health, education and social services. However implemented, the Act will challenge all professional services to examine their own ethical and referral codes and to consider how the best interests of children can be met in a more coherent way. The first step on this path to collaboration will undoubtedly be a definition of boundaries so that they may then be passed with impunity and without asset stripping.

WORKING TOGETHER

The concept of joint working with children with special needs has long been an important principle of any service, whether within health, education or social services. But, as the Department of Health's review of English local authorities' childcare statements (HMSO, 1990d) succinctly noted,

> Simply asserting the need for cooperation does not of course produce it (although it may well be a necessary state in achieving it), and research and inspections have repeatedly indicated that 'departmentalism' at the local level is a persistent obstacle to effective working with children and families. (p. 31)

Similarly, the House of Commons Select Committee's Report on the Education of Under-fives (House of Commons Education, Science and Arts Committee, 1989) commented that 'There is no evidence on a national scale of the high degree of cooperation necessary to achieve the best use of existing resources . . . or a clear collective view of the shape of the desired comprehensive services.' Evidence to the same committee by the Association of County Councils found that about 33 per cent of their membership had some form of central coordinating mechanism, designed to cross boundaries and produce the 'clear collective' view advocated by the Select Committee. But the ACC did not refer to either child health or the voluntary sectors, a fact underlined by the National Children's Bureau's Report *Working Together* (Pugh, 1988). This survey found that coordination between all the stakeholders in young children's services was very variable, with joint management indicated in only about 15 per cent of cases.

However, there is ample informal evidence of individual and indeed service commitment to developing new ways of working, which cross boundaries and permit sharing of expertise in the best interests of children. The Department of Health (1990d) report on childcare policy statements quotes one authority which has shown a consistent attempt to break down agency barriers. The concept of cooperation is built into every stage of the policy statement, which includes a *separate* section setting out how the authority works with other departments and agencies. This lists major 'domains' for collaboration as:

(a)   general interagency working;
(b)   education;
(c)   housing;
(d)   health;
(e)   recreational services;
(f)   borough solicitor;
(g)   voluntary and consumer groups;
(h)   probation service and police.

The list is not comprehensive, but it represents an attempt to achieve a clearly thought-out and articulated policy for making collaboration work; for breaking across boundaries and for specifying some of the *contexts* for collaboration—for example, joint planning teams and working groups—which are essential ingredients in achieving true collaboration.

Planning for the 1990s, and for a growing awareness of the interdependence of all services working for children, will produce some major challenges. The Department of Health (1990a), in *The Care of Children: Principles and Practice in Regulations and Guidance*, notes that 'the various departments of a local authority (eg health, housing, education and social services) should co-operate to provide an integrated service and range of resources *even when such co-operation is not specifically required by law*' (p.19). But the same guidance also comments that 'Co-operation between organisations, departments *and individuals* is crucial in the provision of protection for vulnerable children and also in ensuring proper use of available resources.' In effect, planning systems around total services will be ineffective without the willingness of individuals to work within strategic frameworks and to work more flexibly with their counterparts in other agencies.

Changes in local government and within the local accountability of a number of services (in particular education, through local management of schools and the ability of schools to opt for grant-maintained status) mean that *individuals* are likely to take on new significance as virtual 'ecosystems' within their own agency. The longer-term impact of local management of schools will almost certainly be the fragmentation and disempowerment of the LEA as the coordinator and planner of services. Similar changes in the health service (with the emergence of budget holding GPs and hospital trusts) are likely to reduce the overall influence of the District Health Authorities (DHAs). In the social services, the purchaser/provider mode in both children's services and community care will necessitate new relationships with the private and voluntary sector, and the introduction of the concept of 'value for money' and 'purchaser/ provider' into professional deployment.

Will it really matter? The government White Paper on *Caring for People* (Department of Health, 1990b) claims that greater individuality in service planning and consumer choice will improve quality of care. The local authority will develop an 'enabler role'. The new concept of 'care management' is defined as 'a progressive separation of the tasks of assessment from those of service provision in order to focus on needs, where possible having the tasks carried out by separate staff' and 'a shift of influence from those providing to those purchasing service' (Department of Health, 1990c). The separation of assessment from provision has theoretically been the cornerstone of the Education Act 1981. Despite its problems, bureaucracy and the endless wrangles about resources, the 'statementing' process provides an opportunity for *joint* assessment of need in conjunction with the consumer, and for reconciliation processes between different professional agencies about the most appropriate provision. But the 'purchaser/provider' role of community care (which in many instances will provide for the same, albeit older, customers as the Education Act 1981) carries problems. Firstly, assessment is a dynamic and continuous process. 'Snapshot' diagnoses are seldom appropriate, and educational progress is best achieved by an interaction between continuous assessment and the child's home and learning environment. A danger of the purchaser/provider model is that marketing will indeed take over, with consortia of independent consultants—be they educational psychologists, social workers, clinical psychologists, speech therapists, etc.—who are usually brought in on the 'send for the fire brigade' principle, and whose essentially one-off, short-term contracts give them little time for the nuances and timescale of good teamwork within the present local education authority (LEA) special needs system.

Attractive as the idea of individual case management may be, the 1990s will pose major challenges for professionals like educational psychologists who have increasingly worked with other professionals (particularly in schools) as well as with individual children. A few individuals are suggesting that the growing constraints on working across LEA resource policies vindicate a more independent stance. *Parents* may have greater choice in selecting an adviser with whom they feel comfortable. Indeed there is growing (albeit mainly anecdotal) evidence that many parents are turning to private assessment by educational psychologists and other professionals. While the paucity of LEA resources and the waiting list for assessment may play major roles, part of the new culture of individuality is being expressed by parents wishing to have control of services and the feeling that private assessment must be more honest (since naturally without resource overtones) than that provided by the local authority.

But a move to more private use of professional services has ominous overtones for the development of genuine interagency services. The principle of a good-quality family support service, like Honeylands at the Royal Devon and Exeter Hospital (Brimblecombe and Russell, 1987; Russell, 1990a), is that *joint* working and information sharing is crucial if parents and children are to be helped. The use of private services, however competent, means that records are likely to be inconsistent; there will be few opportunities for team building; and, above all else, there will be major debates about accountability. Both the Education Act 1981 and the Children Act 1989 focus upon the best interests of the child. The Children Act, in its preamble, highlights 'the child's welfare as the paramount concern', but goes on to emphasize the complementary 'primary importance of parents in the child's welfare'. In some instances there will be clear lines of duty towards children or parents, but in others the lines may be more thinly drawn. In the USA and Canada, parents seem most likely to seek private assessment and support if they are firstly in a position to employ their own professional advisers and understand the process for using an independent opinion—and where they have a very clear idea of the service they want. Should educational psychologists, and other professionals with relevant expertise, allow themselves to be drawn into parents' battles for particular provision? The Higashi school for autistic children in Boston, USA, or conductive education in Budapest, or a residential school for specific learning difficulties in the Home Counties *may* provide a unique learning experience for the child concerned. But is it also part of the new market economy for psychologists to remind parents of the existence of other options, or constantly reiterate their independence from both parent and LEA in the dispute in question?

TRANSLATING POLICY INTO PRACTICE

Crossing professional boundaries is not only about individual professional practice. It also entails anticipating and indeed creating policy trends and determining the future shape of services. Educational psychology is in many ways a new profession for children with special needs. As one mother of a child with severe learning difficulties commented succinctly at a recent voluntary council seminar, 'when my [16-year-old] daughter was small, the *psychiatrist* had the power. Now it is the psychologist who dots i's and crosses t's on her statement. It's not surprising parents don't see any difference—they're all men with beards and briefcases anyway!' But professionals are not all 'beards and brief-cases', or indeed any of the other stereotypes which attach themselves to what are considered to be powerful occupations. In reality parents (and indeed teachers) often misunderstand the roles—and hence the boundaries—of a range of professional func-tions, because both have the 'hands on' experience of the difficulty but lack access to the wider strategic thinking which determines the professional identity. As Tharp and Gallimore noted (1988),

> Educational reformers tend to focus on ' . . . matters remote from the practices of teaching and school (or) on the daily experiences of teachers before and after they enter the profes-sion. Ignoring such details and their effective implementation puts even the soundest of (educational) reforms at risk'. (p. 3)

In effect, if teachers and parents—the main stakeholders in special education—fail to understand the role of the educational psychologist or indeed the context within which he or she works, then confusion will reign and problems and misconceptions persist.

To some extent misconceptions flourish because of the way in which policy itself develops. Barbara Keogh (1990) notes that:

> an appealing and persistent fantasy of many educational researchers is that policy change is based on empirical findings. The fantasy emerges from the analytic rationalistic tradition, coupled with a genuine motivation by researchers to improve the state of the field. From this perspective policy should follow research and change should be founded on evidence. Examination of major shifts in educational policy suggest quite a different scenario, how-ever. Change results from social-political concerns and most policy decisions precede rather than follow research. The sweeping changes in policy and practice contained in Public Law 94.142 emerged from civil rights issues and had a constitutional rather than empirical foundation. Similarly many of the changes proposed under the regular education initiative were derived from values and beliefs rather than data. (p. 186)

Barbara Keogh's perspective also reflects the culture and context of change in the United Kingdom, where attitudes to parent participation, integration and indeed to multi-professional collaboration arise from fundamental beliefs about human rights, participation and the more open approach to information of the past decade. If, in fact, research and evaluation *follow* changing attitudes to services and the people working in them, then the role of educational psychologists—often seen as thrust to prominence by the 1981 Act statementing processes—will also change and boundaries slip in an almost accidental way. The civil rights perspective means that, according to anecdotal evidence, parents are most likely to seek any private second opinions or professional advocacy from this professional group. Their choice of educational psychologists as advocates and advisers indicates not only the importance of the profession to parents, but also their perceptions of the ability of educational psychology services to influence the system and to achieve what parents want. Indeed, paediatricians and their health services colleagues were regarded and used in the same way in the pre-1981 Act era. Barbara Keogh, reflecting on the process of turning policy into practice, went on to note that:

> policy reflects socio-political conditions and that policy change precedes research is in many ways a good thing . . . Given the slow pace of research, the penchant for researchers for precision of design and rigor of analysis, and the tendency of most researchers to be cautious in inference and generalisation, it seems fair to say that we will not make major progress in educational reform if we wait for comprehensive data sets to drive our decision. (p. 190)

She goes on to speculate that Public Law 94:142 could not have happened if the pace of change had been delayed for verification by research. (Public Law 94:142 is the major US legislation regulating the provision of education to children with special educational needs. It favours integration and provides for these children to be supported in mainstream education.)

Although her observations fit neatly into the UK perspective, they fail to acknowledge the pain and stress of being in the 'front line' of such social change, when the professional agency may have doubts about some policy developments but be unable to wait for verification or external evaluation. In the case of educational psychology, there has been a wide public debate about a shift to resource-led statementing and the dilemma of the independent assessment coming into collision course with the local authority policy on provision. In practice, using the social change model of Barbara Keogh, we do not have time to wait to assess the extent to which economic realities and the impact of local management of schools are limiting and setting boundaries on practice. The perceptions and fears of parents are sufficient to widen the debate and to place a higher premium on the so-called independent (and usually privately commissioned) assessment.

One consequence of such perceptions, whether or not accurate, is that the fantasy becomes part of the perceived truth. If parents perceive the educational psychologist as the 'poodle' of his or her local authority and the restrictive, centrally held budgets under LMS, then artificial boundaries will be created whether or not they are real. The educational psychologist may be felt to be less available and less independent. He or she may be reduced from a developmental to a 'fire brigade' role and in effect become corralled by low expectations rather than by reality.

Perhaps most worryingly, he or she may be seen as more desirable if 'independent' and personally hired by the parents or indeed by the school or service. While the independent second opinion is built into every service in the UK (with independent social workers now becoming more common), the theoretical assumption that 'independence' is synonymous with 'privately financed' is a confusion. The independent educational psychologist can be open and honest and give sufficient time to his or her task. But the new boundaries may become 'ring-fenced' with other professions, which will not automatically exchange records, information or team discussions out of the context of the local or health authority. In effect, freedom from boundaries and a more individual service may actually be self-isolating and confusing, with a multiplicity of 'independent' contractors inevitably competing with each other for clients and resources, and cut off from many of their interprofessional contacts.

THE NEW MARKET PLACE

As noted above, the traditional perceptions of accountability and professional boundaries have been changing over a number of years. Such changes have been not only from within professions but also in the context within which professionals have to work. Geoff Lindsay (1990) notes that a wider-ranging view is now necessary because:

> First, government policies have had radical effects on key institutions with which psychologists have traditionally worked. The reforms in the health service are a case in point. For example the development of hospital trusts, whether they proceed or not or in what number, has caused clinical psychologists to consider their future development vis-à-vis employers. (p. 503)

A comparable radical approach to the funding and organization of the education service has had a similar effect on educational psychologists. LMS has led to the delegation of a large proportion of funding of education from LEA control to school control. While LEAs have retained central control of their psychological services, this could change.

Certainly the recent report by HMI concerning educational psychologists notes that they 'will need to ensure that they are in a strong position to provide positive and flexible responses to meet the challenging demands that will be made upon them in the next few years' (HMI, 1990). Concerns about the future ability of educational psychologists to work across boundaries and on an authority-wide basis are similar to those concerns being expressed by other professional groups affected by the 'changing institutions' referred to above.

Gerald Wistow, in evidence to the Select Committee on Community Care (1990), voices similar views:

> In a more market-orientated economy of community care, there will be much less emphasis on collaboration and joint planning and correspondingly more emphasis on negotiation, bargaining and doing business together. It has of course always been the case that inter-agency relationships are more frequently founded upon processes of bargaining and exchange rather than disinterested and rational planning. However, there may be strong advantages in being much more explicit about the fact. (p. 29)

He saw such explicitness as leading to greater honesty about 'the kind of bargaining chips' each side possessed, but also noted the need for an internal audit by each agency of their own resources, reflecting that: 'Until we can analyse the full range of health and local authorities will be able to bring to this new market place . . . it will be impossible to draw up a final balance sheet on the consequences for inter-service relationships.' (p. 38)

In effect, to make the new interagency services work, each collaborative venture must begin with an internal analysis of the relative resources and conditions of each participant. The same community care report takes the discussion wider, noting that collaboration is often seen as a 'macro' activity between statutory authorities and institutions. In practice collaborative working may depend much more on the 'micro' relationships between individuals in health, education and social services. The report highlighted the importance of assessment as the key trans-boundary activity, but expressed concern that 'the potential for conflict with professionals who do have that expertise [to carry out assessment] but have not been assigned a lead role is a matter of concern' (p. 37). Although collaboration as a positive exercise is widely discussed and promoted within all professions (including educational psychology), the Select Committee took a less sanguine view than some of the ability of current professional agencies to work together. In particular the committee was alarmed at the number of witnesses who emphasized the need to have clear, formal procedures for the reconciliation of professional disputes over 'best services'. Partnership between professionals was obviously not assumed to be universally present and the 'equivalent expertise' advocated by Sheila Wolfendale (1987, 1988, 1989) for *parents*' views was not regarded as applying to professional colleagues!

CHILDREN IN NEED AND THEIR FAMILIES—A NEW APPROACH

> Better co-ordination does not necessarily require a unified service. The purpose may be served by a network of facilities linked through common admission policies or close working relationships. What is important—*and what the provisions of the Children Act should help to secure*—is that the pattern of co-ordination should take full account of local needs and opportunities and should be supported by local policies and management structures. (Rumbold, 1991, p. 30)

The implementation of the Children Act 1989 will not only formally acknowledge the most fundamental review of childcare legislation in this century. It will also have radical implications for a wide range of professionals (including educational psychologists) who may not have seen themselves as playing a primary role in the enactment of duties relating to general childcare issues. The Children Act, as I have already noted, is an Act for the *whole* authority—housing, education, leisure and recreation as well as social services. The Act is based upon five basic principles:

(a) the welfare of the child;
(b) partnership with parents (with an emphasis upon voluntary and participative agreements rather than formal procedures);
(c) a recognition of the importance of families, and of supporting them in their caring role;
(d) the centrality of the views of the child and parents. Local authorities have a duty to ascertain and take due account of these wishes and feelings;
(e) corporate responsibility—the local authority and health authority have to work together.

The emphasis on responsiveness to consumer views (and the need to work cooperatively in assessing such views) and to consumer needs, and on acting upon them, has overtones of the 1981 Act. The same Act gives early warning signs about the problems of developing a sense of corporate identity for children and families without clarification of roles, duties, resources and professional identities.

The potential of the Children Act is perhaps best illustrated in the new definition of 'children in need' (Section 17) as:

(a) those unlikely to achieve or maintain or have the opportunity for achieving or maintaining a reasonable standard of health or development without the provision of services;
(b) those whose health or development is likely to be significantly impaired or further impaired without the provision of such services;
(c) those who are disabled.

The range of the wording is such that a local authority would have considerable scope to widen or restrict the number of children for whom it provided services. Children in need, once identified, have greater rights to services such as day care than children not in need. The local authority has a *duty* to support the former, a *power* to support the latter. But there are major questions about who will be regarded as being 'in need'. There are no formal statutory assessment procedures, as under the Education Act 1981. Assessment orders within the more voluntary partnership envisaged by the Children Act will be a last resort, and linked to risk of significant harm. Children with disabilities are, however, clearly spelt out, albeit with the old, rigid and distinctly non-developmental definition of the National Assistance Act 1978.

In order to identify children in need, local authorities will be required to keep a register of such children. The draft guidance expresses a hope that such a register will be jointly instituted by health, education and social services. But issues about referrals, the label of 'register of disabilities' and anxieties about false positives will pose new dilemmas for education and indeed for the health services. Traditionally psychologists have not been closely involved with their social services counterparts. Sonia Jackson at the University of Bristol (1987) and others have highlighted the parlous inattention to education as a key component in decision making about placements for children in care. But the Children Act offers opportunities to cross that particular boundary. Local authorities must now provide for children with disabilities 'services to minimise the effect of their disabilities and give them the opportunity to lead lives which are as normal as possible'. Historically social services have played a small role in providing services for children with disabilities—the history of health service leadership left a legacy of anxiety about the extent to which children with special needs could be integrated within ordinary children's services—and the statutory and public duties relating to child abuse have deflected hard-pressed care in many instances. But the Children Act, as the Rumbold Committee notes, offers an opportunity for a common agenda for all children.

The register may be seen as stigmatizing, negative and inappropriate for the 1990s. But unless children with special needs are identified at an early stage, early intervention cannot be offered, and problems may proliferate and only emerge when the child is actually in school. The register (with its accompanying duties of social services to inform parents about all local services, as well as to provide day care and other support services) does offer an opportunity for joint planning. At least, it may ensure that social services departments take a more proactive role in Section 5 assessments. It should also ensure that educational psychology services could achieve what Fish aspired to (1985), namely the input of psychological services into day care, playgroups and other non-LEA provision from a very early age.

The current preoccupation with difficult behaviour as the major issue in management of day-care services indicates a gap in the provision. But social services will have to acknowledge the unique contribution of educational psychological services to identification, assessment and problem solving on traditional social services territory. Equally LEAs will have to acknowledge the intense, personal and effective resource which educational psychologists can offer, with appropriate management and other support, in much more diverse settings in the early years. One consequence of LMS and the reduction in funds held centrally in LEAs is that the practice of educational psychologists working within other agency settings is actually likely to decrease—with the 'send for a fire brigade' approach being invoked when existing provision has broken down. But processes and procedures of the Children Act may at least ensure that the more careful assessment of 'children in need' will promote better mutual consultation and planning around individual children.

An important aspect of the Children Act, on which educational psychologists will have a unique perspective, is that of talking to children and ensuring that they participate in decision making. Indeed, the rights of the child are so enshrined in the Act that children can refuse permission for a medical examination if they are considered to understand the nature of the request and be able to give such informed consent. The notion of consent is a vexed one. A child with severe learning difficulties might very well be able to consent to treatment—or resist it—if somebody could sign in Makaton. An educational psychologist, knowing a child in the school context, may well be the most likely 'expert witness' in terms of deciding whether that child has consented to a particular intervention, or to assess the level of comprehension of a complex decision about lifestyle, custody, etc. which has to be made.

Most importantly, in terms of statutory procedures and the formal assessment orders which may be sought at the end of the line when there are serious doubts about the welfare of the child, the educational psychologist may—and probably should—be one of the professionals more frequently summoned to court as an important expert witness on the child's needs. Although appearing in court may not seem immediately relevant to definitions of boundaries, the US experience is that influential professionals—frequently the educational psychologist—spend an increasing amount of time in court solving other people's boundary and resource problems. For example, an educational psychologist may be called as a witness not only about a particular programme of study, or choice of school, but about the additional needs for physiotherapy or speech therapy, for family support or for referral to specialist services such as audiologists. The parents, who will increasingly call upon educational psychologists, will see the psychologist as their advocate and as representing the interests of the whole child.

THE NEW CHANGE AGENTS—PARENTS AS PARTNERS

Perhaps the greatest potential for positive change in resolving interprofessional boundary issues has come through the changing role of parents. They have the unique role (and opportunity) to facilitate, to interrelate and ultimately to challenge where and how they receive services. But the cost of such change can be heavy. In the new era of theoretical empowerment, parents acquire responsibilities and duties as well as opportunities.

The Warnock Report (1978) heralded a new era for 'parents as partners' in special educational procedures. The concept of parent participation was written into the Education Act 1981, with its emphasis on collaboration and informed consent. If the rhetoric has not always matched the reality, the failure has been not in lack of intent but rather in the timescale of acknowledging that voluntary and statutory services must work together to provide parents with the advice, training, support and respect needed in order to become full partners. The work of Sheila Wolfendale (1988), Robert Cameron (1989) and others, who have developed new strategies for helping parents to use their expertise and observational skills during assessment, has reflected what Warnock forecast as a 'sea change' in attitudes and expectations—not just about disability and special needs, but about the feasibility of families contributing directly to the assessment process. The new partnership goes wider than assessment. The 1986 and 1988 Education Acts have been hailed as 'empowering' parents in other directions. Research from Plowden onwards has shown the importance of bringing parents into schools.

But there are threats as well as opportunities in some of the new procedures. John Tomlinson (1988), writing about parental power and the National Curriculum, reflected that 'parents now may be asked to adopt the role of inquisitor and monitor of the education service, teachers and schools, and to use the new complaints procedures all in the exercise of consumer sovereignty' (p. 8). Circular 22/89, on assessment and statements, clearly states the need to develop a new 'frankness and openness' between parents and professionals. The same circular notes the 'close co-operation' between parents and the statutory services,

> with a thorough understanding by each of the participants of the part which they and others play in the procedures. Authorities may need to give thought to arrangements which assist families and maintain effectiveness in relationships with the various services. (p. 8)

In effect, *all* professional groups will need to give careful consideration to the conditions for effective partnership, and to ensure that parents are supported in exercising their new powers, if Tomlinson's fears of 'inquisitorial monitoring' are to be avoided.

The outlook, despite parental concerns about the implications of the National Curriculum, open enrolment, LMS and decline of resources, is not all negative. The DES White Paper, *Better Schools* (1985), emphasizes that quality in education must be everyone's business. But the 'business' is more complex than it has been for many years. The tension between centrally directed education policy and devolution to individual schools (which may be less benevolent and harder to challenge on policy issues than LEAs) must have repercussions for parents, whether or not they are exercising their own personal powers under the 1981 and 1988 Acts. Many parent organizations wonder whether parents of children with special educational needs will have the time or energy to assume new responsibilities as governors and managers of schools, where the partnership may assume the new role of a quasi-business enterprise, with parents possibly employing professional advice as well as using it.

Most importantly, the ability of the LEA to advise and orchestrate a range of complex support and advisory services may be greatly limited. Attainment targets, programmes of study and assessment are intended to offer parents, schools, LEAs and the government clearer and comparable information about the achievements of pupils and schools in a way which can improve performance individually and collectively. However, the assessment arrangements of the 1988 Act are essentially 'in school', and many parents of children with severe learning difficulties are critically aware of the significance of the need for multi-professional assessment, the *joint* endeavour, to ensure their children develop to their full potential. Boundaries must be crossed if the 1981 Act is to be effective.

Despite criticisms from the House of Commons Select Committee (1987) and the Institute of Education's DES-funded research into the implementation of the 1981 Act (Goacher *et al.*, 1988), most parents would agree that things have got better. The 'effective relationships with the various services' endorsed by Circular 22/89 are being improved. Parents are playing a more active role and there is growing commitment to seeking their views actively. Many parents have commented on the greater specificity of the USA's 'individual educational programmes', with their clear curricular statements.

A parental campaign to have such a curricular component in the 1981 Act's statement of special educational needs was rejected as the Bill went through Parliament. The 1988 Act restores this balance, with statements having a clear curriculum relevance and with any modifications or exemptions to be clearly specified.

Now, however, many parents fear that the curriculum content of the statement may be over-cautious and that (despite government reassurances) the inherent flexibility of the National Curriculum may not be tested. The new arrangements may seem particularly threatening to children who are in full or part-time mainstream placements. Schools and their governors that are preoccupied with the new curriculum may be less sympathetic to children with very specific learning difficulties. Scarce resources may not be stretched to include such children, who may be seen as lowering overall academic achievements at a particular school. Governors (unless particularly well informed about special educational needs) may resist the acceptance of children with any special needs unless the financial resources and teaching implications are fully explored.

Parents may therefore find themselves seeking professional advocates in terms not only of challenging the LEA but of actually negotiating their child's programme of work and fair share of resources *within the school*. If one consequence of LMS and SSLMS is an 'archipelago' system, in which individual schools (and their governors) function more as a federation than as a whole authority, not only will professionals like educational psychologists have to establish 'diplomatic relations' with a widely disparate and sometimes slightly hostile network of individual schools, but they will rely even more on the customer parents to inform and advise them on the nature of a particular establishment or service and the needs of children.

DEVELOPING A WHOLE-SCHOOL POLICY—PARENTS AND PROFESSIONALS IN TANDEM

Parental involvement as described by Sheila Wolfendale (1989) and others will be ineffective unless there is clarity about the role and contribution of parents. The National Curriculum Council (1989) envisages an 'atmosphere of encouragement, acceptance, respect for achievements and sensitivity to individual needs' (p. 7) occurring only if there is 'continuous communication with parents and mutual parent–teacher support' (p. 8). The same report from the Task Group looks to '*home–school partnerships* which enable families to support the teaching programmes for the child with special educational needs' (p. 8). To achieve such partnerships it will be essential to have coherent school and interprofessional policies.

Parent involvement and parent advocacy will never be easy. Circular 22/89, in Section 20, stresses the need 'for parents to have written guidelines to assist them in their contribution to assessment' (p. 8). It emphasizes that such information should be in 'straightforward plain language' and that parents should have a right to bring 'an adviser or friend and translators for support at meetings' (p. 15) if they so wish. The assessment procedures to be introduced for the 1988 Act with regard to the National Curriculum will similarly need to acknowledge the personal anxieties and concerns of parents—and to acknowledge that links to the child's wider home and social environment will be crucial in achieving progress.

There are some important lessons, however, to learn from the positive initiatives of early intervention programmes with children with special needs and their families. A major consequence of the initiatives in the education of children from disadvantaged backgrounds has been the strong relationship between home background and early learning. Corresponding research into the impact of the birth of a disabled child upon family lifestyles and expectations and of parental involvement in early educational strategies have shown the need to acknowledge family stress, to provide a counselling element in all professional services and to develop parental competence and confidence in bringing up a child who is 'different'.

Robert Cameron (1989), considering 'teaching parents to teach children', has noted the importance of acknowledging that parents have two primary educational roles when a child has a disability or special education need. Firstly parents need to understand how to teach a child everyday life skills. Secondly they need help in managing difficult or disruptive behaviour which the child may acquire. Since the mid-1970s, the Portage home-teaching model has become increasingly popular, and it has been estimated (Cameron, 1989; Russell, 1990b) that there are now over three hundred schemes in the United Kingdom. Portage is characterized by focusing upon helping parents to teach children with special needs within their own homes, and by involving families in selecting their own education goals.

As Cameron (1989) and others have emphasized, the central feature of Portage is the home teaching, which has three key features, namely:

(a)   using direct contact people (especially parents) to teach the child;
(b)   using an individual teaching programme which is based upon a realistic assessment of the child's existing skills;
(c)   providing *positive* monitoring and recording procedures.

One of the major successes of a good Portage scheme is that it permits information to travel between parents and professionals and provides a detailed database on a child which can be utilized by subsequent service providers. A major criticism of current special needs programmes is that they frequently fail to manage the transfer of relevant information between families and different networks of professionals. Portage additionally provides a 'key worker' approach in offering support to parents through a familiar individual. It offers, therefore, an important model for transcending traditional boundaries and including parents not only in strategy but also in implementation of intervention and assessment for children with special needs.

In 1986 a group of parents organized a conference for professionals on assessment and the 1981 Act. All the professionals were required to go through 'The Maze', which introduced them to a parents'-eye view of assessment, its pitfalls and its problems. 'The Maze' has now been published by Camden Elfrida Rathbone as a resource to be used during the assessment process. The project clearly demonstrates the importance of acknowledging that assessment is not

> just about the allocation of scarce resources. The Maze is concerned with another dimen-
> sion . . . There is nothing really frightening about listening to parents talk about their
> children, hearing what they want for them and acting on what they have to say. Doing that
> will make it possible to design services sensitive to the needs of young people and their
> families. (Nelson, 1989).

Listening to parents is, in effect, the most important access point to both the 1981 and

1988 Education Acts. It is also a salutary reminder that, in the civil rights context of the 1990s, parents may actually be as much part of the solution as part of the problem. Many boundary issues in professional practice will resolve themselves if it does prove possible to establish new partnerships with parents. And, in terms of increasingly scarce resources, the consumer can influence the elected members who control budgets and release resources. We neglect the potential of parents to be part of the professional network at our peril.

REFERENCES

Association of County Councils (1989) *Evidence to the House of Commons Education, Science and Arts Committee's Enquiry into the Nursery Education*. ACC.

Brimblecombe, F. and Russell, P. (1987) *Honeylands: Developing a Support Service for Families with Handicapped Children*. National Children's Bureau.

Cameron, R. (1989) 'Teaching parents to teach children: the Portage approach to special needs', in Jones, N. (ed.), *Special Educational Review*, vol. 1. Basingstoke: Falmer Press.

Court, D. (chair) (1976) *Fit for the Future*. Report of the Committee on Child Health Services. Department of Health/HMSO.

Department of Education and Science (1985) *Better Schools*. London: HMSO.

Department of Health (1990a) *The Care of Children: Principles and Practice in Regulations and Guidance*. HMSO.

Department of Health (1990b) *Caring for People*. HMSO.

Department of Health (1990c) *Community Care in the Next Decade and Beyond*. HMSO.

Department of Health (1990d) *Child Care Policy: Putting It in Writing*. A Review of English Local Authorities' Child Care Policy Statement. SSI/HMSO.

Fish, J. (chair) (1985) *Equal Educational Opportunities for All?* Report of the Committee of Inquiry into Special Educational Provision. ILEA.

Goacher, B., Evans, J., Welton, J. and Wedell, K. (1988) *Policy and Provision for Special Educational Needs: Implementing the 1981 Education Act*. London: Cassell.

HMI (1990) *Educational Psychology Services in England, 1988-9*. DES.

House of Commons Education, Science and Arts Committee (1987) *Enquiry into the Implementation of the 1981 Act*. HMSO.

House of Commons Education, Science and Arts Committee (1989) *Enquiry into Nursery Education*. London.

Jackson, S. (1987) 'The education of children in care'. Bristol Papers in Applied Social Studies No. 1, University of Bristol.

Keogh, B. (1990) 'Narrowing the gap between policy and practice', *Exceptional Children*, **57**(2).

Lindsay, G. (1990) 'Accepting the challenge', *The Psychologist*, 3 (11), 485.

Pugh, G. (1988) *Services for Under-Fives. Developing a Coordinated Approach*. National Children's Bureau.

National Curriculum Council (1989) *A Curriculum for All: Special Educational Needs in the National Curriculum Council*. York: National Curriculum Council.

Nelson, S. (1989) *The Maze* (series of cards). London: Camden Elfrida Rathbone.

Rumbold, A. (chair) (1991) *Starting with Quality*. Report of Committee of Inquiry into the Quality of Educational Experience Offered to 3 and 4 year olds. London: HMSO.

Russell, P. (1990a) 'Honeylands: developing a service for families', *Children and Society*, Spring 1990, **4** (1).

Russell, P. (1990b) 'Policy and practice for your children with special educational needs: changes and challenges', in Wolfendale, S. (ed.) *Support for Learning*. Slough: NFER.

Tharp, R. G., and Gallimore, R. (1988) *Rousing Minds to Life*. Cambridge University Press.

Tomlinson, J. (1988) 'Curriculum and market: are they compatible?', in Haviland, J. (ed.) *Take Care, Mr Baker!* London: Fourth Estate.

Warnock, M. (1978) *Special Educational Needs*. Report of the Committee of Enquiry into Special Educational Needs. DES/HMSO.

Wistow, G. (1990) Evidence quoted in *Community Care Planning and Collaboration*. Eighth Report of the House of Commons Social Services Committee on Community Care. HMSO.

Wolfendale, S. (1987) *Primary Schools and Special Needs: Policy, Planning and Provision*. London: Cassell.

Wolfendale, S. (1988) *The Parental Contribution to Assessment*. Developing Horizons No. 10. Stratford-upon-Avon: National Council for Special Education.

Wolfendale, S. (ed.) (1989) *Parental Involvement—Developing Networks between School, Home and Community*. London: Cassell.

Chapter 12

Educational Psychologists and Europe

Geoff Lindsay

In this chapter I shall look at the future for educational psychology with special reference to the changing scene in Europe. I shall focus particularly on the developments within the European Community, but also take note of the exciting changes in Eastern Europe.

While there is a general socio-political sea change in Europe, there are specific issues which apply to educational psychology. In particular, the European Directive on the Recognition of Qualifications has implications for all psychologists. Therefore, in this chapter I shall first discuss this directive in particular, and secondly the issue of the comparability of training across Europe. Thirdly, I shall consider the development of ethical codes and disciplinary procedures within the UK, following the setting up of the Register of Chartered Psychologists, and the relationship between the UK practice in this field and that of other countries in Europe.

THE EUROPEAN DIRECTIVE

On 1 January 1991 the EC Directive on the Recognition of Professional Qualifications (89/48/EEC) came into operation. This is concerned with the recognition of higher education diplomas. Its intention is to remove the barriers which have hitherto existed and prevented or hindered movement between member countries. Specifically, a person trained in a profession or occupation in one EC member state should not be prevented or hindered from practising that profession or occupation in another EC member state. This is a very important, indeed momentous, piece of legislation. It should enable British educational psychologists to practise in other parts of the EC; similarly, educational psychologists from France, Germany and Spain, for example, should be able to practise in the UK.

That, at least, is the idea behind the legislation. But, as with all legislation based upon principle, it is important to consider two main questions. First, what are the actual corollaries, the specific implications of the directive? Second, how will the principle be turned into actuality?

Main provisions of the directive

The directive specifies to which professions and occupations it applies. Article 1 defines these by a series of criteria. Professional psychology, including educational psychology, is included. The core of the directive is in Article 3, the essence of which is that a person who has qualified in one member state should not be prevented from practising the same profession in another member state simply on the grounds that his or her qualifications were not from the second state. However, the host member state (that is, the state to which the professional has migrated) may make certain stipulations. If, for example, the applicant's period of training was of a lesser duration than that expected in the host state, the applicant may be required to provide evidence of professional experience also. Overall, this period required must not exceed four years.

In some cases there may be significant differences between the training in the two countries. In this instance the host country may require the applicant 'to complete an adaptation period not exceeding three years or take an aptitude test'. The directive makes provision for the migrant to choose which route to take. However, there is also provision for each country to decide, for each profession, that only one option is to be allowed.

Note that there is no requirement for a language test. McPherson (1989) suggests that this is because

> ostensibly the Commission thinks it inconceivable that someone not fluent in the language of the host Member State would wish to practise there (personal communication). A more cynical interpretation is that a language test would enable professions of Member States to subvert the intention of the Directive by requiring migrants to be fluent, e.g. in Parisian patois or Glasgow patter. (p. 382)

Article 6 addresses the 'good character or repute' of the applicant. This is to be demonstrated by 'the production of documents issued by competent authorities in the Member State of origin or the Member State from which the foreign national comes showing that these requirements are met.' (Article 6). If no system exists for the production of these, the applicant must make a declaration on oath, or a comparable declaration.

Article 7 requires that the migrant, once accepted, should be able 'to use the professional title of the host Member State corresponding to that profession'. Article 8 requires that the applicant be given a decision within four months. The remaining articles are concerned with the operation of the directive, including the need for a review of its working.

IMPLICATIONS FOR EDUCATIONAL PSYCHOLOGISTS AND THE PROFESSION

As was stated above, the primary aim of the directive is to facilitate freedom of movement. But will this actually happen? There are several issues which must be considered here.

First, the directive is facilitative. It is not forcing educational psychologists to migrate, neither is it providing any incentives so to do. Thus the desire to migrate is a separate issue. When we look at the condition into which the UK education service has fallen over recent years, is it likely that there will be a mass influx of educational psychologists from other member states? The much publicized attempts to attract teachers into LEAs in the South-East had some, limited, effects, but were associated with hard-selling advertising and enticement campaigns. On the other hand, the shortage of EPs in other countries may lead to an exodus from the UK.

Second, there is the language issue. It is not a requisite that the migrant EP should speak the language of the host country—but clearly there will be 'market forces' which will tend to ensure this is the case. Given the infamous lack of bi- and multilingual inhabitants of the UK (apart from those who have themselves immigrated, or whose previous generations immigrated) the number of UK psychologists able to migrate without further language development is surely limited. There is a higher preponderance of multilingual psychologists in other countries.

Third, there are problems in defining comparable learning and experience. This is not a simple matter even within the UK. For example, Scottish training of educational psychologists differs from that in the rest of the UK. Also, a significant minority of clinical psychologists specialize in work with children, yet generally these are not considered eligible for posts in an educational psychology service; nor are educational psychologists, in general, considered eligible to specialize with children in the NHS. The section on training (below) shows the variations that exist across Europe.

Fourth, there is a need for either an adaptation period or examination. The British Psychological Society (BPS), which is recognized in the UK as the competent authority to consider applicants on behalf of the government, has argued strongly for the former. It has urged the government not to allow an applicant a choice between adaptation and examination, arguing that 'there is always within the training of professional psychologists an extensive component of on-the-job or within placement supervised experience', and that assessment methods 'always have within them a key component of demonstrating that this candidate can perform competently in the natural area in which psychological senses are to be delivered' (Response of the BPS to the Department of Trade and Industry, dated 14 February 1990; reprinted as Newman, 1990). This is a very reasonable stand for all professional psychology, as with other culturally related professions, where the context is of such importance. Of course, the same arguments apply to UK educational psychologists wanting to work in, for example, Spain.

Fifth, there is the question of the standing of the migrant while undergoing 'adaptation'. In his report to the Sixth General Assembly of the European Federation of Professional Psychological Associations (EFPPA), McPherson (1990) presenting the report of the Task Force on the Directive, argues that 'during an adaptation period a professional psychologist should normally be in employment (or have full honorary status) as a psychologist and should be regarded as a trainee rather than as a full member of the profession' (p. 7). This task force also argues that even if an applicant is considered to be fully qualified to be recognized in the host country (that is, he or she does not require an adaptation period), the need for some form of acclimatization will almost certainly exist. In such cases, they argue,

National Associations should, in the interest of good practice, encourage all migrant professional psychologists to spend a period working under the guidance of an experienced member of the profession of the Host State before starting to work independently and should take any steps necessary to facilitate such arrangements. (McPherson, 1990, p. 6)

Sixth, there are potential problems with the issue of 'character and repute' of migrant psychologists. On the one hand the protection of the public requires relevant information to be passed to the host country, but on the other hand each of us as psychologists expects some reasonable privacy. What kind of information should be passed? How should this be determined? How will each country decide—on its own or agreed criteria? In his report to the Sixth General Assembly of the EFPPA, McPherson suggests a formula whereby a National Association might be asked:

> X has applied to be regarded as qualified to practise as an educational psychologist in the UK. Is your Association aware of any factors, such as proven professional misconduct, which in your mind should cause us to prevent or limit his or her right to practise? (adapted from McPherson, 1990)

Of course, this requires that all associations would agree to answer such a question.

These are some of the issues to be addressed now that the directive is operative. Most of the administrative load in the UK falls upon the British Psychological Society, the competent authority. In other member states it may be the BPS's equivalent or a government department advised by that body.

In the following two sections I shall consider in more detail the issues of patterns of training and ethics.

PATTERNS OF TRAINING

The training of educational psychologists in the United Kingdom is regulated by the British Psychological Society (BPS). This body discharges this responsibility in two ways. First, it defines the training and experience required of individual psychologists in order to become eligible for membership of the Register of Chartered Psychologists, and more specifically to be able to use the title Chartered Educational Psychologist. Second, the BPS evaluates and accredits first degree courses in psychology, as well as post-graduate training courses in educational psychology.

The present requirements for a person to be eligible for membership of the register are:

(a)   graduate basis of registration (essentially a first degree in psychology of at least dual honours standard);
(b)   qualification as a teacher;
(c)   minimum of two years' teaching experience with children and young people;
(d)   post-graduate training in educational psychology of two years (normally, at present, a one-year full-time Master's course and one year's supervised practice, or internship).

However, Scotland has different requirements. Rather than a teaching qualification or experience, the requirement is for three years' training in educational psychology, normally a two-year master's course followed by one year of supervised practice. This difference reflects different historical tradition and views north and south of the border, particularly concerning the importance of the teaching experience. This element has been questioned by many over the past twenty to thirty years, but the importance placed upon it by the Association of Educational Psychologists, the relevant union outside Scotland, has helped to maintain its being a requirement.

The enactment of the European directive has caused the BPS to consider its qualification again. In continental Europe, there is no clear parallel with British educational psychologists, and in many countries the patterns of training for all professional psychologists are different from those in the UK. The situation in three countries will be described to show the difference that exists.

In Norway, recognition as a psychologist is enshrined in law and the basis of accreditation is the passing of the *cand. psychol.* examination at a Norwegian university. The training course lasts for six or six and a half years and is an integrated programme, including both academic and practical work. Also, the amount of specialization is less than in the UK, where three- or four-year degree psychologists will enter completely different professional training programmes according to whether they wish to become educational psychologists, clinical psychologists, occupational psychologists, etc. This is not the Norwegian way:

> The work of a professional psychologist today encompasses such a wide specter [*sic*] of tasks that an educational program for professional psychological work can not avoid including a certain degree of specialization. On the other hand it is important to stress that specialization at the expense of professional breadth could lead to unfortunate limitations in the professional competence of the psychologist. This means that the degree in psychology must be organized as a theoretical and practical training in which the functions of the practice of general psychological work are focused on to a larger degree than specialization for certain types of problems and areas of work.
>
> The educational program for psychologists must be so broad that the psychologist can handle the most frequent psychological problems in work with individuals, groups, and environments, and if necessary refer the client to a specialist. Breadth must be taken care of in the basic education program, while specialist competence must for the most [part] be provided through special programs for advanced education. Both for professional reasons, and to assure cooperation, the curriculum must also include an introduction to related subject areas. (Norwegian Psychological Society, 1990, p. 3)

In Spain, there is currently a state of development, but the essence is a five-year programme offering a broadly based approach. The first cycle is academic, the second includes practical exercises in a range of centres. Recognition by the title *Liceaciado en Psicologia* is available at this point, but there is also a third cycle which offers more specialized experience. However, these areas do not correspond to UK professional psychology categories, but include, for example, sports psychology, consumer behaviour, intervention in social sciences, and drug addiction treatment (Prieto, 1990).

The Netherlands' system differs again. It lasts for between four and six years, but the second part, leading to the doctoral degree (*doctorandus*), includes specialized practicum, one of which is school psychology. On award of the doctoral degree, the person is granted the professional title *Psycholoog* (psychologist: the award of the degree of *doctor* requires the formal submission and defence of a research thesis subsequent to this stage). Further, post-doctoral training is being developed by the universities in conjunction with the Netherlands Institute of Psychology. A post-doctoral training programme in clinical psychology already exists, and similar programmes in educational psychology and other areas are to follow (Dijkhuis, 1990).

It can be seen that the patterns of training across Europe are highly varied. This poses clear difficulties when a psychologist wishes to move to another European country. How can a person from elsewhere in Europe be considered competent to perform the duties of an educational psychologist in the UK? How will such psychologists' qualifications be assessed for equivalence? Alternatively, how will a UK-trained psychologist be considered on application to another country?

As with issues of ethical codes, there is an inevitable tension when harmonization is sought. On the one hand, clearly comparable training programmes would greatly help judgments of equivalence. But on the other hand, each country has its own social and legal history. Given this situation, the EFPPA set up a task force on training at its Fifth General Assembly in Rome, 1988. The report to the Sixth General Assembly in Luxembourg, 1990, took the position of recommending general principles to direct training in all areas of professional and applied psychology. In other words, at least for the immediate future, there is to be no attempt to specify exact requirements applicable to each country. Rather a quality assurance model is to be followed.

The main elements of the report accepted by the Sixth General Assembly are as follows:

1   Preparation for autonomous professional practice of psychology comprises at least two components: a core programme and an advanced professional training in psychology. The core programme is concerned with the knowledge and skills relating to psychology as a scientific discipline and is common to all branches and specialisms within psychology. In the advanced component the student will acquire the knowledge and skills which are necessary for independent practice in a chosen field of professional psychology.
2   Both components should be provided within a university or equivalent institution of higher education. In some countries with an established tradition of doing so, professional training may be provided by an affiliated professional school or training programme.
3   Together the two components should last at least six years with the distribution between the core programme and advanced training being determined by each country according to national circumstances. However, at least half of the time should be devoted to the core programme. At all levels one should aim at optimal integration of the core programme and the professional training.
4   All training should be accredited in ways acceptable to the relevant national association.
5   Entry to autonomous professional practice should be restricted to those who have completed both components.
6   The core programme in psychology should provide a broad introduction to psychology. It should include the traditional subdisciplines of psychology, ranging from the biologically oriented approaches to those that are cognitively and socially oriented, and including developmental, methodological, philosophical and ethical issues.
7   Professional training should cover the theoretical knowledge, skills, competencies and research abilities required in the applied fields of psychology as set out below:

Theoretical knowledge
a   A variety of different theoretical models should be taught because no single model is able to cope satisfactorily with the range of problems that present to the professional psychologist.
b   Theoretical models must be considered critically so that students are fully aware of their limitations as well as their advantages.
c   Theoretical teaching needs to be integrated with practice.

Skills and competencies
a   Substantial practical training is essential.
b   Practical training should include experience in a variety of settings, methods and approaches. It should include work with individuals, groups and organisations as well as practice in assessment, programme development and evaluation.

    c Ethical considerations should be taken into account in training.

    d Practical training needs to cover communication skills as well as the transmission of psychological skills to others through teaching, supervision and consultation.

    e Like other aspects of training, practical skills need to be tested and examined.

Research training

    a Because of the importance of evaluating practice as well as the need to develop new models, techniques and intervention programmes, an appreciation of the methods of applied research is essential.

    b Students should have the experience of conducting an original and independent research project as part of their training (thesis).

8 National associations have an obligation to ensure that the education and training provided is consistent with their codes of practice and ethical standards.

9 It is recommended that national associations should encourage and promote, keep a record of, and if possible accredit, courses for the training of professional psychologists. (Committee on Training and Education in Psychology, 1990)

Further work will take place over the next two years. The UK system maps on to these requirements quite well, but of course there are changes in train in the British higher education system. The BPS has also set up a task force on the future of professional psychology, which is considering the issue of the future developments of *all* types of professional applied psychology—not only those that currently exist in the UK (such as educational) but new ventures (such as health psychology). Patterns of training, organization, employer base and operation are all being examined.

By the time of the Seventh General Assembly of the EFPPA in 1992 it is to be hoped more countries will have achieved the basic set of standards outlined above. But the actual nature of the training programmes is likely still to vary to meet the characteristics of each nation's set-up, such as its employer base. In the interim, and for the foreseeable future, comparability of qualifications will not be easy to judge. The BPS has a committee charged with this responsibility, for European psychologists and those from anywhere else. Its task is not easy.

ETHICAL CODES

One of the hallmarks of a profession is that its members are expected to behave in an ethical manner. In order to achieve this objective there are two requirements which are necessary, but not sufficient. First, there should be a set of guidelines, which inform the professional how to behave, or alternatively how not to behave. Although this distinction may seem a minor issue of semantics and emphasis, the implications can be very important. Second, there should be a regulatory procedure to check on behaviour and to provide a means for sanctions if the ethical guidelines are breached.

The development of a European perspective on the application of psychology raises the issue of the generalizability and consistency of such ethical guidelines and regulatory procedures across relevant countries.

The United Kingdom situation

In the United Kingdom the body which has the responsibility for these matters is the BPS. This organization is the learned society and professional body which covers all areas of psychology, and is open to all types of psychologist (such as educational, clinical, research and occupational). The BPS is incorporated by Royal Charter, which charges it, as two of its objects,

> 3 (ii) to promote the advancement and diffusion of a knowledge of psychology pure and applied and especially to promote the efficiency and usefulness of Members of the Society by setting up a high standard of professional education and knowledge; [and]
> 3 (iv) to maintain a Code of Conduct for the guidance of Members and Contributors and to compel the observance of strict rules of professional conduct as a condition of membership. (British Psychological Society, 1988, p. 1)

In addition, since December 1987, the BPS has been allowed by its Royal Charter to maintain a register of chartered psychologists. These are the members of the society who fulfil certain additional requirements and demonstrate an advanced training in an area of psychology. One such group comprises educational psychologists, who will have undertaken post-graduate training.

Code of conduct

The BPS Code of Conduct covers five general areas of professional behaviour, namely: general, competence, gaining consent, confidentiality and personal conduct (British Psychological Society, 1985).

Each area contains guidelines relating to some specific aspects of the domain in question. For example, one clause from the section on personal conduct states:

> 5.2 [they shall] not exploit the special relationship of trust and confidence that can exist in professional practice to further the gratification of their personal desires.

This code of conduct is the benchmark against which members of the BPS might judge the minimum standards of acceptable behaviour. In addition, subsections of the Society have developed additional codes specific to their own circumstances. Thus the Division of Educational and Child Psychology (DECP) has for many years had its own code of professional conduct applicable to that subset of members of the BPS who are also members of the DECP.

More recently, the society has taken the view that it is preferable to have only one code of conduct for all members, and for sub-systems to develop guidelines for good practice. This, of course, has the opposite emphasis to that of the code. Whereas the code describes basic standards below which psychologists should not fall, such guidelines promote standards to which psychologists should aspire.

Disciplinary procedures

These are set out in the statutes of the BPS (British Psychological Society, 1988). They cover all members of the society. However, their main use is likely to be against those members who operate as professional psychologists, in any field, and who are on the register of chartered psychologists.

The disciplinary procedures have two main components, which reflect distinct phases in the process. First there is a stage of *investigation*, then there is a stage of *discipline*.

The Clerk to the Investigatory Committee, normally but not necessarily a permanent officer of the BPS, is responsible for the administration of complaints. The clerk's first task is to check that the complaint is clear and bring it to the attention of the investigatory committee. This comprises four senior members of the society, including the president and honorary general secretary.

This committee has the task first of all to determine whether there is an *a priori* justification to investigate. If this is the case, the investigating committee then sets up an *investigatory panel*, which contains members who have expertise in the specific area under investigation. This investigating panel will take whatever steps it considers appropriate to gain evidence. They may wish to ask the subject of the complaint to give his or her comments on the allegations.

If the panel decides there is substantiation for the complaint, its deliberations and recommendations are reported to the investigatory committee. This committee then makes its recommendations to the chair of the disciplinary board.

If the chair of the disciplinary board agrees with the report of the investigatory committee, a disciplinary committee is formed from among members of the board. The board comprises four non-psychologists, all senior members of other chartered or comparable bodies, and three past presidents of the society. The chair is always a non-psychologist, as must be the chair of any disciplinary committee. Also, the majority of the disciplinary committee must be non-psychologists.

Comment

The types of complaint that might be made vary in several respects. The register and these procedures are primarily to protect the public, but another psychologist might be the complainant. The issue might be any that is covered by the code, such as competence or professional behaviour. Thus one complaint might be about poor quality of work, another might concern inappropriate sexual behaviour, a third might relate to scientific fraud. In some instances there might be a court case also, such as that of alleged sexual abuse of a child. The range of penalties open to the disciplinary board varies from reprimand to removal from the register.

EUROPEAN PERSPECTIVE ON CODES OF CONDUCT

In the previous section I discussed the implications for training of the Directive on the Recognition of Qualifications. But there are also important implications for professional practice, including the issue of ethical codes and disciplinary procedures.

The Fifth General Assembly of the EFPPA, held in 1988, recognized that the development of freedom of movement between member states would pose important questions on these matters. Assuming a psychologist's qualifications were recognized and approved as a mark of training, experience and competence, how would ethical behaviour be judged?

The EFPPA instructed the task force on ethics to consider these matters, and in particular the ethical codes in force in different countries. This task force has considered the ethical codes of a number of member societies, and an interim report was made for the Sixth General Assembly in Luxembourg, September 1990 (Lindsay, 1990).

The task force set itself three questions:

(a)   Is there the basis for a common European ethical code?
(b)   Is it useful to have such a code?
(c)   How should a common ethical code be achieved?

Examination of the ethical codes from a number of countries revealed that there was indeed much in common in their content. This is shown in Table 12.1, where the codes of six European countries and the code for the American Psychological Association are presented. An attempt has been made here to break down each code into the more specific area that it covers.

Inspection of the table shows that many categories appear in the codes of most of the countries examined. In particular, the central issues of relationships with clients and colleagues, competence, confidentiality, making statements (including advertising) and reporting research and other findings are general. Those that are less general appear to reflect particular circumstances of the countries, rather than differing views of questions of ethics (for example, fees and remuneration).

However, while the content may be similar the style of the codes varies. In this table I have used categories derived mainly from the Scandinavian code. However, in many other cases the area covered by a particular category may be subsumed under another heading. Interestingly, the UK code is the most discrepant. It comprises five main sections: general, competence, gaining consent, confidentiality and personal conduct. 'Relationships with clients', for example, is subsumed under the last of these categories. Also, some codes comprise two sections: the principle, and examples of its meaning. Finally, some associations have supplementary codes and/or guidelines. The BPS has several of these.

The findings of this generally high level of similarity across codes is encouraging. It indicates a common set of views on ethical behaviour amongst the psychological communities in Europe, and in the United States. This in itself, together with the general imperative to develop a single code, encouraged the EFPPA task force to conclude that a common code was both feasible and potentially useful.

The problem, however, is in its derivation, given the different styles, organizations and arrangements of the codes we examined. The task force recommended that there should be a two-stage process. First, a meta-code should be drawn up. This would essentially be the same as the analyses I have presented here, but in greater detail. All EFPPA member associations would be urged to ensure their codes contained all the constituent elements, in whatever arrangement the association decided. A later stage would be the production of a single code which all associations would accept.

In addition to this harmonization of ethical codes, there is the issue of comparability of disciplinary procedures. This has not been examined yet, but is likely to take place once the ethical codes are equivalent. Given this present state, I can only speculate on such developments, but I would consider strict comparability less easy to achieve given the different legal and quasi-legal structures in different countries. Once more, it is more likely that the first stage will be an examination of the different procedures, leading to a set of agreed general principles. This might include comparable disciplinary stages, and similar tariffs of penalties.

As UK and European psychologists we should also be prepared to look elsewhere for useful models, and the history of practice in North America is of interest here. For

Table 12.1 *Content of Ethical Codes of Six European Countries and the United States*

	Scandinavia	Germany	Spain	Hungary	Austria	UK	US
1 Responsibility, general principles	✓	✓	✓	✓	✓	✓	✓
2 Competence	✓	✓	✓	✓	✓	✓	✓
3 Relationships with clients	✓	✓	✓	✓	✓	✓	✓
4 Confidentiality	✓	✓	✓	✓	✓	✓	✓
5 Psychological methods, investigations and statements, including research reports	✓	✓	✓	✓	✓	✓	✓
6 Public statements, advertising	✓	✓	✓	✓	✓		✓
7 Professional relationships	✓	✓	✓		✓	✓	✓
7a Relationships with employers					✓		
8 Research, teaching	✓	✓	✓	✓	✓		✓
9 Professional designation, title, qualifications	✓	✓	✓	✓		✓	✓
10 Training		✓	✓				
11 Fees and remuneration				✓	✓		
12 Working conditions						✓	✓
13 Personal conduct						✓	✓
14 Obtaining consent						✓	✓

example, the American Association of State Psychology Boards has a long history in the field of disciplinary procedures, almost fifty years, from which we might learn (Edwards and Reaves, 1990).

CONCLUDING COMMENTS

The start of a new era was heralded by the year 1991. The possibility for greater movement of professionals, including educational psychologists, provides an exciting scenario, in the context of a greater 'Europization' of the different states.

In this chapter I have explored some of the issues which are particularly relevant to educational psychologists, but of course this discussion must be considered within the wider context of general political change. There are no single, common patterns of practice or training for educational psychologists across Europe. However, there are common issues that face educational psychologists and their counterparts in other countries. Probably the most important is the general question of how to facilitate the development of children in the context of their families and schools. All European countries are, to varying degrees, multicultural and multi-ethnic. In some cases there are long-standing conflicts between sub-groups. In other instances, recent demographic trends (such as immigrations) have led to tension. But for the future there is a clear need to overcome these difficulties. The breaking down of national boundaries must be reflected by a similar reduction in intracountry distinctions between populations. The *rapprochement* of East and West provides an exciting example of positive developments on the political scene.

Educational psychologists have an important role in providing rigorous assessments of children's needs, and helping with the attainment of optimal support for these children's development. This may include direct programme planning, parental support, inservice training of teachers, advice to education authorities and in some cases direct child advocacy. Psychologists may be advising on the provision of support, or providing the intervention themselves.

Although there are differences remaining between us at the level of detail, there is a common purpose. Over the next decade, I would hope that we learn, collaboratively, to examine each other's practice.

I see the current changes in Europe as important opportunities and challenges. If taken up correctly, these will lead to a greater and more important role for educational psychologists and indeed other psychologists, working together across national boundaries for the betterment of children and adults.

REFERENCES

British Psychological Society (1985) 'A code of conduct for psychologists', *Bulletin of the British Psychological Society*, **38**, 41–3.
British Psychological Society (1988) *The Royal Charter Statutes and Rules*. Leicester: British Psychological Society.
Committee on Training and Education in Psychology (1990) *Optimal Standards for Professional Training in Psychology as Recommended by EFPPA Member Associations*. Report to Sixth General Assembly of EFPPA. Mondorf-les-Bains, Luxembourg.
Dijkhuis, J.J. (1990) *Psychologists in the Netherlands: Their Training and Professional*

Regulation. Report to the Sixth General Assembly of EFPPA. Mondorf-les-Bains, Luxembourg.

Edwards, H.P. and Reaves, R.P. (1990) 'Enforcing ethical behaviour: disciplinary processes in the US and Canada'. Paper presented to the Sixth General Assembly of EFPPA. Mondorf-les-Bains, Luxembourg.

Lindsay, G.A. (1990) 'Task force on ethics'. Report presented to the Sixth General Assembly of EFPPA. Mondorf-les-Bains, Luxembourg.

McPherson, F. (1989) 'Psychologists and the EEC (11): the provisions of the Directive on the Recognition of Qualifications', *The Psychologist*, **2** (9), 382–3.

McPherson, F. (1990) 'Task force on the European directive'. Report to the Sixth General Assembly of EFPPA. Mondorf-les-Bains, Luxembourg.

Newman, C. (1990) 'E.C. directive: comment by the British Psychological Society', *News From EFPPA*, **4** (3), 34–6.

Norwegian Psychological Society (1990) 'Standards for the Norwegian Cand. Psychol. degree'. Report to the Sixth General Assembly of EFPPA. Mondorf-les-Bains, Luxembourg.

Prieto, J.M. (1990) 'Studying psychology in Spain'. Report to the Sixth General Assembly of EFPPA. Mondorf-les-Bains, Luxembourg.

Name Index

Ainscow, M. 61
Apter, S.J. 60
Argyris, C. 29, 111, 118, 131, 132
Aries, P. 153
Association of County Councils 171
Association of Educational Psychologists 101, 188
Aubrey, C. 72

Baldridge, J. 104
Banks, J. 143
Bardon 8–9
Barker, R.G. 52, 54, 56, 58, 62, 64, 65
Barrett, W. 50
Barrow, J. 141
Barton, L. 25
Bell, C.H. 23, 24
Bennett, N. 59, 63
Bennis, W.G. 106
Bijou, S.W. 51
Black, A. 63
Blake, R. 104
Blau, T.H. 168
Blom-Cooper, L. 158
Bloom, B. 9, 26
Bloom, B.S. 60–1
Bloom, J. 93
Blundell, D. 59, 63
Bonoma, T.V. 104
Booker, R. 142
Booth, T. 144
Born, R. 124
Boyan, C. 126
Boydell, T. 89
Bradley, H. 146
Brimblecombe, F. 173

British Psychological Society 11
Bromley, E. 76
Bronfenbrenner, U. 55, 56, 59, 61, 62, 65
Brophy, J. 59, 60
Brophy, J.E. 21
Bryans, T. 141–2, 142
Bryne, E.M. 139
Brzezinska, H. (Myers et al.) 108
Burden, R. 100
Burke, W. 109
Burns, T. 106
Burt, C. 25, 36, 39
Bush, T. 104, 105, 107
Byrne Whyte, J. 91

Cameron, J. 5
Cameron, R. 179, 182
Cameron, R.J. 23, 24, 26
Caplan, G. 20, 22, 27, 78, 100
Carello, C. 58
Carkhuff, R.R. 28
Carrington, B. 141
Ceci, S.J. 168
Chazan, M. 2
Checkland, P. 56
Checkland, P.B. 53, 59, 65
Cherry, C. (Myers et al.) 108
Claxton, G. 9
Cline, T. 88, 143
Coard, B. 143
Cohen, M.D. 105–6
Conoley, C.W. 22, 27
Conoley, J.C. 22, 27, 60
Cooke, D. 168
Cooper, D. 138
Court, D. 170

Cowne, L. 109
Croll, P. (Galton et al.) 63
Cullen, C. 168
Cummins, J. 143, 144, 145
Curtis, D. (Baldridge et al.) 104
Cutting, M.C. 26

Daly, B. 71–2
D'Amato, R. 8, 13
Davis, G. 149
Dean, R. 8, 13
Delefes, P. 63
Department of Education and Science (DES) 25, 36, 99, 120, 180
Department of Health 171, 172
Desforges, C. 50
Desforges, M.F. 145, 149
Dessent, T. 36, 37, 114
DeVault, M.L. 61
Dijkhuis, J.J. 189
Dill, W. 111
Dowling, E. 100
Doyle, W. 54, 58

Ecker, J. (Baldridge et al.) 104
Ecob, R. (Mortimore et al.) 40, 114, 140, 141
Edwards, H.P. 196
Egan, G. 28
Egan, K. 51
Egeth, H. (McCloskey et al.) 154
Ekehammer, B. 58
Etzioni, A. 99–100
Evans, Dennis 87
Evans, J. (Goacher et al.) 146, 147

199

Subject Index